Advances in Theory and Practice of Emerging Markets

Series Editor

Yogesh K. Dwivedi, EMaRC, School of Management
Swansea University Bay Campus
Swansea, UK

Emerging Markets (EMs) exhibit a number of unique characteristics (i.e. unique challenges and opportunities) in terms of socio-economic, demographic, cultural, political, and regulatory. Examples of such unique challenges and opportunities includes diversity and fragmentation of markets, differential market growth rate in terms of urban vs rural, evolution of institutions, political instability, distinct cultural heritage, inherent corruption, and unusual technological diffusion trends. Unique characteristics of EMs makes this context different from developed countries, causing implications for both theory and practice. It necessitates substantial adaptations of theories developed and approaches employed in the Western world for investigating problems specific to such markets. As such, doing research in the EMs context for establishing new conceptual and theoretical paradigms from multidisciplinary perspectives is vital for making the global economy more equitable and sustainable.

This book series aims to publish scholarly work from a variety of disciplines (for example, information systems, electronic government, marketing, digital and social media marketing international business, human resources, public administration, entrepreneurship, operations and supply chain management, health care management, finance, accounting, economics, innovation, science policy, built environment, energy production and consumption, agriculture extension and management, biodiversity conservation and management, sustainable development) focusing on the issues prominent in Emerging Markets such as India, China, Brazil, Russia and South Africa in a book series.

The series will strive to publish conceptual, theoretical, and empirical works relating to the contexts of Emerging Markets. This series will contain four sub-series including: monographs, handbooks, edited volumes, and text books. The Research Monographs and Handbooks sections will focus on the state-of-the-art of both established and emerging topics specifically in the contexts of Emerging markets. Doctoral research produced from the institutions based in one of the EMs countries would also be considered for publication in the monograph category of the series. Monographs will be considered both in the form of relatively shorter pieces and traditional more extended works. This series would also encourage and invite academics and researchers to publish text books specific to EMs context.

Jeremiah Arigu Emmanuel
Ramanie Samaratunge • Daniel Prajogo

Social Enterprises and Impact Investors

Partnerships that Sustain Emerging Countries

Springer

Jeremiah Arigu Emmanuel
Monash Business School
Monash University
Clayton, VIC, Australia

Ramanie Samaratunge
Monash Business School
Monash University
Clayton, VIC, Australia

Daniel Prajogo
Monash Business School
Monash University
Clayton, VIC, Australia

ISSN 2522-5006 ISSN 2522-5014 (electronic)
Advances in Theory and Practice of Emerging Markets
ISBN 978-3-031-59453-3 ISBN 978-3-031-59454-0 (eBook)
https://doi.org/10.1007/978-3-031-59454-0

This Springer imprint is published by the registered company Springer Nature Switzerland AG
The registered company address is: Gewerbestrasse 11, 6330 Cham, Switzerland

Preface

This book explores how social enterprises and impact investors can use inter-organisational partnerships to pursue complementary social and economic interests in emerging countries. But how and why do they work so well? It is because these organisations are hybrids in matching social and commercial focus: the combination of a solid business orientation and social mission creates social value and has a sustainable impact and profit. Studies have used the concept of organisational compatibility and resource complementarity to examine buyer-supplier relationships in business. For this to work, however, enterprises and investors must be able to determine the presence and nature of those qualities, which is the aim of this book. A major African nation, Nigeria, provides empirical evidence for how this can be done successfully, and how lessons learned can be applied to other emerging countries.

This study provides knowledge for enterprise practitioners wanting collaboration with impact investors. Understanding how missions can be aligned will guide potential enterprises to model a hybrid organisational structure that can attract potential investors. Investors, in turn, can be guided in structuring their investment portfolios to attract the right enterprises. From the view point of government, policymakers and institutions wanting to create a sustainable funding platform for hybrid organisations will also find this study helpful for policy guidance.

Clayton, VIC, Australia

Jeremiah Arigu Emmanuel
Ramanie Samaratunge
Daniel Prajogo

Contents

List of Figures

List of Tables

Abbreviations

ADB	African Development Bank
AUM	Asset Under Management
BoP	Bottom of the Pyramid
BVN	Bank Verification Number
CAC	Cooperate Affairs Commission
CBN	Central Bank of Nigeria
CAMA	Companies and Allied Matters Act
DEC	Development Exchange Centre
DFIs	Development Finance Institutions
DGGF	Dutch Good Growth Fund
EIA	Environmental Impact Assessment
ESG	Environmental, Social and Corporate Governance
FDI	Foreign Direct Investment
FAFIN	Fund for Agricultural Finance in Nigeria
GDP	Gross Domestic Product
GNP	Gross National Product
GIIN	Global Impact Investing Network
GESS	Growth Enhancement Support Scheme
IFC	International Finance Corporation
ICSEM	International Comparative Social Enterprise Model
IIs	Impact Investors
MFBs	Microfinance Banks
MSMEs	Micro, Small and Medium Enterprises
MoU	Memoranda of Understanding
NBS	National Bureau of Statistics
NSIA	Nigerian Sovereign Investment Authority
NGOs	Non-Governmental Organization
OECD	Organisation of economic community development
PEBEC	Presidential Enabling Business Environment Council
RSSF	Real Sector Support Fund
SAP	Structural Adjustment Programmes

SET	Social Exchange Theory.
SEs	Social Enterprise
SMEs	Small and Medium Enterprises
SMEDAN	Small and Medium Enterprise Development Agency
TRASI	Tools and Resources for Assessing Social Impact

Chapter 1
Social Enterprise and Impact Investing

1.1 Introduction

This book examines collaborations between social enterprises (SEs) and impact investors (IIs) to learn how they are guided by organisational compatibility and resource complementarity when they seek to establish partner fit in pursuit of their different social and economic interests. It also seeks to understand organisational-level and institution-wide factors that influence pre-investment actions undertaken by SEs and IIs prior to their establishment of partner fit. These actions are based on their levels of compatibility in organisational logics and complementarity of resource strength.

SEs and IIs have attracted more global attention since 2008, when the resources of government and philanthropy collectively proved inadequate for addressing intractable social problems in a sustainable manner (Power et al., 2012; Trivedi, 2010; Trivedi & Stokols, 2011). Since then, impact investing has spread rapidly across the developed world in tandem with interest in social enterprises, attracting investors who specialise in funding organisations that are interested in finding innovative solutions to critical social problems in their home countries (Bandini, 2016; Roundy et al., 2017; Verkerk, 2013). This new form of partnership between SEs and IIs has attracted significant attention of practitioners and academics (Bandini, 2016; Mair & Martí, 2006). This is mainly due to a broad-based consensus amongst stakeholders that SEs and IIs are crucial for addressing the enduring concerns of people at the bottom of the socio-economic pyramid (BoP)—those who have the most extensive social problems (Defourny & Nyssens, 2010; Jamali et al., 2016; Littlewood & Holt, 2018).

Scholars have described SEs and IIs as organisations or individuals who deploy resources innovatively within the environment of entrepreneurial opportunities to provide solutions to a range of societal problems such as poverty, unemployment, inequality, gender, sustainability and climate change (Bansal et al., 2019;

J. A. Emmanuel et al., *Social Enterprises and Impact Investors*, Advances in Theory and Practice of Emerging Markets,
https://doi.org/10.1007/978-3-031-59454-0_1

Bugg-Levine et al., 2012; Greenwood & Freeman, 2017; Martin & Lohin, 2017; Rahdari et al., 2016; Thurman, 2016; Zahra et al., 2009).

1.2 Key Definitions

Social Enterprises

Social enterprises are entities associated with community funding and entrepreneurship (Peredo & Chrisman, 2006; Peredo & McLean, 2006), social change agents (Drayton, 2002; Waddock & Post, 1991), institutional entrepreneurs (Mair & Marti, 2009), social ventures (Dorado, 2006; Sharir & Lerner, 2006), entrepreneurial operations between profit and not-for-profit organisations (Frumkin, 2009), and social innovation (Alvord et al., 2004; Phills et al., 2008). Although there is no consensus definition of a social enterprise, based on empirical data collected across 721 SEs from 43 countries (Defourny et al., 2021), the International Comparative Social Enterprise Model (ICSEM) project teams have identified three models: a social business, a social cooperative, and an entrepreneurial non-profit enterprise. Aligning with the empirical evidence from Defourny et al. (2021), this book defines SEs as organisations that combine a strong business orientation and a social mission to create social value while also making a—necessary—sustainable profit.

Impact Investing

The Global Impact Investing Network (GIIN) defines impact investing as "investments made into companies, organisations, and funds with the intention to generate social and environmental impact alongside a financial return" (2015: 55). The purpose is to explore how private resources could be harnessed to tackle the world's greatest problems, with positive externalities across social and environmental impacts (Roundy et al., 2017; Santos, 2012). The Rockefeller Foundation envisions impact investing as offering "a bridge between traditional philanthropy, which incubates innovation and mobilizes attention to exciting solutions, and the private-sector capital markets that ultimately hold the wealth required to advance these solutions" (Bugg-Levine & Goldstein, 2009: 32). Drawing on this perspective, this book argues that the exciting solutions that private capital holds for difficult social problems are embedded in the knowledge of how investment funds can be matched with the right investee.

1.3 Collaboration Between SEs and IIs

This study defines SEs and IIs as hybrid organisations with blended motives: they have been established to achieve sustainability through market-driven approaches. This broad definition positions SEs and IIs on a spectrum of economic and social missions (Dees, 1998). SE and II partnerships accurately fit Hockerts' (2015) description as organisations primarily pursuing a social mission that depends largely on commercial revenue to sustain their operations. Since this dual objective may not necessarily align with all investors' interests, tensions can arise if organisational goals are not compatible with shared complementary resources (Battilana et al., 2012). It is therefore argued that, when IIs and SEs set out to collaborate through the alignment of compatible organisational logics and share complementary resources, potential conflict can (and indeed must) be mitigated, because the collaboration process aims to match organisations most likely to work harmoniously towards achieving a common goal of social and economic interests.

The achievement of SEs' dual motives also entails that they incorporate and balance contradictory organisational structure, mission, goals and objectives that fall between non-profit and for-profit organisational forms (Pache & Santos, 2013; Santos et al., 2015; Smith et al., 2013). However, although SEs hold enormous potential to bring about social change and transformation, they still suffer from a range of funding challenges (Burkett, 2010; Castellas et al., 2018; Lyon & Owen, 2019), which underpins their need for collaborating with IIs for financing. The literature further suggests that SEs, depending on their nature, size and goals, require a broad array of material and non-material resources, such as support networks, financial assistance, innovation and knowledge, and strategic cultural and institutional resources, in order to function (Montgomery et al., 2012). Finding and attracting the right resources demand that SEs engage in collaborative entrepreneurship to harness these once they are identified and engaged.

This book focuses on SEs, whose commercial competence has been proven to enhance their exchange value, and thus balancing the power dynamic with IIs is critical for a sustainable relationship (Clark, 2015). Hence the lens of social exchange theory is used to determine the type of resources exchanged between SEs and IIs and its influence on their collective decision to establish partner fit (Huybrechts & Nicholls, 2013; Nicholls & Huybrechts, 2016).

1.4 Better Understanding of SE and II Partnerships

Despite the important role of SEs and IIs in addressing complex societal challenges, Agrawal (2018: 300) observes that "much less research has been undertaken on the actions and processes on impact investing firms". The lack of knowledge about the impact investing process here points to a significant knowledge gap in how IIs engage with organisations within their mandate: "the lack of knowledge about the field and lack of knowledge production on the field pose an increasing risk of failure for both investors and the investees" (Agrawal & Hockerts, 2019b: 3). Limitation in knowledge also cuts across contextual environments in both developed and emerging economies (Ngoasong et al., 2015; Phillips & Johnson, 2019), particularly from the perspective of goal alignment towards collective social and economic impacts (Ormiston et al., 2015). According to Höchstädter and Scheck (2015), little is understood about the mechanisms underpinning the organisational-level motives through which investors deliver social and environmental impacts via investee business operations.

The literature also reveals a strong connection between organisation-level factors and a knowledge gap on macro-level factors that influence the collaboration experience between SEs and IIs. This is why Munro and Belanger (2017: 47) argue that "the more that research can increase the SE community's understanding of the external environment, the better equipped SEs will be to strategically align themselves for success". It has also justified the need for country-specific empirical studies (Defourny et al., 2011; Ngoasong et al., 2015; Ratten, 2014). An in-depth study is therefore required to empirically explore the following issues:

- The limited empirical research about the collaboration process between impact investors with organisations within their mandate, and with SEs in particular
- The lack of understanding about the motivations underpinning impact investors' drive for social and environmental impact distinct from other organisations
- The limited knowledge about contextual influence on impact investing across developed and emerging economies and
- The risk of potential failure between investor and investee that is linked to inadequate knowledge about collaboration prospects and outcomes

1.5 Nigeria as the Case

This research takes Nigeria as a case of examining the partnership building between SEs and IIs for a number of significant reasons. First, according to a survey by GIIN in 2015, Nigeria has remained a strategic destination for impact capital flow despite its economic recession since 2015 (IIF, 2019). Impact-investing transactions in Nigeria by 2019 were 3.9 times greater in value compared to Ghana, with about $4.7 billion transactions in Nigeria and $1.2 billion transactions in Ghana (IIF, 2019). Nigeria also has the largest economy in West Africa but with a limited presence of a non-DFI (development finance institution) impact-investing community (GIIN, 2015; Hurst, 2015). The learning experience of SEs already in dyad relationship with IIs can model and promote a dramatic experience for SEs struggling to attract IIs financing in Nigeria, in Africa more widely, and in other regions of the world. However, despite the benefits that impact funds hold for the development of SEs in Nigeria, there is limited empirical research that examines how their collaboration with IIs has evolved (George et al., 2016; Ngoasong et al., 2015;

Rivera-Santos et al., 2015). This supports the call for more empirical research on SEs in Nigeria (Julian & Ofori-Dankwa, 2013; Kolk & Van Tulder, 2010; Rivera-Santos et al., 2015; Zoogah & Nkomo, 2013).

Second, Nigeria is currently facing significant challenges in financing SEs due to a downward trend in Overseas Development Assistance (ODA), with a huge decline in funds from traditional sources, such as government and private individuals (Kirigia et al., 2011). As a result, the Nigerian government is facing enormous challenges of increasing poverty, unemployment, and other critical social problems. Recent government strategies are now focused on private-sector small and medium-size enterprises, or SMEs, of which it is estimated that 84% are to be categorised as underserved organisations, with a finance gap of US$140–170 billion (Omidyar Network, 2013). Recent World Bank studies also reveal that low access to financing has remained one of the biggest problems bedevilling SMEs in frontier nations like Nigeria (Wang, 2016).

Third, the term "social enterprise" is not very popular in Nigeria. A GIIN survey observed that social enterprise in this country was still in its infancy (Wilson et al., 2015), and IIs therefore identified hybrid SMEs with blended motives as a large target for impact investing because of their important role in economic growth (financial returns) and job creation (social impact) (Ebitu et al., 2016). Rivera-Santos et al. (2015: 81) observed:

> Recognising that social entrepreneurs may not self-identify as social enterprise in some context, despite their having all the characteristics of social enterprise in the literature, has implications for data collection strategies, as it has become relatively common for researchers to rely on self-perception to identify social entrepreneurs.

Fourth, despite these challenges, Nigeria still offers tremendous opportunities and prospects for impact investing (IIF, 2019). GIIN (2015) has targeted 72,838 hybrid SMEs in Nigeria as potential recipients of impact capital, given their social impact and economic role in employment creation and the provision of goods and services to underserved populations, particularly in rural areas. For the purposes of this study, therefore, hybrid SMEs constituted the main target of IIs in Nigeria, and this study draws on the experiences of hybrid SEs with dyadic relations with IIs in Nigeria to explain how they collaborate to establish partner fit.

1.6 The Key Objectives of This Study

Research has noted that IIs differ from other investors in terms of personal values, motivations, and processes that are contextually determined (Roundy et al., 2017). Unique contextual factors also determine how SEs and IIs collaborate and how they arrive at their decision to establish partner fit (Bierly III & Gallagher, 2007; Miller & Wesley, 2010), from both micro-organisational-level and macro-environment-level influences. Some scholars posit that experience from previous collaboration may engender credibility and trustworthiness in the eyes of potential partners

(Bennett et al., 2008), with the possibility for replication across both emerging and developed countries. Therefore, our book is focused on achieving the following key objectives:

- To provide empirical evidence on the nature of collaboration between SEs and IIs in establishing partner-fit in the pursuit of their socioeconomic involvement in the Nigerian economy
- To discover the differences between IIs and other investors in terms of values, motivations and processes
- To investigate the influence of contextual factors in determining the collaboration between SEs and IIs, and what influences decisions to establish partner-fit and
- To ascertain the learning outcomes from the collaborative experience between SEs and IIs.

In order to achieve these objectives, our book will address the following overarching research question: *How are SEs and IIs guided in determining their organisational compatibility and resource complementarity towards achieving partner fit in Nigeria?* This question is elaborated with a number of sub-questions:

- In the process of collaboration, how do SEs and IIs establish partner fit in pursuit of their social and economic interests in Nigeria?
- At the micro-organisational level, what factors influence collaboration and partner selection between SEs and IIs?
- How does the Nigerian macro-environment influence the collaboration process between SEs and IIs, and what factors enable or constrain the establishment of partner fit between them?
- What is the perceived learning experience from the collaboration and partner selection between SEs and IIs with dyadic relations?

1.7 Theoretical Foundations

In addressing the knowledge gap on how SEs and IIs collaborate, this study uses the theoretical lens of partner fit to examine how SEs and IIs determine the right partner in pursuing their collective social and economic interests (Bierly III & Gallagher, 2007; Thorgren et al., 2012). Related research on partner fit has used the concepts of organisational compatibility and resource complementarity, which explain the alliances between buyers and suppliers (Manotungvorapun & Gerdsri, 2016), in order to gain the understanding of how organisations select partners to increase their inter-firm collaboration (Dhurkari & Nandakumar, 2015; Sarkar et al., 2001; Solesvik & Encheva, 2010).

Organisational compatibility refers to the resemblance between partners in their organisational culture, management and operating style (Sarkar et al., 2001). Institutional theory scholars have observed that motivated hybrid organisations can build bridges by aligning or accommodating competing logics (Micelotta et al.,

2017), which gives them the advantage of disrupting dominant logics to create, modify or transform society (DiMaggio, 1988; Greenwood & Suddaby, 2006; Hampel et al., 2017; Marti & Mair, 2009). Institutional logic theory is used to capture the complexity associated with hybrid organisations (Bielefeld, 2009; Dacin et al., 2011; Greenwood et al., 2011), unlike dominant organisational theories that separate organisations from societal contexts and rely on market mechanisms to explain firm actions (Friedland & Alford, 1991; Lounsbury & Boxenbaum, 2013; Thornton & Ocasio, 2008).

Complementarity occurs when partners leverage resources and complementary skills to jointly create additional value between them (Hamel, 1991; Hamel & Prahalad, 1993; Mindruta et al., 2016). Proponents of social exchange theory posit that every social interaction has benefits that can be derived by the parties involved, and that, for a relationship to generate mutual benefits, trust, mutual commitment and reciprocity are required (Blau, 2017; Clark et al., 2014; de Jesus et al., 2017). Clark's (2015) empirical study further affirms that SEs' relationship with funding partners is predominantly characterised by reciprocity and strong interpersonal relationships. This is contrary to several assumptions within the literature that relationships are mainly characterised by power imbalance (Mogapi et al., 2019; Ozanne et al., 2016; Smith et al., 2013). Social entrepreneurship literature has also acknowledged the imperative for "lone actors to pursue strategic partners that fill both such voids" (Montgomery et al., 2012: 377), and either "compensate for weakness" or "act as complementors" (VanSandt et al., 2009: 423).

In understanding how SEs and IIs establish their partner fit in pursuing their social and economic interests, we integrate the theories of institutional logics and social exchange and apply them in the context of organisational compatibility and resource complementarity that guide the organisational decision-making process. Integration of sociological and psychological theories to examine collaborative entrepreneurship in hybrid organisations is not coincidental to this study. Just as SEs and IIs need to collaborate to address the world's most difficult problems, Mayer and Sparrowe (2013) argue, scholars may need to draw insight from different theories to address what no single theory on its own can address. By implication, this study demonstrates that social exchange and institutional logic can mutually fill the knowledge gap on procedural organisational behaviours and institutional complexities, since each will hold promise to inform the other. Just as institutional logic fills a theoretical gap regarding the influence of values, practice and cultural context on exchange behaviour of organisations, social exchange theory helps specify the process and mechanisms through which patterns of social collaboration can shape and reproduce organisational identities and practices constitutive of institutional logic (Pirkey, 2016).

1.8 Philosophical Background of the Method of the Study

This research uses qualitative methods based on a critical realist (CR) philosophical perspective. CR philosophy is used because of its preference for qualitative methods in understanding social events (Hu, 2018). In management studies, CR is suitable for explaining competing theories of complex social events (Wynn Jr & Williams, 2012). It has also emerged as a useful philosophy for theory development in entrepreneurial research (Kitching et al., 2015; Martin & Wilson, 2016; Ramoglou & Tsang, 2016). Based on these principles, data have been collected through semi-structured, in-depth interviews from six SEs and six IIs, linked in a dyadic form, to reveal how they established partner fit.

Dyadic data analysis has been used to demonstrate the importance of mutuality in understanding parties in a dyadic relationship as a key component of social networks (Blau, 1964; Heider, 2013; Homans, 1958). Qualitative dyadic analysis has also been used due to the nascency of social entrepreneurial research: it aims to capture the deeper reality of participants' experience, underpinned by CR philosophy (Delbridge & Edwards, 2013; Fleetwood, 2005; Ryan et al., 2012), which understands business relationships as "real" affects, such that their properties are legitimate objects of analysis in line with dyadic affective modes of analysis in social networks (Ferris et al., 2009; Ryan et al., 2012).

1.9 The Rationale of This Study

This book is timely because it brings several insights and makes contributions to the entire group of stakeholders in the social entrepreneurship and impact investing space.

For academia, the study expands knowledge of social exchange and institutional logic theories drawn from previous studies. Using institutional logic theory, previous studies have mainly focused on tensions that arose because hybrid organisations were pursuing competing social and economic interests (Agrawal & Hockerts, 2019a; Bruneel et al., 2016; Mogapi et al., 2019; Reay & Hinings, 2009). This study expands knowledge on how hybrid organisations with dyadic relations can collaboratively pursue dual purposes with minimal tensions. In social exchange theory, previous studies have been focused on dyadic social exchange relationships in mainstream business settings, involving mainly tangible resources (Hald, 2005; Jap, 1999; Spekman, 1988; Tanskanen, 2015; Zeitz, 1980). This study extends knowledge of social exchange theory to include hybrid inter-organisational relations, involving both tangible and intangible resources, in order to determine the level of power dynamic between them.

The study thus makes several contributions. Firstly, the combination of social exchange (Blau, 2017; Emerson, 1976; Homans, 1958) and institutional logic perspectives (DiMaggio, 1988; Greenwood & Suddaby, 2006) has allowed the study to demonstrate a novel insight that extends business partner selection literature on organisational compatibility and resource complementarity (Dhurkari & Nandakumar, 2015; Manotungvorapun & Gerdsri, 2016) to the hybrid organisational context. The institutional logics perspective provides a deeper understanding of how organisations with dual purposes align their unique purposes in a compatible fashion with minimal conflict. Social exchange theory is used to broaden understanding of the types of resources needed for the dual motives of social and economic business that partners can exchange, highlighting the power dynamics between them. The study provides a new narrative that makes cross-disciplinary contributions to management theory regarding inter-organisational dyadic relationships (Greenwood & Freeman, 2017; Mayer & Sparrowe, 2013; Micelotta et al., 2017).

Secondly, examining how SEs and IIs establish partner fit (Bierly III & Gallagher 2007; Bordia et al., 2017) by aligning complementary resources and compatible organisational logics demonstrates the applicability of these concepts in establishing partner fit in an emerging economy (Battilana et al., 2009; Thorgren et al., 2012; Micelotta et al., 2017; Zhao & Lounsbury, 2016). The contribution hinges on the fact that social entrepreneurship as a contextual phenomenon needs to be understood from theory application in different contexts. This insight modifies knowledge from research streams that view relationships between SEs and their funding partners as mainly characterised by power imbalance (Agrawal & Hockerts, 2019a; Glänzel & Scheuerle, 2016). The study provides empirical evidence of the types of resources exchanged between hybrid organisations with dual purposes at the organisational level (Bordia et al., 2017; Di Domenico et al., 2009). For example, complementary resources such as financial resources and technical expertise from IIs were complemented with different types of resources from SEs, such as innovative, viable and scalable business models, and fixed assets. These resources also define exchange value between the partners.

Practitioners will gain insights into how SEs and IIs collaborate to establish partner fit from emerging country examples and this sheds light on the contextual influence on social entrepreneurship intentions (McCallum & Viviers, 2020; UNDP, 2015). The contextual environment of social entrepreneurship in Nigeria highlights the presence of an institutional void (ineffective or absence of formal and established governing structures) and how SEs and IIs with dyadic relations navigate these macro-institutional influences to achieve their unique intentions. Institutional voids in the Nigerian environment cut across the absence of global standards of macro-institutional requirements for impact investing practice. This highlights emerging-country perspectives in solving difficult social problems and sheds greater light on impact investing practices in other regions of the world, including their unique challenges (Agafonow, 2015; Doherty et al., 2014; Jamali et al., 2016; Kerlin, 2012). A shift from the dominant literature focus on developed economies' experience (Aidis et al., 2008; Milligan & Schöning, 2011) is a sure pathway to developing the field of social entrepreneurship. This knowledge will continue to deepen understanding of how SEs and IIs select the right partners across regions. The influence of politics, corruption, tax uncertainty and other barriers that constitute impediments for SEs' collaboration with IIs from a Nigerian perspective is a vital insight that is required to develop the field of social entrepreneurship.

References

Agafonow, A. (2015). Value creation, value capture, and value devolution: Where do social enterprises stand? *Administration & Society, 47*(8), 1038–1060.

Agrawal, A. (2018). Impact investing: Framework and future research avenues. *Social Business, 8*(3), 293–317.

Agrawal, A., & Hockerts, K. (2019a). Impact investing strategy: Managing conflicts between impact investor and investee social enterprise. *Sustainability, 11*(15), 4117.

Agrawal, A., & Hockerts, K. (2019b). Impact investing: Review and research agenda. *Journal of Small Business & Entrepreneurship, 33*(3), 1–29.

Aidis, R., Estrin, S., & Mickiewicz, T. (2008). Institutions and entrepreneurship development in Russia: A comparative perspective. *Journal of Business Venturing, 23*(6), 656–672.

Alvord, S. H., Brown, L. D., & Letts, C. W. (2004). Social entrepreneurship and societal transformation: An exploratory study. *The Journal of Applied Behavioral Science, 40*(3), 260–282.

Bandini, F. (2016). Social enterprises. In *Principles and practice of impact investing: A catalytic revolution* (1st ed.). Routledge.

Bansal, S., Garg, I., & Sharma, G. D. (2019). Social entrepreneurship as a path for social change and driver of sustainable development: A systematic review and research agenda. *Sustainability, 11*(4), 1091.

Battilana, J., Leca, B., & Boxenbaum, E. (2009). How actors change institutions: Towards a theory of institutional entrepreneurship. *Academy of Management Annals, 3*(1), 65–107.

Battilana, J., Lee, M., Walker, J., & Dorsey, C. (2012). In search of the hybrid ideal. *Stanford Social Innovation Review, 10*(3), 51–55.

Bennett, R., Mousley, W., & Ali-Choudhury, R. (2008). Transfer of marketing knowledge within business-nonprofit collaborations. *Journal of Nonprofit & Public Sector Marketing, 20*(1), 37–70.

Bielefeld, W. (2009). Issues in social enterprise and social entrepreneurship. *Journal of Public Affairs Education, 15*(1), 69–86.

Bierly, P. E., III, & Gallagher, S. (2007). Explaining alliance partner selection: Fit, trust and strategic expediency. *Long Range Planning, 40*(2), 134–153.

Blau, P. M. (1964). *Exchange and power in social life*. Transaction Publishers.

Blau, P. (2017). *Exchange and power in social life*. Routledge.

Bordia, P., Restubog, S. L. D., Bordia, S., & Tang, R. L. (2017). Effects of resource availability on social exchange relationships: The case of employee psychological contract obligations. *Journal of Management, 43*(5), 1447–1471.

Bruneel, J., Moray, N., Stevens, R., & Fassin, Y. (2016). Balancing competing logics in for-profit social enterprises: A need for hybrid governance. *Journal of Social Entrepreneurship, 7*(3), 263–288.

Bugg-Levine, A., & Goldstein, J. (2009). Impact investing: Harnessing capital markets to solve problems at scale. *Community Development Investment Review, 2*, 30–41.

Bugg-Levine, A., Kogut, B., & Kulatilaka, N. (2012). A new approach to funding social enterprises. *Harvard Business Review, 90*(1/2), 118–123.

Burkett, I. (2010). *Financing social enterprise: Understanding needs and realities*. Foresters Community Finance.

Castellas, E. I.-P., Ormiston, J., & Findlay, S. (2018). Financing social entrepreneurship: The role of impact investment in shaping social enterprise in Australia. *Social Enterprise Journal, 14*(2), 130–155.

Clark, S. (2015). *Social enterprise-business partnerships: Exploring the influence of institutional logics upon social enterprise partnership experiences and decision-making* (Doctoral dissertation). Retrieved from https://eprints.utas.edu.au/23155/1/Clark_whole_thesis.pdf

Clark, S., Woods, M., & Adams, D. (2014). *Balancing social and commercial objectives within business organisations: What can we learn from social enterprise?* Paper presented at the Proceedings of the International Association for Business and Society, pp. 268–279.

Dacin, M. T., Dacin, P. A., & Tracey, P. (2011). Social entrepreneurship: A critique and future directions. *Organization Science, 22*(5), 1203–1213.

de Jesus, I. C., Bruni, A. L., Oliveira, S. R. G., & Araújo, E. A. C. (2017). *Dyadic relationships of trust and knowledge sharing in cooperation networks between micro and small enterprises for innovation* (Paper presentation). ICSB World Conference Proceedings, Washington.

Dees, J. G. (1998). *The meaning of social entrepreneurship*. Kauffman Foundation and Standford University. Retrieved from https://community-wealth.org/content/meaning-social-entrepreneurship

Defourny, J., & Nyssens, M. (2010). Conceptions of social enterprise and social entrepreneurship in Europe and the United States: Convergences and divergences. *Journal of Social Entrepreneurship, 1*(1), 32–53.

Defourny, J., Kuan, Y. Y., & Kim, S. Y. (2011). Emerging models of social enterprise in Eastern Asia: A cross-country analysis. *Social Enterprise Journal, 7*(1), 86–111.

Defourny, J., Nyssens, M., & Brolis, O. (2021). Testing social enterprise models across the world: Evidence from the "International Comparative Social Enterprise Models (ICSEM) project". *Nonprofit and Voluntary Sector Quarterly, 50*(2), 420–440.

Delbridge, R., & Edwards, T. (2013). Inhabiting institutions: Critical realist refinements to understanding institutional complexity and change. *Organization Studies, 34*(7), 927–947.

Dhurkari, R. K., & Nandakumar, M. (2015). Measures of complementarity and compatibility in strategic alliances for innovation: A review of literature. *The International Technology Management Review, 5*(4), 182–201.

Di Domenico, M., Tracey, P., & Haugh, H. (2009). The dialectic of social exchange: Theorizing corporate—Social enterprise collaboration. *Organization Studies, 30*(8), 887–907.

DiMaggio, P. (1988). Interest and agency in institutional theory. In L. G. Zucker (Ed.), *Research on institutional patterns: Environment and culture*. Ballinger Publishing Co.

Doherty, B., Haugh, H., & Lyon, F. (2014). Social enterprises as hybrid organizations: A review and research agenda. *International Journal of Management Reviews, 16*(4), 417–436.

Dorado, S. (2006). Social entrepreneurial ventures: Different values so different process of creation, no? *Journal of Developmental Entrepreneurship, 11*(04), 319–343.

Drayton, W. (2002). The citizen sector: Becoming as entrepreneurial and competitive as business. *California Management Review, 44*(3), 120–132.

Ebitu, E. T., Glory, B., & Alfred, U. J. (2016). An appraisal of Nigeria's micro, small and medium enterprises (MSMEs): Growth, challenges and prospects. *British Journal of Marketing Studies, 4*(5), 21–36.

Emerson, R. M. (1976). Social exchange theory. *Annual Review of Sociology, 2*(1), 335–362. https://doi.org/10.1146/annurev.so.02.080176.002003

Ferris, G. R., Liden, R. C., Munyon, T. P., Summers, J. K., Basik, K. J., & Buckley, M. R. (2009). Relationships at work: Toward a multidimensional conceptualization of dyadic work relationships. *Journal of Management, 35*(6), 1379–1403.

Fleetwood, S. (2005). Ontology in organization and management studies: A critical realist perspective. *Organization, 12*(2), 197–222.

Friedland, R., & Alford, R. R. (1991). Bringing society back in: Symbols, practices, and institutional contradictions. In W. W. Powell & P. J. DiMaggio (Eds.), *The new institutionalism in organizational analysis* (pp. 232–267). University of Chicago Press.

Frumkin, P. (2009). *On being nonprofit: A conceptual and policy primer*. Harvard University Press. Retrieved from https://www.hup.harvard.edu/catalog.php?isbn=9780674018358

George, G., Corbishley, C., Khayesi, J. N., Haas, M. R., & Tihanyi, L. (2016). Bringing Africa in: Promising directions for management research. *Academy of Management Journal, 59*(2), 377–393.

GIIN. (2015). *The landscape for impact investing in West Africa*. Retrieved from https://thegiin.org/knowledge/publication/westafricareport

Glänzel, G., & Scheuerle, T. (2016). Social impact investing in Germany: Current impediments from investors' and social entrepreneurs' perspectives. *Voluntas: International Journal of Voluntary and Nonprofit Organizations, 27*(4), 1638–1668.

Greenwood, M., & Freeman, R. E. (2017). Focusing on ethics and broadening our intellectual base. *Journal of Business Ethics, 140*, 1–3.

Greenwood, R., & Suddaby, R. (2006). Institutional entrepreneurship in mature fields: The big five accounting firms. *Academy of Management Journal, 49*(1), 27–48.

Greenwood, R., Raynard, M., Kodeih, F., Micelotta, E. R., & Lounsbury, M. (2011). Institutional complexity and organizational responses. *Academy of Management Annals, 5*(1), 317–371.

Hald, K. S. (2005). *Managing inter-organizational relationships: Using the force of partner attraction*. Copenhagen Business School. Retrieved from https://research-api.cbs.dk/ws/portalfiles/portal/58880103/4.pdf

Hamel, G. (1991). Competition for competence and interpartner learning within international strategic alliances. *Strategic Management Journal, 12*(S1), 83–103.

Hamel, G., & Prahalad, C. K. (1993). Strategy as stretch and leverage. *Harvard Business Review, 71*(2), 75–84.

Hampel, C., Lawrence, T., & Tracey, P. (2017). Institutional work: Taking stock and making it matter. In R. Greenwood, C. Oliver, & T. B. Lawrence (Eds.), *The SAGE handbook of organizational institutionalism* (pp. 558–590). SAGE Publications Ltd.

Heider, F. (2013). *The psychology of interpersonal relations*. Psychology Press.

Höchstädter, A. K., & Scheck, B. (2015). What's in a name: An analysis of impact investing understandings by academics and practitioners. *Journal of Business Ethics, 132*(2), 449–475.

Hockerts, K. (2015). How hybrid organizations turn antagonistic assets into complementarities. *California Management Review, 57*(3), 83–106.

Homans, G. C. (1958). Social behavior as exchange. *American Journal of Sociology, 63*(6), 597–606.

Hu, X. (2018). Methodological implications of critical realism for entrepreneurship research. *Journal of Critical Realism, 17*(2), 118–139.

Hurst, G. (2015). *Impact investing powers up east African economies*. Institutional Investor. Retrieved from https://www.institutionalinvestor.com/article/b14z9w8yhzj3b6/impact-investing-powers-up-east-african-economies

Huybrechts, B., & Nicholls, A. (2013). The role of legitimacy in social enterprise-corporate collaboration. *Social Enterprise Journal, 9*(2), 130–146.

IIF. (2019). *Nigeria and Ghana Impact investing and policy landscape*. Retrieved from https://thegiin.org/assets/IIF%20Study%20on%20Impact%20Investing%20Full%20Report.pdf

Jamali, D., Mohanna, N., Sherif, D. H., & El Sayeh, S. (2016). A comparative study of social enterprises: North vs. south perspectives. In R. Larattta (Ed.), *Social enterprise-context-dependent dynamics in a global perspective*. IntechOpen.

Jap, S. D. (1999). Pie-expansion efforts: Collaboration processes in buyer–supplier relationships. *Journal of Marketing Research, 36*(4), 461–475.

Julian, S. D., & Ofori-dankwa, J. C. (2013). Financial resource availability and corporate social responsibility expenditures in a sub-Saharan economy: The institutional difference hypothesis. *Strategic Management Journal, 34*(11), 1314–1330.

Kerlin, J. A. (2012). Defining social enterprise across different contexts: A conceptual framework based on institutional factors. In B. Gidron & Y. Hasenfeld (Eds.), *Social enterprises*. Palgrave Macmillan.

Kirigia, J. M., Nganda, B. M., Mwikisa, C. N., & Cardoso, B. (2011). Effects of global financial crisis on funding for health development in nineteen countries of the WHO African region. *BMC International Health and Human Rights, 11*(1), 4.

Kitching, J., Hart, M., & Wilson, N. (2015). Burden or benefit? Regulation as a dynamic influence on small business performance. *International Small Business Journal, 33*(2), 130–147.

Kolk, A., & Van Tulder, R. (2010). International business, corporate social responsibility and sustainable development. *International Business Review, 19*(2), 119–125.

Littlewood, D., & Holt, D. (2018). Social entrepreneurship in South Africa: Exploring the influence of environment. *Business & Society, 57*(3), 525–561.

Lounsbury, M., & Boxenbaum, E. (2013). Institutional logics in action. In *Institutional logics in action, part A (Research in the sociology of organizations).* Emerald Group Publishing Limited.

Lyon, F., & Owen, R. (2019). Financing social enterprises and the demand for social investment. *Strategic Change, 28*(1), 47–57.

Mair, J., & Martí, I. (2006). Social entrepreneurship research: A source of explanation, prediction, and delight. *Journal of World Business, 41*(1), 36–44.

Mair, J., & Marti, I. (2009). Entrepreneurship in and around institutional voids: A case study from Bangladesh. *Journal of Business Venturing, 24*(5), 419–435.

Manotungvorapun, N., & Gerdsri, N. (2016). Complementarity vs. compatibility: What really matters for partner selection in open innovation? *International Journal of Transitions and Innovation Systems, 5*(2), 122–139.

Marti, I., & Mair, J. (2009). Bringing change into the lives of the poor: Entrepreneurship outside traditional boundaries. In *Institutional work: Actors and agency in institutional studies of organizations* (pp. 92–119). Cambridge University Press.

Martin, R., & Lohin, R. (2017). Impact investing: Tracking the adoption of a financial (and social) innovation. *Rotman Management*, 64–69.

Martin, L., & Wilson, N. (2016). Opportunity, discovery and creativity: A critical realist perspective. *International Small Business Journal, 34*(3), 261–275.

Mayer, K. J., & Sparrowe, R. T. (2013). Integrating theories in AMJ articles. *Academy of Management Journal, 56*(4), 917–922.

McCallum, S., & Viviers, S. (2020). Exploring key barriers and opportunities in impact investing in an emerging market setting. *South African Journal of Business Management, 51*(1), 1–11.

Micelotta, E., Lounsbury, M., & Greenwood, R. (2017). Pathways of institutional change: An integrative review and research agenda. *Journal of Management, 43*(6), 1885–1910.

Miller, T. L., & Wesley, C. L. (2010). Assessing mission and resources for social change: An organizational identity perspective on social venture capitalists 'decision criteria. *Entrepreneurship Theory and Practice, 34*(4), 705–733.

Milligan, K., & Schöning, M. (2011). Taking a realistic approach to impact investing: Observations from the world economic forum's global agenda council on social innovation. *Innovations: Technology, Governance, Globalization, 6*(3), 155–166.

Mindruta, D., Moeen, M., & Agarwal, R. (2016). A two-sided matching approach for partner selection and assessing complementarities in partners' attributes in inter-firm alliances. *Strategic Management Journal, 37*(1), 206–231.

Mogapi, E. M., Sutherland, M. M., & Wilson-Prangley, A. (2019). Impact investing in South Africa: Managing tensions between financial returns and social impact. *European Business Review, 31*, 397–419.

Montgomery, A. W., Dacin, P. A., & Dacin, M. T. (2012). Collective social entrepreneurship: Collaboratively shaping social good. *Journal of Business Ethics, 111*(3), 375–388.

Munro, M. M., & Belanger, C. (2017). Analyzing external environment factors affecting social enterprise development. *Social Enterprise Journal, 13*(1), 38–52. https://doi.org/10.1108/SEJ-06-2016-0021

Ngoasong, M., Paton, R., & Korda, A. (2015). *Impact investing and inclusive business development in Africa: A research agenda* (pp. 1–22). The Open University. Retrieved from https://oro.open.ac.uk/42157/1/ikd-working-paper-76.pdf

Nicholls, A., & Huybrechts, B. (2016). Sustaining inter-organizational relationships across institutional logics and power asymmetries: The case of fair trade. *Journal of Business Ethics, 135*(4), 699–714.

Omidyar Network. (2013). *Accelerating entrepreneurship in Africa*. Retrieved from https://www.omidyar.com/insights/accelerating-entrepreneurship-africa-report

Ormiston, J., Charlton, K., Donald, M. S., & Seymour, R. G. (2015). Overcoming the challenges of impact investing: Insights from leading investors. *Journal of Social Entrepreneurship, 6*(3), 352–378.

Ozanne, L. K., Phipps, M., Weaver, T., Carrington, M., Luchs, M., Catlin, J., et al. (2016). Managing the tensions at the intersection of the triple bottom line: A paradox theory approach to sustainability management. *Journal of Public Policy & Marketing, 35*(2), 249–261.

Pache, A.-C., & Santos, F. (2013). Inside the hybrid organization: Selective coupling as a response to competing institutional logics. *Academy of Management Journal, 56*(4), 972–1001.

Peredo, A. M., & Chrisman, J. J. (2006). Toward a theory of community-based enterprise. *Academy of Management Review, 31*(2), 309–328.

Peredo, A. M., & McLean, M. (2006). Social entrepreneurship: A critical review of the concept. *Journal of World Business, 41*(1), 56–65.

Phillips, S. D., & Johnson, B. (2019). Inching to impact: The demand side of social impact investing. *Journal of Business Ethics, 168*, 1–15.

Phills, J., Deiglmeier, K., & Miller, D. (2008). Rediscovering social innovation. *Stanford Social Innovation Review*. Retrieved from https://ssir.org/articles/entry/rediscovering_social_innovation

Pirkey, M. (2016). *Being, doing, & creating community: Social exchange & the microfoundations of institutional logics* (Paper presentation). Academy of Management Proceedings. https://doi.org/10.5465/ambpp.2016.10979abstract

Power, G., Wilson, B., Brandenburg, M., Melia-Teevan, K., Lai, J., & Gowda, R. (2012). *A framework for action: Social enterprise & impact investing*. United Nations Global Compact. Retrieved from http://www.unglobalcompact.org/docs/issues_doc/development/Framework_Social_Enterprise_Impact_Investing.pdf

Rahdari, A., Sepasi, S., & Moradi, M. (2016). Achieving sustainability through Schumpeterian social entrepreneurship: The role of social enterprises. *Journal of Cleaner Production, 137*, 347–360.

Ramoglou, S., & Tsang, E. W. (2016). A realist perspective of entrepreneurship: Opportunities as propensities. *Academy of Management Review, 41*(3), 410–434.

Ratten, V. (2014). Encouraging collaborative entrepreneurship in developing countries: the current challenges and a research agenda. *Journal of Entrepreneurship in Emerging Economies, 6*(3), 298–308.

Reay, T., & Hinings, C. R. (2009). Managing the rivalry of competing institutional logics. *Organization Studies, 30*(6), 629–652.

Rivera-Santos, M., Holt, D., Littlewood, D., & Kolk, A. (2015). Social entrepreneurship in sub-Saharan Africa. *The Academy of Management Perspectives, 29*(1), 72–91.

Roundy, P., Holzhauer, H., & Dai, Y. (2017). Finance or philanthropy? Exploring the motivations and criteria of impact investors. *Social Responsibility Journal, 13*(3), 491–512.

Ryan, A., Tähtinen, J., Vanharanta, M., & Mainela, T. (2012). Putting critical realism to work in the study of business relationship processes. *Industrial Marketing Management, 41*(2), 300–311.

Santos, F. M. (2012). A positive theory of social entrepreneurship. *Journal of Business Ethics, 111*(3), 335–351.

Santos, F., Pache, A.-C., & Birkholz, C. (2015). Making hybrids work: Aligning business models and organizational design for social enterprises. *California Management Review, 57*(3), 36–58.

Sarkar, M. B., Echambadi, R., Cavusgil, S. T., & Aulakh, P. S. (2001). The influence of complementarity, compatibility, and relationship capital on alliance performance. *Journal of the Academy of Marketing Science, 29*(4), 358–373.

Sharir, M., & Lerner, M. (2006). Gauging the success of social ventures initiated by individual social entrepreneurs. *Journal of World Business, 41*(1), 6–20.

Smith, W. K., Gonin, M., & Besharov, M. L. (2013). Managing social-business tensions: A review and research agenda for social enterprise. *Business Ethics Quarterly, 23*(3), 407–442.

Solesvik, M. Z., & Encheva, S. (2010). Partner selection for interfirm collaboration in ship design. *Industrial Management, & Data Systems, 110*(5), 701–717.

Spekman, R. E. (1988). Strategic supplier selection: Understanding long-term buyer relationships. *Business Horizons, 31*(4), 75–81.

Tanskanen, K. (2015). Who wins in a complex buyer-supplier relationship? A social exchange theory based dyadic study. *International Journal of Operations & Production Management, 35*(4), 577–603.

Thorgren, S., Wincent, J., & Örtqvist, D. (2012). Unleashing synergies in strategic networks of SMEs: The influence of partner fit on corporate entrepreneurship. *International Small Business Journal, 30*(5), 453–471.

Thornton, P., & Ocasio, W. (2008). Institutional logics. In R. Greenwood, C. Oliver, & R. Suddaby (Eds.), *The SAGE handbook of organizational institutionalism* (pp. 99–128). SAGE Publications Ltd.

Thurman, P. W. (2016). *Entrepreneurship and sustainability: Business solutions for poverty alleviation from around the world*. Routledge.

Trivedi, C. (2010). A social entrepreneurship bibliography. *The Journal of Entrepreneurship, 19*(1), 81–85.

Trivedi, C., & Stokols, D. (2011). Social enterprises and corporate enterprises: Fundamental differences and defining features. *The Journal of Entrepreneurship, 20*(1), 1–32.

UNDP. (2015). *Impact investment in Africa, trends, constraints & opportunitites*. Retrieved from https://www.undp.org/sites/g/files/zskgke326/files/migration/africa/14aae1f27ec1834e6e96d4a6af4a75de5956e746f588c7accc93c84bde98d725.pdf

VanSandt, C. V., Sud, M., & Marmé, C. (2009). Enabling the original intent: Catalysts for social entrepreneurship. *Journal of Business Ethics, 90*(3), 419–428.

Verkerk, M. J. (2013). Social entrepreneurship and impact investing. *Philosophia Reformata, 78*(2), 209–221. https://doi.org/10.1163/22116117-90000553

Waddock, S. A., & Post, J. E. (1991). Social entrepreneurs and catalytic change. *Public Administration Review, 51*, 393–401.

Wang, Y. (2016). What are the biggest obstacles to growth of SMEs in developing countries?–An empirical evidence from an enterprise survey. *Borsa Istanbul Review, 16*(3), 167–176.

Wilson, K. E., Silva, F., & Ricardson, D. (2015). *Social impact investment: Building the evidence base*. Retrieved from https://sites.duke.edu/casei3/files/2013/03/OECD-social-impact-investment.pdf

Wynn, D., Jr., & Williams, C. K. (2012). Principles for conducting critical realist case study research in information systems. *MIS Quarterly, 36*, 787–810.

Zahra, S. A., Gedajlovic, E., Neubaum, D. O., & Shulman, J. M. (2009). A typology of social entrepreneurs: Motives, search processes and ethical challenges. *Journal of Business Venturing, 24*(5), 519–532.

Zeitz, G. (1980). Interorganizational dialectics. *Administrative Science Quarterly, 25*(1), 72–88.

Zhao, E. Y., & Lounsbury, M. (2016). An institutional logics approach to social entrepreneurship: Market logic, religious diversity, and resource acquisition by microfinance organizations. *Journal of Business Venturing, 31*(6), 643–662.

Zoogah, D. B., & Nkomo, S. (2013). Management research in Africa. In *Management in Africa: Macro and micro perspectives* (Vol. 53, p. 9). Routledge.

Chapter 2
Social Enterprises and Impact Investing: Progress and Challenges

2.1 Introduction

This chapter reviews the literature pertaining to social enterprise and impact investing. First, we explore how interaction between social enterprises (SEs) and impact investing (II) emerged as a new hybrid model and provide examples of this. Existing funding models for SEs are reviewed to ascertain the uniqueness of impact investor funds and the criteria that guide their decisions on investment in SEs. By so doing, we clarify differences between hybrid SEs that are for-profit and those that are not-for-profit. The different goals of SEs and IIs are also examined to determine how these organisations collaborate to create social impact in a society, drawing upon practitioner and academic research. The second part reviews relevant theories on inter-organisational collaboration between hybrid organisations. It focuses on the theoretical frame that guides the establishment of partner fit, using the concept of organisational compatibility from institutional logics and resources complementarity from social exchange theory. Finally, we present the research questions and conceptual model for the study.

2.2 The Emergence of Social Enterprises

The literature on social enterprise and social entrepreneurship is relatively new, but their foundation has an established history. Social enterprise dates back over a century (Dart, 2004), while social entrepreneurship emerged in the 1990s (Ianes, 2020; Waddock & Post, 1991). The foundation of entrepreneurship literature, however, dates back to the 1700s (Schumpeter, 1934; Smith, 1776). Social entrepreneurs as change agents who seek opportunities to effect social change through diverse market circumstances have been behind social enterprise and social entrepreneurship

J. A. Emmanuel et al., *Social Enterprises and Impact Investors*, Advances in Theory and Practice of Emerging Markets,
https://doi.org/10.1007/978-3-031-59454-0_2

emergence (Nicholls, 2010). SEs gained widespread recognition as a tool for addressing social and environmental problems, such as poverty, inequality and unemployment (Mair & Marti, 2006; Meyer, 2021; Seelos et al., 2011; Wry & York, 2017).

From a geographical point of view, SEs emerged almost at the same time in the US and Europe but with no connection between them until the mid-2000s (Defourny & Nyssens, 2010). In the US, the social enterprise initiative was first launched by the Harvard Business School in 1993, and was supported by several large universities and foundations operating mainly in the not-for-profit sector. In Europe, the emergence of social enterprise was associated with the development of cooperatives in Italy, which later gained recognition in the work of the EMES (L'Emergence des Entreprises Sociales), the European Research Network founded in 1996. The conception of social enterprise across the two continents envisioned social enterprise from different perspectives. The US vision was "entrepreneurial activity with a search for social value creation, strong link with social innovation, use of market resources, promotion of managerial practices, emphasis on the individual characteristics of the entrepreneur, whatever the statute of the organisation non-profit or for-profit, public or private", while Europe's vision was "entrepreneurial activity with a search for social value creation, use of a mix of resources (market, public and voluntary), importance of the governance structure and of the existence of a democratic decision process" (Petrella & Richez-Battesti, 2014: 150). The outcome of the emergence of social enterprise on the two sides of the Atlantic, although embodying controversy over differing aspects of social enterprise, is that they both saw the development of two different schools of thought, championed by two groups of scholars (Borzaga & Defourny, 2001; Defourny & Borzaga, 2001; Defourny & Nyssens, 2010). This study describes the work done by these two schools, based on the work carried out by Defourny and Nyssens (2010).

2.3 'Earned Income' School of Thought

The 'earned income' school of thought conceptualises social enterprise as non-profit organisations seeking alternative funding strategies to support social mission accomplishment (Defourny & Nyssens, 2010; Petrella & Richez-Battesti, 2014). SEs under this category engage in commercial activities to resolve their funding challenges that emerge from cutbacks in public grants, reduction in official development assistance (ODA) in the case of developing countries, and difficulties in generating funds through private donations from individuals or foundations. These approaches have been used by all social enterprise organisations that engaged in commercial or for-profit activities. A typical example of social business, Grameen Bank, developed by Muhammad Yunus in Bangladesh, provides a good approach. According to Yunus (2009), a social business is a type of business that does not distribute all its profit to shareholders and does not depend on donations and public subsidies to carry on its social mission. The notion of social business is currently a new organisational model used by multinational organisations to help people at the "bottom of the pyramid" (in welfare and well-being) access the market (Reficco & Márquez, 2012; Shams et al., 2021). SEs examined in this research fall into the second category of profit-oriented businesses.

2.4 "Social Innovation" School of Thought

The "social innovation" school of thought has its origins in the Schumpeterian conception of entrepreneurs as individuals who possess unique personal qualities to pursue their social mission with great sense of dynamism and creative leadership style (Petrella & Richez-Battesti, 2014). This school holds a strong view of the social entrepreneur as a change maker, a skilful and creative leader, motivated by a social mission. The social entrepreneur is seen as the key driver of social change, rather than an organisation or a business model. This conception has gained support from foundations such as Schwab, Skoll and Ashoka since the beginning of the 1980s, focusing mainly on developing the professionalism of social entrepreneurs with non-profit status (Petrella & Richez-Battesti, 2014). The work of Thorgren and Omorede (2018), showcasing passionate entrepreneur leaders in Africa, furnishes a good example of social entrepreneurs from the social innovation school.

Despite the differences between these two schools, Defourny and Nyssens (2010) observe convergence in their common vision that cuts across criteria, such as the search for social value creation or impact. Both schools view social entrepreneurship as a mission-driven business, gaining increasing attention across business schools and foundations (Defourny & Nyssens, 2014). Others view it as social innovation, employed by all types of enterprise and using market resources, managerial and technical competencies to achieve "double" or triple bottom line vision (Emerson, 2006). The overall purpose is creating blended value that balances and better integrates social and economic goals and strategies.

2.5 Social Entrepreneurship from Academic and Practitioner Perspectives

This section reviews academic and practitioner perspectives of social entrepreneurship in view of widespread perceptions that there is more practitioner-led than academic research (Clarkin & Cangioni, 2016; Ormiston et al., 2015). From the academic viewpoint, the history of social entrepreneurship has its origins in entrepreneurship, a word that originates from the French word "entreprendre", meaning "to take into one's own hands" (Roberts & Woods, 2005: 44). As far back as the eighteenth century, businessman Richard Cantillon described entrepreneurs as "undertakers" who engage in market exchanges at a risk with the intention of making profit (Cantillon, 1997). Cantillon's work created the foundation for three key economic scholarly works on entrepreneurship. The first emanates from a German tradition, and built on the work of Joseph Schumpeter (1934) on innovation. The second was from the Chicago tradition of Knight (1921), focusing on risk. The third is from the Austrian tradition of Israel Kirzner (1973, 1979) and explores "alertness to opportunity".

The term "social entrepreneurship" was first introduced by Banks (1972), and academic research around the construct began in the early 2000s (Haugh, 2007). The definition of social entrepreneurship from an academic viewpoint revolves around a process that combines innovation, opportunity and risk to achieve a predetermined outcome; however, there has been a lingering wish to seek a consensus definition that explains the process of achieving this outcome (Roberts & Woods, 2005). This hinges on the geographical (and hence cultural) bias in social entrepreneurship research (Dato-on & Kalakay, 2016), which means different things to people across regions. Many scholars undertook literature reviews aiming to arrive at an acceptable definition (Bacq & Janssen, 2011; Dacin et al., 2011; Short et al., 2009), but to date there is no consensus definition about the concept of social entrepreneurship (Dato-on & Kalakay, 2016).

The concept of social entrepreneurship has gained wider popularity among academics (Grieco, 2015), but lack of a theoretical framework and definition has left the subject at the infant stage for over two decades (Peredo & McLean, 2006; Seelos et al., 2011; Zahra et al., 2009). The difficulty in defining social entrepreneurship is rooted in the fact that its conceptual entities vary significantly according to geographical context, because countries perceive social entrepreneurship differently (Grieco, 2015). This difference has its roots in the social, political and economic conditions influencing the attributes of social entrepreneurs, which either encourage or discourage entrepreneurial behaviours. Many scholars (George et al., 2016; Grieco, 2015) argue that one fruitful avenue for understanding social entrepreneurship is to measure their emergence and development across different geographical contexts. Noya and Clarence (2013) argue that social entrepreneurship is fine-tuned by the institutional and cultural contexts in which it is created, while the difficulties faced are specific to those contexts.

From a practitioner perspective, it is well documented that the impetus for the growth and development of social entrepreneurship globally is linked to the economic recession of the 1970s (Sobotka et al., 2011) and the global financial crises of 2008 (Kotz, 2009; Poon, 2011; Taylor, 2009), which were periods when the world looked to practitioners to bring together business practice and the passion of social entrepreneurs to solve the world's most difficult problems. The implications of the crises inspired policy-makers and concerned citizens to turn to private entrepreneurs for innovative and sustainable solutions to poverty that was rooted in the inequality in the distribution of global wealth (Nicholls, 2008; Shaw & de Bruin, 2013). Roberts and Woods (2005) note that academics, and indeed policy makers, looked to practitioners to make sense of what social entrepreneurs do and the type of people who engage in social entrepreneurship. This reinforces Höchstädter and Scheck's (2015) observation of the paucity of academic research on social entrepreneurship, because impact investing discourse, which gained popularity at the time of the global financial crises, was driven mainly by practitioners.

Corroborating the implications of the 2008 financial crisis that inspired practitioners' action (Roberts & Woods, 2005) and subsequent academic interest, social entrepreneurship represents an innovative concept currently enjoying wide practitioner and academic attention and with a wider social impact. Based on a comprehensive review of literature on social entrepreneurship from 2007 to 2018, Gupta et al. (2020) argue that one way to further develop the field is to apply theoretical lenses across different contexts, as carried out in this research. This study, therefore, adopts an understanding of social enterprise as defined by the OECD (1999: 3):

> Any private activity conducted in the public interest organised with entrepreneurial strategy, but whose main purpose is not the maximization of profit but the attainment of certain economic and social goals, and which has the capacity for bringing innovative solutions to the problems of social exclusion and unemployment.

At the field level, it is notable that both academics and practitioners are currently faced with the challenge for moving the field of social entrepreneurship to a more advanced level. Roberts and Woods (2005) note that the challenge from an academic perspective is how to turn an inherently practitioner-led field into a more rigorous research-based and objective discipline, whereas practitioners are concerned about raising more awareness, support and robust participation among stakeholders.

In terms of geographical location, the academic discourse on social entrepreneurship has advanced in developed countries (Steiner et al., 2019), while desperate voices on developing countries' experience still lag behind in the discourse, due to insufficient empirical data from the African continent (Littlewood & Holt, 2018). The empirical data needed to contribute to social entrepreneurship discourse lies in doing empirical research that draws data from Africa's unique macro environment, shedding light on the concept of social entrepreneurship.

In tandem with the dearth of literature on the influence of Africa's institutional environment on social entrepreneurship literature, the concept remains emergent in Sub-Saharan Africa, despite the region's large-scale socio-economic problems (Sesan, 2006). When the 2008 global recession brought a sharp decline in foreign aid to Africa, governments and foundations could no longer address difficult social problems (Kirigia et al., 2011). Impact investing, which emerged in 2008 as a sustainable, innovative approach for dealing with complex social issues across regions, has been projected as the most significant opportunity to transform Sub-Saharan Africa and the developing world (GIIN, 2015). However, research has revealed that only a few SEs have been able to attract IIs in developing countries, while many SEs are yet to understand how collaboration between social enterprise and IIs has evolved (Bugg-Levine & Emerson, 2011).

2.6 The Concept of Impact Investing

Impact investing (II) emerged in 2008 following a meeting held by investors and philanthropists in Bellagio, Italy. Similar to social enterprise, the emergence of II has been linked to the inability of government resources, charitable foundations, grants and corporate donations to sustain social ventures. Impact investing was then conceived as "…one of the most innovative ways to bring the resource of the world's financial markets to the world's seemingly intractable problems" (Clarkin & Cangioni, 2016: 135). This study draws on the definition of II by GIIN (2015: 55): "Investments made into companies, organisations, and funds with the intention to generate social and environmental impact alongside a financial return".

Impact investing has emerged to provide the capital needs of organisations that embrace innovative solutions to difficult societal problems with social or environmental and financial returns (Brandstetter & Lehner, 2015; Nicholls & Daggers, 2016; OECD, 2019; UNDP, 2016). It was to be a bridge between philanthropy and capital markets. This study therefore argues that the exciting solutions that private capital holds for difficult social problems are embedded in ethical decisions of impact investing that match investment funds with the right investees.

II aims to address the widespread financial fraud that characterised large financial institutions during the 2008 global financial crisis (Sarah, 2016; Afonso & Blanco-Arana, 2022), giving rise to "a broader movement gaining momentum in contemporary market economies, one demanding more ethical and socially inclusive capitalism" (Dacin et al., 2011: 1204). This view further highlights the importance impact investors (IIs) accord to their social screening process, i.e., what kind of practices inform "excluding or including companies" from an investment portfolio based on a range of social and environmental or financial criteria (Michelson et al., 2004)? The screening process, according to Šimić (2015), is the act of filtering incoming investment proposals from SEs to determine the most viable and attractive opportunities. Essentially, impact investing emerged towards the end of the twentieth century (Clarkin & Cangioni, 2016) as a seed to promote social innovation and entrepreneurship that have direct impacts on the public (Engelmark et al., 2015).

Despite the potential of impact investing, surprisingly there remains limited number of studies on it (Agrawal, 2018; Agrawal & Hockerts, 2019b). Lack of knowledge about the field and the need for knowledge production are critical to increasing collaboration between stakeholders. The next section provides an overview of research trends on impact investing to serve as a guideline to exploring the huge opportunities that abound in the sector.

2.7 The Rise of Impact Investing

Studies on impact investing cut across institutional, firm and individual levels of analysis. At the institutional level, Nicholls (2010) uses an institutional lens to examine the degree of institutional complexity of the field within the financial world and the challenges it faces in gaining acceptance. Institutional environment factors, such as taxation laws, market norms, geographic location, literacy rate, inflation and the quality of public service, play a major role in influencing impact investing strategies, decisions and cost (Castellas et al., 2018; Glänzel & Scheuerle, 2016; Goldszmidt et al., 2011). The institutional void in developing economies is much higher compared to developed countries (Mair & Marti, 2009; Stephan et al., 2015), which creates impact investing opportunities, but at the same time hampers commercial, entrepreneurial activities for profit-first IIs (Mair & Marti, 2009; Mair et al., 2007, 2012). Research on the institutional influence on II is centred around the perspective of institution-level factors because they shape the decision-making process of investors. For example, this study focusses on the macro environment-level factors that comprise social, economic and political factors. Knowledge of these factors creates awareness and better understanding of the opportunities and risks of investing in any geographical location.

At the organisational level, knowledge of elements such as innovation at firm-level, sector-specific knowledge and organisational form (Wood & Hagerman, 2010), opportunity recognition (Lehner, 2013) and due diligence practice (Cumming et al., 2019; Reeder et al., 2014; Serrano-Cinca & Gutiérrez-Nieto, 2013) are important elements that guide the intending action of IIs. Such an approach may potentially mitigate the risk of possible tension and mission drift, particularly in relation to pre- and post-investing periods. Scholars have been called on to examine how these elements affect impact investing practice, particularly the different organisational form that determines how competing logics align with investing decision processes (Agrawal & Hockerts, 2019b). Another important research driver is the stakeholders—the community that constitutes the ecosystem for impact investing. Several stakeholders exist around impact investing. These include banks (Burand, 2012; Jackson, 2013; Scholtens, 2006), individual investors with high net worth (Bolton & Savell, 2010; Brett, 2013; Demel, 2012; Tzouvelekas, 2014), institutional investors (Ganesh, 2017), intending beneficiaries (Corrigan, 2011; Oh et al., 2013) and the state or government (Bonini & Emerson, 2005; Tjornbo & Westley, 2012)—all engage with and influence investment processes and decision-making. Jackson (2013) groups these actors into four categories: asset owners—those who own capital; asset managers—those who deploy capital on behalf of asset owners; the demand side—those who receive and utilise capital such as SEs; and service providers—those who assist in making the process work, such as intermediaries, capacity-building organisations, consultants, and others.

The current research focus is on the relationship between the supply side and demand side of the actors. Phillips and Johnson (2019) note that the demand side is not yet meeting the supply side of impact investing—meaning there are more impact

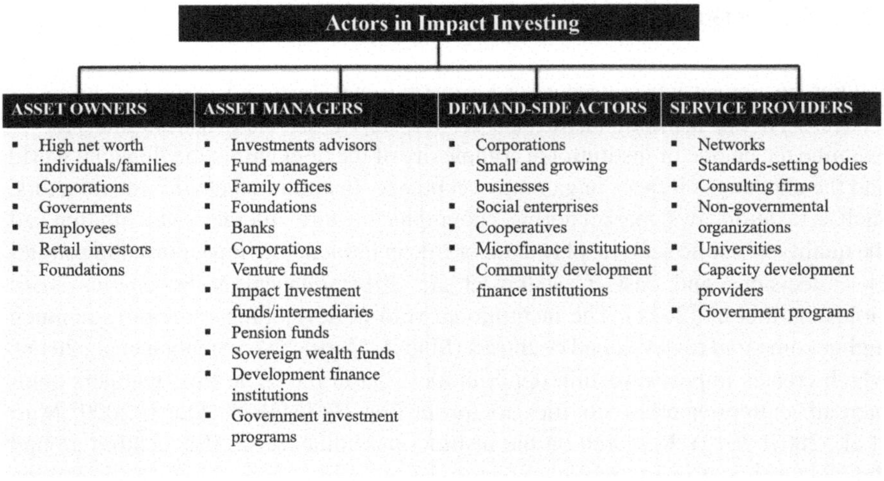

Fig. 2.1 Actors in impact investing. (Source: Phillips and Johnson (2019, p. xi))

funds than the number of SEs can absorb. Some barriers attributed to the wide gap between demand and supply from a study of SEs in Canada shows that a lack of knowledge about the market and inadequate financial literacy contribute to early setbacks. Figure 2.1 provides a list of actors within the four categories of impact investing actors for knowledge creation.

From the list of actors in Fig. 2.1, we note that the demand side, which comprises SEs, will mainly collaborate or interact with asset managers who constitute the supply side of the ecosystem. It is important to know the characteristics of IIs, since this knowledge will guide potential investees in structuring their organisations to attract the right capital for their social and commercial interests. IIs are characterised according to their intentionality for social and/or environmental impact, drawn from "entrepreneurial alertness" (Drnovšek et al., 2018). Another important attribute of IIs is their approach to mitigating potential risk through behaviours described as due diligence (Cumming et al., 2019). Due diligence is discussed in detail below.

2.8 Intentionality for Social and Environmental Impact

The intention of IIs has been defined as a conscious, planned action that emanates from a state of mind that directs and guides business investors toward a specific action (Boyd & Vozikis, 1994; Caseau & Grolleau, 2020). It is a well-orchestrated, vision-driven behaviour underpinned by rational and analytic thinking and aimed at achieving a vision. IIs specifically identify socially- and/or environmentally minded organisations as their target for delivering impact. IIs not only allocate financial resources to their target projects but also provide managerial and technical expert resources geared toward the success of their investee organisations (Yap, 2018).

Their intention to deliver these dual outcomes guides their decisions in selecting the right social enterprise to create the desired or intended positive impacts. These actions define their intentional behaviours, rooted in perceived desirability and perceived feasibility of target investment (Drnovšek et al., 2018). That is why impact-first investors are deliberate in their intention for impact, whereas financial-first investors may not be deliberate in their approach to social impact. The intention for impact is a key component of the definition of impact investing as a theory of change (Jackson, 2013).

2.9 Investing with Expectation of a Return

A simultaneous expectation of social and financial return is an outstanding feature of impact investing (Brandstetter & Lehner, 2015). Because they are intentional about the impact of their investment across social and economic impacts, IIs naturally expect a financial return from their investment. When they invest in debt, equity or hybrid finance, the level of financial returns varies between market-rate returns, below-market-rate returns or market-beating; the rate of return reflects both investor appetite for risks and the corresponding motive for engaging with the market (Ormiston et al., 2015). Institutional investors, in particular, are often guided by the dimensions of risk and return when selecting investment portfolios and opportunities (Brandstetter & Lehner, 2015). Generally, evaluating social innovation from the perceived risk factor is an important strategy that IIs adopt in mitigating the potential loss in their investment strategies (Krlev et al., 2013).

2.10 Due Diligence Practices

Due diligence refers to any "…action taken to ensure that an activity is safe" (Jones & Moncur, 2020: 3). Due diligence from an impact investor's perspective entails background checks, credit checks, site visits, cross-checks and account monitoring, including third-party proof on funding projects (Cumming et al., 2019). Due diligence is what investors do either openly or secretly prior to or during the life circle of a project and is aimed at reducing the potential impact of risk on expected returns from an investment. Due diligence is necessary before selecting a project (establishing partner fit with SEs), because the success of impact investing is tied to the social and commercial success of investee SEs (Austin, 2000; Huybrechts & Nicholls, 2013). The process of due diligence is difficult and costly, but it is an unavoidable issue for IIs, who must maintain institutional legitimacy (Agrawal & Hockerts, 2019b; Chong & Kleemann, 2011). Due diligence is underpinned by the need to "reflect on how the different elements of the ability of the entrepreneur and entrepreneurial empathy can be measured and screened during due diligence as these qualities may affect the investment at a later period" (Agrawal & Hockerts, 2019b:

Table 2.1 Risk in impact investing

Risk factor	Description
Early stage of the market	Risks might arise from the market's small size, the short track record of performance, small portfolio and deal sizes and fund managers little experience with dual return objectives
Ecosystem risk	The impact investment market depends on infrastructure, e.g. policy support and measurement systems, which adds risk
Mission drift	Investee might drift away from the intended mission without the approval of investors
Combination of investment capital	Impact investment combine grant and investment capital. This combination risks not achieving the expectations and intentions of the respective funders
Moral hazard	Similar to traditional investment but extended by the failure of not delivering on the impact mission. Additionally, funders aim at helping the investee but also have to maintain rigor with respect to loss recognition
Legal risk	In addition to legal and regulatory challenges at the beginning of a business, there may also be changes to different regimes over time or changes to transferring the business as it grows. Difficulties in scaling the business or changing ownership will introduce a challenge to the growth of impact investments, but with the help of local management teams, it will be easier to manoeuvre within local regimes
Reputational risk	An impact investment must constantly balance the dual imperative of generating positive social impact and profit. However, these two objectives can also create tensions. In pursuit of more profit, a business may be inclined to target relatively better-off customers, raise prices to take advantages of the lack of competition or take cash out of the business rather than invest in innovation to enable even broader customer reach

Source: Saltuk and Idrissi (2012, p. 27)

20). Carrying out due diligence enables the investor to understand the different types of risks involved in a given project and learn how to value each risk to optimise the outcome for a given investment. In particular, risks associated at the investee and portfolio level can be grouped into social and financial risks (Agrawal & Hockerts, 2019b). Saltuk and Idrissi (2012) have compiled a list of possible risk factors associated with impact investing (Table 2.1, below). The table explains briefly the type of risk associated with either start-up, early-stage or growth-stage enterprises and cuts across ecosystem risk, mission drift, combinations of investment capital, moral hazard, legal risk and reputational risk.

2.11 Impact Investing in Developed and Emerging Economies

Since its inception, impact capital has continuously flowed across developed and developing countries globally. Although there are more challenging social problems in developing countries (Cetindamar & Kozanoglu, 2014; GIIN, 2015; Santi &

Sennett, 2016), developed nations also face well-known social problems, such as climate change, unemployment, homelessness, and disadvantage issues (Agrawal, 2018; FASE, 2016; Flatau, 2017; Wong & Yap, 2019). Figure 2.2 reveals the organisational representation of impact asset under management (AUM) covering all the continents with perceived social challenges. AUM is the total value of impact investment focused funds that are managed by investment firms that aim to generate social, economic, and environmental outcomes.

According to Fig. 2.2, most impact investing organisations are based in developed markets, i.e. USA and Canada 50%, Western Northern and Southern Europe 31%. 6% of the organisations in emerging markets are mostly based in sub-Saharan Africa, 3% in Latin America and the Caribbean, and 2% in Southeast Asia. 92% of impact AUM is housed by organisations based in developed markets, while only 8% of impact AUM accounted for organisations based in emerging markets (Hand et al., 2022). While several impact investing opportunities exist in emerging markets such as Latin America, South Asia, Africa, Eastern Europe and South-East Asia, most impact funds were noticed as active in the US domestic market (Hand et al., 2022). This can be attributed to an aligned, market-based solution for social problems (Tansey et al., 2017). It is important to point out here that IIs are social entrepreneurs with humanity at heart. Although they often target below-market return on investment, with a specific focus on social impact, they will not invest in a social enterprise without first ascertaining its viability and competence to deliver social or environmental impact with a financial return (Battilana, 2018). SEs need to have the relevant capability and competence to capture existing opportunities in national and

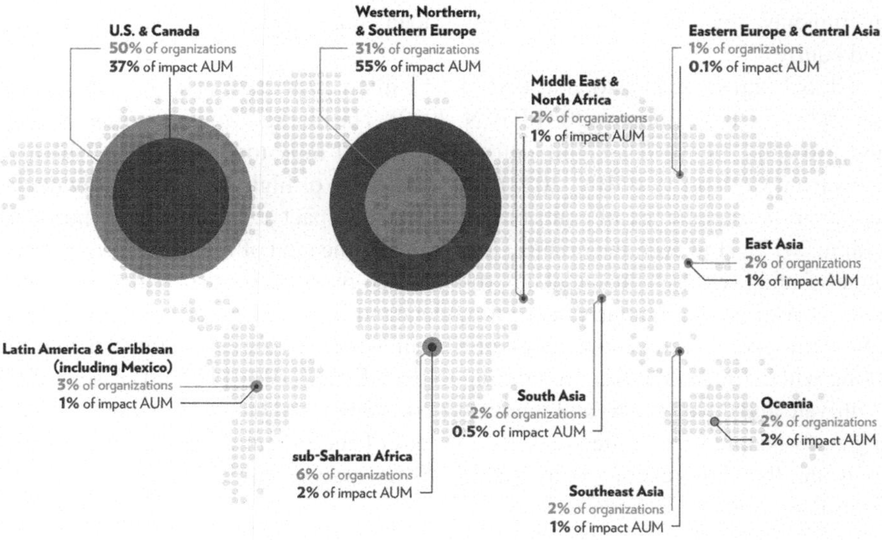

Fig. 2.2 Overview of impact investing organisations and impact AUM by location. (Source: Hand et al. 2022: 4)

international markets (Cetindamar & Kozanoglu, 2014). Although the opportunities for impact investing abounds in emerging and developing economies, a survey by GIIN West Africa found that inadequate flow of impact funds across developing economies can be linked to the fact that

> Many early-stage enterprises and SMEs are informal and lack the strategy, structure and records that would qualify them as investor-ready. Small Scale and Medium Enterprises (SMEs) across the continent often lack governance and management skills and robust business systems, leading to gaps in operation management and financial planning or accounting. (Santi & Sennett, 2016: 338)

Given the nature and characteristics of social enterprise in developing countries, we must explore research trends on impact investing to ascertain impact-investing expectations from social enterprise. WEF (2014) and Wood (2012) observed that, despite high risks and expensive investment environment, institutional investors have demonstrated interest in impact investment across developing markets. The reasons for the upsurge of investors' interest in most emerging markets may be linked to progress made on impact investing in some developing countries. The OECD (2016) offers evidence of how non-state actors (SEs) are delivering social impact to the needs of the "bottom of the pyramid" in developing countries (Table 2.2, below).

Table 2.2 reveals the type of impact-investing organisations operating in Africa, the typical financial products they provide and the sectoral focus and names of the investors. Despite the presence of these investor types, Kickul and Lyons (2016) argue that success in impact investing in Africa depends mainly on the capability of social entrepreneurs to access diverse funding sources. IIs often target socially responsible organisations where they can deploy different types of investment instruments that range across grants, loan guarantees, quasi-equity, bonds and equity.

Global impact assets stood at USD 1.64 trillion as at 2022 and are expected to generate USD6.0 trillion by 2031 (GIIN, 2022). The market, which is still maturing and growing, recorded a significant psychological milestone despite the disruptions from COVID 19 (GIIN, 2022). Globally, 90% of high-net-worth individuals agree on the expediency of contributing to social impact across regions (Martin & Lohin, 2017). However, the premise for achieving the goal of impact investing rests on advancing research on social enterprise development across such different contexts. This study particularly seeks to understand how collaboration between SEs and IIs impacts on the competency of SEs in achieving the goal of social impact along with a financial return. According to the OECD (2016: 112), it is essential to "cultivate and develop new and innovative companies and business models, including ones adapted to the needs of the bottom-of-the-pyramid population". In the long run, this will generate more viable SEs to catalyse supportive resource flows from IIs.

Table 2.2 Investing in developing countries: examples from Africa

Organisation type	Type of financial product	Typical sector focus	Investors
Foundations	Equity, debt, grant, quasi-equity for seed stage and market building Typical deal size (direct investment): USD 50,000–1 million	Access to basic services (food, health, education), social/human development and market-creating initiatives (associations, accelerators, competitors, networks, etc.)	Gatsby Charitable Foundation Omidyar Network Shell Foundation Africa Enterprise Challenge Fund Bill & Melinda Gates Foundation
Dedicated early-stage impact funds	Equity, debt, quasi-equity inventory finance and grants for relatively early stages of enterprise Typical deal size: USD 50,000–2 million	Access to basic service (food, health, education, water, energy) and social/human development	Acumen Fund Tony Elumelu Foundation LGT Philanthropy Root Capital Gatsby Charitable Trust
Development finance institutions	Equity, debt, mezzanine quasi-equity and guarantees. Fund investment: USD 50–200 million Direct Investment: USD 5–50 million	Infrastructure project, agriculture, social—governmental and environmental initiatives	IFC CDC Group Swiss Investment Fund for Emerging Markets (Sifem) AFDB Dutch Development Agency French Development Agency
Institutional investors	Direct Investment: providing coinvestments through debt (banks) or invest in funds (pension and insurance funds) Deal size: USD 1–200 million	Project (agriculture, energy, water, transportation, telecom) and growth stage of financial services, retail, and real estate	South Africa Public Investment Corporation Teachers Insurance & Annuity Association (TIAA CREF) Equity Bank, Kenya JP Morgan

Source: OECD (2016)

2.12 Impact Investing Opportunities from Emerging Economies' Perspectives

Research reveals that only a few SEs have been able to attract impact investing in some emerging economies, while a large number of SEs are yet to understand how IIs engage with SEs in addressing intractable social problems (Bugg-Levine & Emerson, 2011; Diouf, 2015). Bugg-Levine et al. (2012) observe that a lack of funding opportunities became a major constraint faced by SEs, yet there has been a growing interest in those SEs believed to generate financial returns that will make them attractive to the right IIs; they further argue that

> … financial engineering can make it possible to channel investment from the financial markets to organisations known as social enterprises, which have traditionally looked to charity for much of their funding. With the right financial innovations, these enterprises can access a much deeper pool of capital than was previously available to them, allowing them to greatly extend their social reach. (p. 4)

According to Curatolo et al. (2017), impact investing happens when an investor provides a social enterprise or a for-profit with a business purpose with the capital required to develop or nurture that business. While impact-investing opportunities abound in regions of great need (OECD, 2019) and are capable of generating sustainable development greater than traditional aid and public-sector investment interventions (Santi & Sennett, 2016), several factors, perceived to be contextual in nature, have continued to hinder them from attracting the right IIs.

To be investment-ready, a social enterprise needs to have the capacity and the capability to seek and attract impact investment by demonstrating attributes that characterise an investment-ready firm (Curatolo et al., 2017). Several scholars have thus argued that better insight into how SEs collaborate with IIs to gain much-needed financing can be enriched when empirical data and knowledge from emerging economies that are currently insignificant are incorporated into developing a richer and more inclusive understanding of the field (Littlewood & Holt, 2015; Martin & Osberg, 2007; Rivera-Santos et al., 2015). This study contributes to setting the pace of harnessing the great opportunities for impact investing in emerging countries. At the third Financing for Development Conference held in Addis Ababa, Ethiopia, in 2015, African countries were encouraged to prioritise domestic capital formation, including mobilisation of external resources to address huge funding gaps (UN, 2015). The Agenda for Action called on businesses and investors to apply creativity and innovation in addressing sustainable development challenges, in particular the use of impact investing mechanisms and solutions (UNDP, 2015). It was widely noted that Africa potentially offers the most exciting and largely untapped impact-investing opportunities. Figure 2.3 provides a snapshot of impact-investing development globally, with the most considerable opportunities in the African continent.

Sub-Saharan Africa, as an emerging market, has been labelled the region with the highest impact-investing opportunities, with 34% of fund managers surveyed investing in the region (Drexler et al., 2013). A survey by GIIN (2016) identified

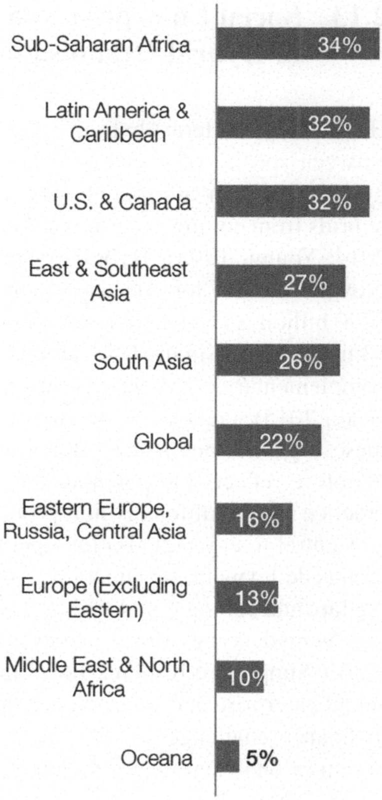

Fig. 2.3 Global survey of IIs' focus based on geographical location. (Source: Drexler et al. (2013, p. 14))

Nigeria, Ghana and other West African countries as potential destinations for impact investment. African countries alone have been reported to be worth US$60 billion in impact-investing deals (GIIN, 2015; UNDP, 2015). The key motivation behind impact investing in African economies has been summarised by Nadine Kettaneh, the Managing Partner of Willow Impact Investors: "impact investors support social entrepreneurs and their business aiming to illustrate concrete example of a financially sustainable and for-profit social enterprise" (Drexler et al., 2013: 3, 6). Despite the huge opportunities for impact investing, regulatory problems, corruption, infrastructure deficits and political instability are among the major factors that need to be overcome in order to harness the full potential of impact investing (Drexler et al., 2013; Intellecap, 2017; Ngoasong et al., 2015). Ironically, countries with the most significant barriers in these areas often offer the biggest opportunities for social, environmental and financial impact (Drexler et al., 2013). For example, Sule (2019: para.9) argued: "there are more impact investment funds than there is investable social enterprise in Nigeria". This shows there remains a lack of attractive SEs in Nigeria and other African countries, leading to a major setback in IIs' collaboration with SEs, and linked to lack of awareness or lack of commitment on the part of key stakeholders.

2.13 Social Enterprise and Impact Investing as Examples of Hybrid Organisations

Historically, the term "hybrid" is associated with biology and describes cross-overs between species of plants or animals (Jäger & Schröer, 2014). In social science, hybrid has been associated with post-colonial studies that characterise cultural hybrids from composition in non-Western or migration life-forms (Jäger & Schröer, 2014; Young, 1995). Hybrid organisations have emerged from the context of a growing market for social and environmentally conscious products to be worth \$290 billion, as well as a market for socially responsible investments with growth to \$3 trillion assets in the USA alone (Haigh et al., 2015). Popularity in the growth of complementary organisations seeking to meet growing market opportunities (Haigh et al., 2015), created by social, environmental and economic challenges, has led these organisations to be categorised as hybrid. The term "hybrid organisation" therefore reflects the potential for such enterprises to blend traditional for-profit practice with traditionally non-profit practices (Battilana, 2018; Haigh et al., 2015).

Central to any organisation operating as a hybrid is the duality of social impact alongside financial sustainability. Studies reveal that "creative integration of social welfare and commercial logics by balanced entrepreneurs may foster the emergence of new models and effort to catalyse supportive resource flows" (Wry & York, 2017: 455). "Supportive resource flow" in this context highlights inadequate capital for social enterprise and the wide perception that impact investing may offer a solution to finance challenges of SEs. In order to tap into this benefit, SEs need to gain organisational legitimacy to attract funding, particularly from IIs with blended motives. Note, however, that social entrepreneurs may hold different identities (for-profit or not-for-profit) that align with social welfare and commercial logic, and this shows legitimacy-seeking behaviour and explains how institutional logic contributes in the organisational form of social entrepreneurship (Wry & York, 2017). The next section examines terminologies associated with hybrid organisations, irrespective of operational field and organisational identity.

2.14 Blended Value Framework for Impact Investing and Social Enterprise

Blended value is the conventional wisdom and legal definition that clearly separate "doing well" from "doing good" (Bonini & Emerson, 2005). It is common to hear organisations say "we want to be seen to be "doing well" and "doing good"". This is the language that sets hybrid organisations apart from traditional non-profit organisations and purely commercial enterprises. A typical example of social impact can be likened to the provision of 170 million boxes of economically valuable cookies sales to Girls Scout versus the social impact of employing 1.4 million people by Walmart (Bonini & Emerson, 2005): Walmart employing 1.4 million people demonstrates social impact in employment creation, with a significant impact on the number of people removed from the list of job seekers. Blended value or dual motivation from the perspective of hybrid organisations also represents a corporate-level orientation that acknowledges optimum investment to create economic and social value for maximum return (Emerson, 2003).

Blended value is a term used to capture or measure the efficiency of hybrid organisations from pursuing social and economic outcomes. Blended value enables such organisations to capture efficiencies that may not be possible through the pursuit of purely commercial or purely social strategies (Bonini & Emerson, 2005). This study adopts the blended value framework of Kickul, Janssen-Selvadurai and Griffiths (2012) to demonstrate its implications for SEs and impact-investing firms pursuing a social mission side-by-side with economic interests. The blended value approach captures relevant pedagogical themes that distinguish a hybrid organisation from conventional business or traditional non-profit organisation.

2.15 Social Innovation and Opportunity Recognition

Just as impact investing has been conceived as the most innovative way to harness resources of the world's financial markets to address the world's intractable challenges (Clarkin & Cangioni, 2016), social enterprise is likewise understood as an activity characterised by innovation for creating something new rather than a replication of traditional approaches or processes (Austin et al., 2006; Tapsell & Woods, 2008, 2010). There is a connection between SE and II organisations rooted in innovation or the act of creating something new in deviation from existing practices. Collaboration between SEs and IIs becomes necessary since "it is rare to find complex, adaptive, social problems that do not require collaboration among key stakeholders from non-profit, public, and private sectors" (Kickul et al., 2012: 481). Tracey and Phillips (2007) note that SEs interact with a number of stakeholders that range across community, government, foundations and other entrepreneurs. These organisations constitute examples of IIs that collaborate and share resources with SEs for collective social impact. Social innovation between hybrid organisations shows that solutions needed to address difficult problems come through collective innovative contributions from diverse stakeholders and shareholders.

Likewise, opportunity recognition has been framed as "the match between unfulfilled market need and a solution that satisfies the need" (O'Connor & Rice, 2001: 96). An impact investor has been globally recognised as one who creates opportunities for engagement with private capital to address social problems. Such financing complements the traditional international flow of resources, such as aid, foreign direct investment (FDI) deployed to address market failures and institutional barriers (Grafström & Aasma, 2021; Majercakova & Kocisova, 2016). While IIs present innovative finance opportunities to deal with societal challenges, SEs focus on discovering opportunities, presented in the form of poverty, unemployment, inequality, climate and environment, where such resources can be deployed to address burgeoning societal issues. There is scholarly consensus that recognition of opportunity, or identification, is the fundamental element of the entrepreneurial process (Corner & Ho, 2010; Gaglio & Katz, 2001). Opportunity search by SEs and IIs involves a process of rigorous search in the marketplace and under-served segments, including customer needs, economic climate, and advances in technology (Kickul et al., 2012). After identifying unmet needs, organisations capitalise on the gaps and devise or introduce a new innovative product to address such imbalances. According to Kickul et al. (2012), strategic types of opportunity come through leveraging existing partnerships capable of creating collective impact on a defined social problem. Collaboration between SEs and IIs provides a good example of this type of opportunity.

2.16 Financial Sustainability and Business Models

Financial sustainability is the extent to which a hybrid enterprise or social venture can self-fund its activities over a long period of time (Kickul et al., 2012). Financial sustainability from the side of SEs lies in their ability to achieve financial sustainability to the point where they are able to give back equity to IIs. According to Yap (2018), social mission, financial sustainability and impact measurement are the three key characteristics of impact investing. Non-profit SEs often rely on donations, grants, volunteers and a variety of fund sources to start their ventures. Unfortunately, this type of resource keeps such enterprises seeking support indefinitely. These are reasons why hybrid SEs emerge to leverage on alternative sources of funding, such as impact investing other than aid, donations, etc., to achieve sustainability. As hybrid organisations, they must generate sufficient revenue while maintaining their social mission as a priority (Kickul et al., 2012). Studies show that hybrid organisations like SEs and IIs are likely to experience tension and mission drift due to incompatibility of goals, which may impact their financial sustainability (Santos et al., 2015). This study is also challenging that notion through the study of SEs and IIs with dyadic relations to demonstrate how they could establish partner fit to collaborate with minimal tension. Collaboration through alignment of compatible logics is believed to avert potential tension and conflict. It is not enough to argue that both SEs and IIs are hybrid organisations since there must also be a theoretical explanation for matching SEs and IIs whose specific approaches to solving social problems align. Understanding how social enterprise business models fit into investment goals of potential funders is one pathway for examining the compatibility of investors and investees.

According to Kickul et al. (2012), SEs utilise a variety of business models to fulfil their mission, with most contemporary examples coming from the USA and the UK. Studies reveal that SEs in developing countries have good examples of sustainable and scalable entrepreneurial efforts that characterise business models (Langman, 2005; Terjesen, 2007). Using Osterwalder and Pigneur's (2010: 14) definition, a business model "describes the rationale of how an organisation creates, deliver, and captures value". Business models from the perspective of hybrid social enterprise explain how a social idea can be monetised to generate sustainable revenue. It is the financial structure of the enterprise with embedded social impact. However, beyond the monetisation of an idea, it also entails the evolution and the exchange of value (Kickul et al., 2012). Exchange of value is critical in this study, since knowing the type of valuable resources exchanged between SEs and IIs has remained in contention, but it is a key determinant of power dynamic between these actors. The business model for SEs is understood from its function, characterised by the product and services being delivered to the environment (Grassl, 2012). The business model of SEs can also be determined from their mission orientation, based on the level of integration between not-profit social programmes and for-profit social business, and their proposed target markets (Alter, 2006). The business model of SEs can be derived from a micro typology that describes three types of mission (mission-centric, mission-related and unrelated to mission), three types of integration (embedded, integrated and external), and cuts across a not-for-profit and for-profit operation across five types of target market (Austin, 2000). Figure 2.4 illustrates the micro typology of SEs that IIs seek in order to establish partner fit, depending on the investors' level of appetite or intentions.

The three stages of integration in Fig. 2.4 are the distinguishing characteristics of SEs in existence, ranging from non-profit to for-profit-oriented businesses. The external stage exemplifies a relationship that is one-sided, such as charity donors to not-for-profit SEs. The integrated stage is one characterised by bilateral resources exchange and mutual learning. The embedded stage is characterised by a merger of two enterprise types, where social and financial mission are merged at the level of strategy and implementation, with high efficiency in blending social purpose with

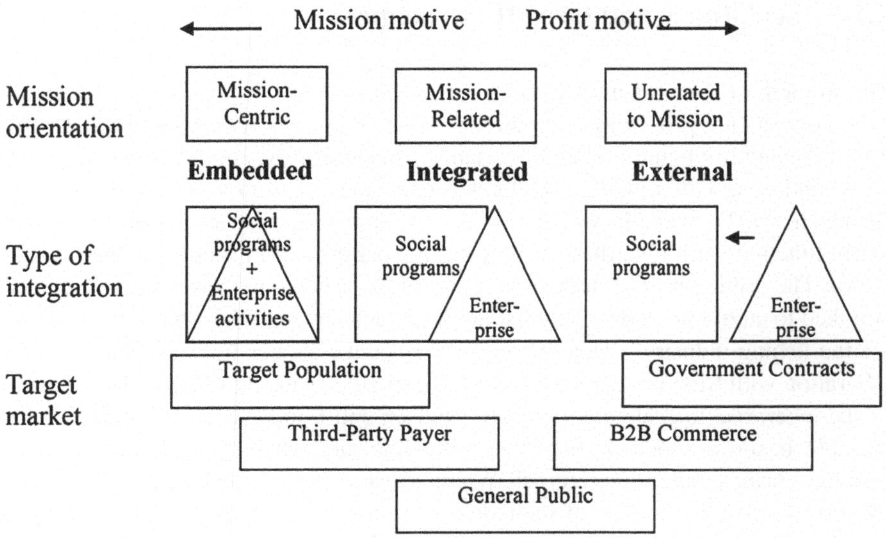

Fig. 2.4 Typology of social enterprises based on mission focus. (Source: Grassl (2012, p. 46))

business outcome (Grassl, 2012). Through the lens of this study, SEs at the external stage will not fit into IIs' mission, because they are unable to generate income and therefore are not sustainable. The embedded and integrated stage falls into the category of SEs with whom IIs seek to establish partner fit, because of the potential for mutual-benefit relationships.

A review of the business model for social enterprise in this section is meant to distinguish between the not-for-profit social enterprise model and the for-profit model or hybrid social enterprise found in current research. These models demonstrate four key elements of the type of action SEs perform in relation to what, how, why and where (Ahokangas, 2014). Some of the key attributes that IIs are keen to see in SEs' business models include advisory boards (the "who" behind the enterprise), management (human resource and technical capabilities), reporting system (financial records), potential income streams, and indicators for social impact, all of which determine the viability of the business model (Kickul et al., 2012).

In line with the focus of this study, recent empirical research has revealed three models of SEs: a social business model, a social-cooperative model, and an entrepreneurial non-profit model (Defourny et al., 2021). One gap identified in the current non-profit entrepreneurial model hinges on lack of sustainability due to inability to generate financial returns from its activities, whereas the social business model being examined here represents the ideal model of focus linked to its financial viability. It is a model deeply rooted in hybrid SMEs that are willing to generate blended value. This type of SE has been described by the founder of social business, Professor Yunus, as a sub-concepts within either profit-making or non-profit organisations (Yunus, 2009).

2.17 Scalability and Growth Strategies

The strength of business models lies in their ability to envisage and provide clarity as to how an enterprise may configure its value creation process (Nielsen & Lund, 2015). Scalability mainly related to financial sustainability, and it is defined as the speed and ease with which a social enterprise can expand in a given environment (Bradach, 2003). Scalability also refers to the ability of a business idea to consistently function well, regardless of how big the organisation becomes (Albert et al., 2006). The driving motive in the scalability of the social enterprise business model is linked to an old proverb: "we must not just teach a man to fish, but to revolutionize the fishing industry". This proverb describes the expectations of IIs from collaboration with SEs: provision of technical expertise is meant to build the capacity of the enterprise to scale continuously. Nielsen and Lund (2018: 66) state that "a scalable business model is one that is flexible and where the addition of new resources brings increasing returns". When investors provide technical support, it is natural to expect replication of such ideas on social enterprise scalability. Scaling a business idea is paramount for IIs, but it may be less important for some SEs whose deeper focus is on accomplishing social missions. This may imply possible tension, since SEs and IIs may disagree on divergent interests that conflict with the mission.

Despite the potential disagreement on scalability, it remains a critical component of a social enterprise business model. According to Nair and Blomquist (2019), successful exit from the "incubator" (early-stage social enterprise) can occur where there is a well-crafted scalable business model. Many early-stage enterprises fail because of a lack of well-thought-out scalable business models primarily rooted in mediocre ideas. Jabłoński (2016) provides examples of primary attributes of a scalable business model in Table 2.3. The idea behind scalability is beyond being sustainable; the business must be effective and efficient, describing how it will expand as application in conventional businesses. Sustainability can only be achieved through viable, effective and efficient scalable strategies.

Other attributes associated with scalable business models include quality of the product or services, innovation behind the product or service, environment acceptance of the product, safety of the product, trust, company image and brand awareness, customer relationship, competence, and social capital (Jabłoński, 2016).

Growth strategy is a clear path description of how the social enterprise will exit. An exit strategy is a term used to describe the method an equity investor uses to recoup or get returns on investment. If a social enterprise demonstrates a good exit plan, it shows the risk for investing in the enterprise is low. Growth strategy is absolutely determined by the investors' target. While some investors are comfortable with small organisations, others are keen to penetrate new markets and expand beyond local boundaries (Kickul et al., 2012). A clear example of growth strategy

Table 2.3 Attributes of scalable business models in social enterprises

L.P	Primary component of a sustainable business model	Scalability mechanisms used for a sustainable business model attribute
1.	Stakeholder network	Seeking synergy, symbiosis and symmetry between various stakeholders in the company
2.	Shareholders structure	Seeking the common goal and common values in the functioning shareholders structure
3.	Key resources	Seeking optimal configuration mechanisms based on own resources
4.	Key corporate governance factors	Seeking a coherent system for the exchange of information, data and knowledge in the process of mutual reporting and supervision
5.	Key corporate social responsibility factors	Seeking correlations between corporate social responsibility factors
6	Key value-based management factors	Seeking correlations between value-based management factors
7.	Key sustainability factors	Seeking correlations between sustainability factors
8.	Financial dividend	Applying the principle of sustainable dividends
9.	Social dividend	Applying the mechanisms creating social capital in conjunction with the expectations of the various groups of stakeholders

Source: Jabłoński (2016, p. 27)

from a social enterprise perspective can be likened to a social enterprise's interest in helping an under-served community access clean water, health or education. In contrast, others have a desire to eradicate poverty globally (Kickul et al., 2012). The point of intersection between scalability and growth hinges on understanding how rapid growth can be achieved without having limitations or obstruction in the road map. Evaluating organisational strategy and linking it to economic feasibility are paramount when designing a business model from the outset.

2.18 Social Impact and Financial Performance

At the heart of social entrepreneurship is the creation of value embedded in a social mission (Alter, 2006; Grimes et al., 2013; Kickul & Lyons, 2016). Every social enterprise should endeavour to demonstrate the effect its activities have on the community and the total well-being of individuals and families. A very good example of social impact enterprise is Work Integration Social Enterprise (WISEs), established through an NGO to create employment opportunity for disadvantaged groups (Ho & Chan, 2010). The enterprise creates opportunity for business training that generates income and improves well-being for its beneficiaries. The process of solving social problems creates beneficial outcomes that bring positive impact and change to achieve the desired impact (Singh, 2016). What is valuable to one may not be valuable to another, meaning it is subjective—it means different things to different people (British Council, 2016).

It has been challenging to determine or measure accurately social impact returns generated by an enterprise (Trelstad, 2008). However, Tuan (2008) has developed approaches for monetising forms of social impact drawn from methodology for cost benefit analysis. Knowing the monetary value of a social impact project is important for funding purposes. McKinsey & Company, in partnership with the Foundation Centre and New York University Stern School of Business, has produced Tools and Resources for Assessing Social Impact (TRASI), an interactive on-line data base software that provides resources and tools for measuring value creation (Kickul et al., 2012). Measuring value creation has become necessary, because it is key to social enterprise financial performance. Making social impact measurable and operational can be achieved through financially measurable indicators.

Financial performance practice is associated with SEs' ability to manage cash flows and understand how to optimally leverage resources within their possession to maximise social impact (Kickul et al., 2012). It is therefore essential for owners and operators of a social enterprise to acquire the basic managerial and financial accounting skills to be able to analyse and interpret key financial statements of the business for reporting purposes. The knowledge of financial measurement and reporting is crucial, because investors at every growth stage of the enterprise will require to know the financial performance of the enterprise: "Financial performance and social impact are of utmost importance to those who fund social ventures (e.g., impact investors)" (Kickul et al., 2012: 485). Hynes (2009) also observes that social value and financial performance of SEs are not mutually exclusive, as they both form the catalyst that pertains to their growth strategies. An important term that connects social impact and financial performance is exchange value. An "exchange value" is the total monetary value a customer is prepared to pay for a particular product because of the usefulness of such a product (Singh, 2016). An exchange value is said to be realised when the product is sold. From the context of social enterprise relations with IIs, exchange value between them will be the expected benefits from the collaboration to each partner (Di Domenico et al., 2009). These benefits can be both social impact and financial outcomes.

2.19 Potential Tension in Collaborations Between SEs and IIs

The unifying attribute between SEs and IIs stems from their hybrid nature, which distinguishes them from traditional not-for-profit and private commercial entities. The two organisations have gained strength from the perceived tensions, which sets them apart from purely commercial and aid-based grants organisations (Jones, 2019). A sustainable relationship between SEs and IIs is believed to be determined differently across organisations, depending on their mission and structure of operation (Miller & Wesley, 2010; Wood & Hagerman, 2010). Tensions between SE and II organisations can arise when there is a mismatch of interests between collaborating parties regarding the social or environmental and economic expectations of the intended relationship. Managing these tensions comes with challenges under various circumstances, so that sometimes the most viable option can be an exit from such a relationship (Janowicz-Panjaitan & Krishnan, 2009). Despite the potential for disagreement, some scholars posit they can combine the elements of differences in ways that do not normally exist or conform to orthodox logic of neo-institutional theory (Battilana et al., 2017). In Table 2.4, Jones (2019) sets out likely areas where SEs and IIs could experience tension as they pursue their social and economic goals. This study focuses on four areas of tension relating to SEs' and IIs' pre-investment strategies for inter-organisational alignment (Agrawal & Hockerts, 2019a).

The impact of the inter-organisational relationship between SEs and IIs is greatly moderated by the integration of social mission into their business objectives (Agrawal & Hockerts, 2019a). Establishing partner fit with organisations with

Table 2.4 Potential areas of tension between SEs and IIs

S/N	Category	Tension
1.	Impact outcomes	Mission vs. business
2.	Business outcomes	Sustainability vs. scalability
3.	Resource acquisition	Outcome vs. process
4.	Growth	Hockey-stick curve vs. nonlinear

Source: Adopted and modified from Jones (2019: 17)

conflicting social missions and business objectives, even after due diligence, can result in failed collaboration. The key conflict may arise when social metrics are not well integrated into the existing business practice or established social and economic expectations (Jones, 2019). Establishing partner fit between SEs and IIs can be challenging due to the difficulties in assessing accurately the aspirations and goals of intending partners (Santos, 2012), but with due diligence such obstacles can be minimised.

Another potential area of tension is the business outcome in relation to sustainability and scalability. IIs with commercial motives place high value on profitability as well as scalability of the social enterprise operational model. Finding a social enterprise that balances these motives in their social impact mission is key to a successful inter-organisational relationship. Tension can arise between SEs and IIs when IIs seeking collaboration with SEs do not provide a clear threshold at which financial returns can be considered adequate as a maximum or minimum return on investment (Jones, 2019). This situation makes it difficult for SEs to manage their social mission for sustainability side-by-side with impact-investing goals for scalability.

Studies reveal that investment in social enterprise is a form of resource acquisition that impact investing equates to an outcome in itself, i.e. measuring received funding as successful investment (Jones, 2019). This belief influences IIs or entrepreneurs to see the process for recouping capital as mandatory (Clarkin & Cangioni, 2016). While this belief is important for instilling business-mindedness in SEs, such a mentality can also be detrimental if SEs focus on acquiring the resources regardless of the process, structure and legitimacy of the source (Navis & Glynn, 2011). Instead of rejecting detrimental partnership with such investors, SEs in desperate need of resources may accept such offers due to probable scarcity of finance.

Some proponents of blended financing posit that sources and structure of finance for SEs may vary depending on the growth stage of the enterprise (Jones, 2019). An average impact investor operates a "hockey stick" curve, where they expect sudden growth after initial investment, yet there are other investors who provide "patient capital", targeting early-stage SEs (Deeg & Hardie, 2016). Patient capital is a long-term investment in equity or debt whose providers target receiving benefits in the future, irrespective of the firm's adverse short-term challenges (Deeg & Hardie, 2016). Tension will arise if SEs establish partner fit with IIs who map commercial enterprise growth stages wrongly with impact growth strategy (Deiglmeier & Greco, 2018): for example, when growth-stage IIs establish partner fit with early-stage SEs focusing on sustainability of social impact as against scalability of impact. The context where SEs operate, particularly in emerging countries, is full of uncertainties, such as political instability, infrastructure barriers and economic instability (Jones, 2019). These challenges demand that investors in early-stage SEs wait a little longer, as against high expectation for immediate growth after each and every subsequent investment.

The next sections will demonstrate how the application of institutional logics and social exchange theories will guide collaboration between SEs and IIs to achieve compatible and complementary collaboration.

2.20 Theories of Collaboration Between SEs and IIs

The growing search for knowledge about how IIs engage with their investee SE across contexts has remained a burgeoning question in the field of social entrepreneurship research (Glänzel & Scheuerle, 2016; Hart, 2016; Mogapi et al., 2019; Power et al., 2012; Gupta et al., 2020). Some scholars have started exploring organisation-level and country-specific factors that could influence inter-organisational alignment between IIs and their investee SEs (Agrawal & Hockerts, 2019a; Mogapi et al., 2019). An empirical study by Mogapi et al. (2019) reveals that organisational values aligned around engagement strategy, leadership and sector identification constitute an important guide to the practice of impact. It is believed the studies of institutional entrepreneurs (SEs and IIs), representing men and women who intentionally or unintentionally create new forms of organisations as a way of achieving their interests or the interests of groups they represent (Greenwood et al., 2017), will shed light on how competing interests in hybrid organisations can be aligned to achieve dual motives with minimal tension.

2.21 Integrating Institutional Logics and Social Exchange Theories

This study draws insight from the institutional logics frame and social exchange theory (Thornton & Ocasio, 2008; Van de Ven, 1992; Van de Ven & Poole, 1995) to explore themes, concepts or variables that explain the process through which SEs and IIs collaborate to establish partner fit. Some scholars note that limited knowledge exists on how SEs and IIs collaborate to address social and economic problems across national contexts (Defourny & Nyssens, 2010; Engelmark et al., 2015; Jamali et al., 2016; Kerlin, 2012). Despite the view that revealing how SEs and IIs establish partner fit will require empirical examples, research has not yet embraced the theoretical implication of collaboration between parties in dyadic relationship (Liden et al., 2016). Linked to this is a lack of conceptual tools to operationalise mutuality between parties in dyad. To operationalise mutuality, scholars must design studies that examine two or more parties collaborating or depending on each other to accomplish set goals or mission statements (Kiggundu, 1981; Wageman & Turner, 1999; Tough et al., 2022). This underpins why the current research draws upon empirical data from SEs and IIs with dyadic relations in Nigeria as case examples to demonstrate how mutuality can be operationalised. Integrating institutional logics and social exchange theories will enable the study to demonstrate how organisational compatibility and resource complementarity, respectively, guide the establishment of partner fit between SEs and IIs in Nigeria.

The institutional logics framework has been used consistently by scholars to gain insight into behaviours across hybrid organisations (Agrawal & Hockerts, 2019a). Clark's empirical study (2015: 5) reveals "the commercial competencies of social enterprises were shown to enhance their exchange value, balance out power dynamics between partners, and contribute to the development of relationships that generated shared value". This research extends that line of study by integrating the social exchange framework with institutional logic to demonstrate the type of resources exchanged between SEs and IIs to determine the level of power dynamics between them.

2.22 Institutional Logics Theory: Hybrid Inter-Organisational Relationships

Scholars have observed that resource acquisition needs of SEs have become a critical component in their organisational strategy (Shane & Venkataraman, 2000; Williams et al., 2017; Zhao & Lounsbury, 2016). The need for resources has further introduced a compelling demand for SEs to engage in cross-sector partnerships with different organisations in order to access both tangible and intangible resources (Dentoni et al., 2016; Voltan & De Fuentes, 2016). For example, the current study examines how SEs leverage on IIs' financing and other related support to address difficult societal problems. Yet this comes with some requirement for SEs to set up as two separate legal entities, for-profit and not-for-profit, pursuing commercial and social missions, respectively (Bromberger, 2011, 2013). Alternatively, some adopt a hybrid integrated legal form with double or triple bottom line motives (Battiliana et al., 2012; Hoffman et al., 2012), combining social welfare and commercial logics to overcome resource acquisition barriers (Voltan & De Fuentes, 2016; Wry & York, 2017). The great concern for SEs is pursuing different goals with diverse actors operating different logics and principles, which often makes collaboration prone to tensions and conflict of interest (Purdy & Gray, 2009; Reay & Hinings, 2009), unless missions are aligned and established in trust (Agrawal & Hockerts, 2019a; Dentoni et al., 2016). Approaches to understanding the organisational perspective of dual social and economic interests between SEs and IIs have been explored by scholars as competing institutional logics in hybrid organisations (Battilana & Dorado, 2010; Pache & Santos, 2013; Reay & Hinings, 2009). This interest is shaped through intra- and inter-organisational relationships well grounded in the institutional logics literature (Au et al., 2016; Damayanthi & Gooneratne, 2017; Greenwood et al., 2010; Thornton & Ocasio, 2008; Zeyen & Beckmann, 2011).

Institutional logics, in a broad sense, focuses on how conflicting or competing societal values and belief systems shape individuals and organisational actors (Thornton, 2015; Thornton & Ocasio, 2008). The term "institutional logics" was first introduced by Friedland and Alford (1991) to describe contradictory practices and beliefs inherent in modern institutions across Western societies. Thornton and Ocasio (2008: 101) built on the early development of the concept by Jackall (1988) and Friedland and Alford to define institutional logics as "the socially constructed, historical patterns of material practices, assumptions, values, beliefs, and rules by which individuals produce and reproduce their material subsistence, organise time and space, and provide meaning to their social reality". Competing logics occur when dominant logic in a field is challenged by new logics from emerging actors in a similar field. For example, the conventional business and state failure to address humanity's difficult social problems is being challenged by institutional entrepreneurs (Battilana et al., 2009; Greenwood & Suddaby, 2006; Mair & Marti, 2009), exemplified in the activities of SEs and IIs through the idea of "doing well by doing good" (Henry, 2015). Impact investing scholarship demonstrates that social value creation alongside income generation are competing activities (Agrawal & Hockerts, 2019b), and favouring financial returns over social value creation leads to mission drift (Ebrahim et al., 2014) and can bring about loss of legitimacy (Lehner & Nicholls, 2014).

By definition, institutional logics connect agency action and cognition with socially constructed systems, referred to as institutionalised practice and rules. What becomes acceptable practice as social welfare and commercial logic results from disruptive agency action (SEs and IIs). When their embedded action gets recognition across societies, it becomes institutionalised belief and practice. The pursuit of conflicting logics of social welfare and commercial interest by SEs and IIs highlights a good example of some of the contradictory practices across societies today (Friedland & Alford, 1991; Seo & Creed, 2002). From previous studies, social logic and commercial logic appear the two most common types of competing logics used to analyse hybrid inter-organisational relations (Pache & Santos, 2010, 2013; Saz-Carranza & Longo, 2012). Based on research by Agrawal and Hockerts (2019a), there are differences in the levels of institutional logics acting on impact investing and social enterprise organisations (see Table 2.5).

Based on the level of difference across commercial and social logics shown in Table 2.5, Agrawal and Hockerts argue that organisations with hybrid goals often experience tensions when actors engage in decisions that motivate their commitment to a specific institutional logic. Institutional logic refers to such tension as competing logics that exist when a judgement concerning the primary interest of social or environmental impact by investors is overly influenced by the secondary interest for financial gain and vice versa. Studies reveal that hybrid organisations pursuing competing interests to meet social or environmental and commercial goals often face severe difficulties in balancing the tensions created at the strategic level of the organisation (Bruneel et al., 2016; Davies & Chambers, 2018; Jay, 2013). It is not unlikely that the goal to achieve these multiple dimensions of sustainability—social, environmental and economic, also called the "triple bottom line"—may generate tensions distinctly in SEs and IIs at inter-organisational leadership level (Ozanne et al., 2016; Smith et al., 2013).

Despite competing interests, the institutional logics perspective links to institutions and action to highlight tendencies where new logics are created to change, dissolve or transform existing practices (Voltan & De Fuentes, 2016). While it is notable that inefficient organisational practices may have existed, due to seemingly unproductive strategy that unduly relies on traditions and norms of well-established relationships (Suchman, 1995), there are tendencies for organisations to gain

Table 2.5 Institutional logics of impact investing and social enterprise

Levels of Differences/ institutional logics	Commercial logic	Social logic
Ownership	Group/individual owns the enterprise through investment or equity (Pache & Santos, 2013)	Group/individual protects and spreads the social mission (Pache & Santos, 2013)
Sources of legitimacy	Return on investment, performance, effectiveness, efficiency (Nicholls, 2010)	Hero entrepreneur, beneficiaries, social change, disruptive change (Zahra et al., 2009)
Mission	Efficient allocation of resources; earned income while serving the society (Ruebottom, 2013)	Socially relevant and innovative solutions to serve the society (Zahra et al., 2009)
Central values	Self-interest, consumer rather than the beneficiary, earned income, growth (Tracy & Jarvis, 2007)	Social value creation, equally, social justice (Zahra et al., 2009)
Model of governance	Governance towards defined objectives and performance, linear and rational (Ruebotton, 2013)	A democratic form of governance, high importance on the interest of beneficiaries (Ruebotton, 2013)
Logic behind decision	Profit maximisation and fulfilling fiduciary duty (Battilana & Dorado, 2010)	Social value creation, welfare (Battilana & Dorado, 2010)

Source: Agrawal and Hockerts (2019a, p. 3)

legitimacy as a result of isomorphic and mimetic cultural practices (Meyer & Rowan, 1977; Powell & DiMaggio, 2012). This explains why "institutional theory has often been criticized largely as being used to explain both the persistence and homogeneity of phenomena" (Dacin et al., 2002: 45). Diverging from continuing practices and norms of institutions, social innovators such as SEs and IIs now seek new ideas that address social and economic goals (Mulgan et al., 2007), which they achieve through a deliberate movement from one dominant logic to another that support their cause to initiate institutional change (Lounsbury, 2002; Scott et al., 2000; Suddaby & Greenwood, 2005). However, Martin and Osberg (2015) observe that they often face challenges from devising a means to navigate persistent norms in order to balance related logics that aim to distort existing equilibria. Mogapi et al. (2019) also argue that they indeed demonstrate their hybrid nature by countering orthodox logics and expectations of the neo-institutional field. This underlies the premise for integrating social exchange theory with institutional logics, since it will provide an alternative avenue to reinforce social interaction to challenge, combine or create organisational identities and practice integral to the institutional field (Pirkey, 2016).

2.23 Social Exchange Theory and Inter-Organisational Collaboration

As earlier established, collaboration between social enterprise and impact investing is an inter-organisational phenomenon, since it takes place between independent organisations (Lawrence et al., 2002; Phillips et al., 2000). Social exchange theory is one of the streams of research that focuses on the rationale behind the formation of relationships (Nicholls & Huybrechts, 2016), linked to the importance of aligning shared values and the role of trust between exchange partners for managing power imbalances (Amoako, 2019; Bierly III & Gallagher, 2007; McEvily et al., 2017; Nicholls & Huybrechts, 2016). Dominant research in these areas focuses on economic analyses between buyers and sellers' dyadic relationship. The interest in inter-organisational collaboration arises from the search for a sustainable process of collaboration between SEs and IIs linked to their role in mainstreaming sustainable development across regions. This interest is also anchored in institutional norms, practices, structures and processes guiding relationships between collaborating partners. The norms, in this case, relate to inter-organisational relationships not driven by buyer-supplier arrangements (Jap, 1999; Phillips et al., 2000), although that is important, but primarily driven by mutual commitment to social trust that promotes the sharing of resources to achieve collective goals (Andresen et al., 2014; Carli & Nilsson, 2015). From this perspective, collaboration is perceived as a value system which aligns with the thinking of McGregor (1989) and Sarason (1972) as a relational system that enables individuals in a group to share mutual aspirations with a conscious motive to work together. However, in order to maintain a stable relationship between actors, proponents of social exchange theory posit that trust is essential (Blau, 1964; Cropanzano et al., 2017).

Social exchange theory (SET), as a well-established discipline in social sciences (Blau, 2017; Ekeh, 1974; Emerson, 1976; Homans, 1958; Molm, 2006), is currently receiving renewed attention in management studies (Cropanzano et al., 2017; Cropanzano & Mitchell, 2005; Muthusamy & White, 2005). The theory developed distinctively within organisational studies and social psychology (Cropanzano & Mitchell, 2005). Traditionally the theory views interpersonal interactions from an exchange perspective, involving social cost and benefits traded in relationships, and governed by normative rules and agreements (Di Domenico et al., 2009). The most notable principles of SET have applied to employee motivation (Podsakoff et al., 2000) and intra-organisational relationships occurring between top-level managers and subordinates (Kim & Organ, 1982).

Several studies use SET for its features and the application to individual relationships. This study aligns with previous study by Di Domenico et al. (2009) to extend the application of SET beyond the individual level by also applying it to exchanges between organisations; it further develops SET application to exchange at the organisational level by moving to knowledge of exchange between hybrid organisations.

Focusing on the hybrid inter-organisational relationship between SEs and IIs, the study adopts the definition of collaboration by Miles et al. (2006: 2) as "a process where two or more parties work closely with each other to achieve mutually beneficial outcomes". This definition focuses on a problem-solving strategy driven by collective cooperation. Several scholars perceive inter-organisational collaboration and wide-ranging forms of partnership between SEs and other stakeholders as sustainable practice in social entrepreneurship and social innovation (de Bruin et al., 2017; Shaw & de Bruin, 2013). This explains why organisational scholars are becoming interested in inter-organisational collaboration (Di Domenico et al., 2009; Ryan & O'Malley, 2006). However, scholars who apply SET in explaining alliance partner selection argue that trust is strategic and expedient for establishing partner fit (Bierly III & Gallagher, 2007; Thomas & Skinner, 2010). As important as access to resources is to strategic alliance between organisations, Bierly III and Gallagher (2007) note that relying on trust is critical. But at the same time individual- or firm-level trust can be problematic. Trust has been defined as the "willingness to rely on an exchange partner in whom one has confidence" (Moorman et al., 1993: 82). Trust is an essential core attribute in potential or ongoing interfirm collaborative relationships. The reason is that an organisation with a reputation for being trustworthy can gain competitive advantage, capable of facilitating openness by partners in a future alliance (Bierly III & Gallagher, 2007). Studies on interfirm supply chain relationships have shown that the power of a collaborative supply chain relationship is strongly dependent on partners' level of trust in each other (Thomas & Skinner, 2010). Studies also report how success or failure in an interfirm collaboration can be impacted by two levels of trust—total trust and asymmetrical trust (Thomas & Skinner, 2010).

The conceptualisation of trust within a dyadic relationship has been termed problematic, because it does not account for both sides in a relationship, i.e. it is not ascertained from a dyadic measure of trust level between dyadic partners (Thomas & Skinner, 2010). In other words, the level of trust between dyadic collaborating partners may not be at the same level. Some scholars likewise believe trust compatibility between collaborating partners is essential for a deeper understanding of power dynamics within mutual relationships (Tomlinson et al., 2009). To avoid potential problems that arise from attributing individual construct of trust in a dyadic unit of analysis, Mentzer and Flint (1997) suggest the use of specific and accurate terminology that describes dyadic trust. A new term is required to describe dyadic trust, because inter-organisational collaboration does not depend on, for example, a trusting supplier or a trusting buyer alone—meaning one party cannot alone collaborate by itself, rather it requires collaborative behaviours between a trusting supplier and a trusting buyer.

Based on this, Thomas and Skinner (2010) propose a new term, total trust, comprising a combination of suppliers' and buyers' trust attributes as the appropriate term for trust in dyadic relationships. Total trust therefore is trust that can be termed mutual trust. Mutual trust occurs when two parties trust one another at a roughly equivalent level, and where such level of trust can be jointly perceived by the parties involved (Deutsch, 1958; Zucker, 1987). As mutuality is key to successful dyadic relationships, mutual trust between dyadic partners (Tomlinson et al., 2009), like

SEs and IIs, is paramount to unlock the strength for tension-free collaboration across key areas of interest.

While total or mutual trust between dyadic partners connotes roughly equivalent levels of trust, the tendency for a mismatch in trust level between dyadic partners is referred to as trust asymmetry (Thomas & Skinner, 2010). SET calls the imbalance in the benefits gained from dyadic relationship "exchange asymmetry" (Tanskanen, 2015); asymmetry means "one party in the relationship benefits more than the other" (p. 578). An example of asymmetrical exchange can occur in a situation where a supplier has more trust in an exchange than a buyer has or vice versa (Thomas & Skinner, 2010). Likewise, between collaborating SEs and IIs, one party may have more trust than the other. Asymmetrical trust is essential in a dyadic relationship, because mutual or total trust does not capture or describe the behaviours of collaborating parties in dyad, since dyadic partners' trust level may vary. Thus not all pre-investment processes translate to the establishment of partner fit due to divergence between low and high levels of trust—or trust asymmetry. The presence of asymmetrical trust in exchange relationships between dyadic partners highlights the possibility of weakening the emergence of mutual or total trust in collaborative behaviours in inter-organisational relationships.

Just as trust influences entrepreneurial relationships in mainstream business (Welter, 2012), requiring a trustworthy supplier and a trustworthy buyer, in the same manner the role of trust in hybrid social entrepreneurship relationships cannot be underestimated. Value creation, a key attribute of collaboration in hybrid organisations, viewed as social exchange, and characterised by non-contractual engagement in some situations, emphasises reciprocity that relies mostly on trust (Blau, 2017; Leach, 1961). The interest of social exchange and institutional theorists in exploring conflicting logics and power asymmetry from inter-organisational perspectives holds promising outcomes for sustainable collaboration between hybrid organisations.

2.24 Matching Theory of Collaboration: Compatibility and Complementarity

The theoretical model of this study is built on the premise that organisations are motivated to engage in inter-organisational relationships aiming to create value higher than what organisations can achieve individually (van Fenema & Loebbecke, 2014). Several studies have applied the matching theory of alliance between organisations from the concept of compatibility and complementarity to determine success in alliance formation (Mitsuhashi & Greve, 2009), governance of business relationships involving resources (Chi & Levitas, 2007; Lu et al., 2016; Mindruta et al., 2016) and formation of entrepreneurs' intentions and initiation of economic exchange (Vissa, 2011). These studies in their unique style have showcased how two organisations can be matched based on attributes linked to their compatibility and complementarity. This study extends such a line of research by combining institutional logic and social exchange theories to demonstrate inter-organisational pre-investment collaboration processes, based on compatible logics and complementarity of resource type between SEs and IIs with dyadic relation in Nigeria. This line of thinking aligns with the researcher's interest in critically analysing impact investing inter-organisational relationships with SEs in order to determine how they align social and economic interests to establish partner fit. This interest stems from the notion that "actors who support dissimilar institutional models can overcome conflict and move toward mutually beneficial coexistence" (Mair & Hehenberger, 2014: 1174).

Previous studies on inter-organisational collaboration have focused on the dynamics of managing co-operative relationships between organisations that may pursue competing logics (Dyer & Singh, 1998; Dyer et al., 2018; Powell et al., 1996). Reay and Hinings (2009) argue that competing logics can co-exist across organisations, while rivalry between logics can be well managed by developing collaborative relationships between actors. This background literature is confirmatory of the current realities that inter-organisational collaboration remains built around conflicting interests (Lumineau et al., 2015). However, the approach to collaboration in this study focuses on a "collective" strategy around socio-political and economic arrangements involving inter-organisational cooperation rather than competition (Di Domenico et al., 2009; Phillips et al., 2000). The study is built on the premise that distinct social and commercial logic between SEs and IIs can be aligned in a fashion that allows them to explore inter-organisational resources that allows them to achieve collective interests.

There is a range of theories that provides valuable insights into the concept of inter-organisational collaboration besides social exchange and institutional logic theories. For example, network theorists focus on embedded relations which enable and constrain organisational action governed by relational strategy, rather than contractual mechanisms (Bonnell & Gold, 2015; Knoke, 2018). Resource-based theorists also frame collaboration from the perspective of competitive advantage, which requires firms to re-conceptualise relationships with their competitors to build capability through resource sharing (Doz et al., 1989; Huxham & Vangen, 2013). Most non-profit organisations leverage from this approach to collaboration in advancing their social mission and draw from the resource-dependence concept of inter-organisational relations where power dominance and control remain inevitable (Pfeffer & Salancik, 2003). Institutional theorists, however, view collaboration from the perspective of its potential to transform institutional structures (Lawrence et al., 2002): for example, how societal institutional arrangements affect the emergence of hybrid SEs will be an interesting area to examine in order to ascertain how SEs and IIs collaborate. An interesting question institutional theorists pose for inter-organisational collaboration centres on how organisational structures that seek to balance differentiation and integration can support competing logics for social or environmental and economic value (Smith et al., 2013; Tracey et al., 2011).

This literature thus holds great potential to inform a robust insight into inter-organisational collaboration scholarship. However, approaches to collaboration require inter-disciplinary literature support to gain broader insights from other scholarship. In particular, since this research focuses on establishing partner fit through inter-organisational collaboration between SEs and IIs with dyadic relations, the study draws on the concept of "collaborative entrepreneurship" to provide better insights into how potential tensions from competing logics of social welfare and commercial logic between actors can be resolved to establish sustainable partnerships. The approach of this research is centred on resource scarcity that engenders cooperation for the emergence of strategic mutual cooperation between organisations (Sakarya et al., 2012).

The approach in this study also aims to extend knowledge on both macro- and micro-level logics that create the basis for organisational sense-making in specific societal domains (Vaskelainen & Münzel, 2018). The macro-level logics relate to socio-cultural, political and economic factors that enable or constrain collaboration between actors. Micro-level logics likewise relate to organisational-level factors that determine trust levels between actors. The theoretical lens specifically examines how SEs and IIs accommodate competing interests of social and economic value to establish partner fit for collective interest. According to Montgomery et al. (2012: 377), organisational literature recognises the importance of harnessing vital resources through collective action and that "resource collaboration between diverse actors is paramount in challenging and changing institutional norms and values". By pursuing a dual focus on financial returns and impact, impact investing can be viewed as a complex institution where incompatible logics are incorporated to achieve a cause, despite potential tensions (Greenwood et al., 2011).

Under the conceptual model in Fig. 2.5, the study illustrates how collaboration between SEs and IIs can be achieved amidst enabling or disenabling macro- and micro-institutional complexities. The model draws insight from the concept of partner fit to examine how IIs ascertain or select the right SEs to collaborate with, termed partner fit (Bierly III & Gallagher, 2007; Thorgren et al., 2012). Finding the right partner, which begins with a pre-investment process, is necessary, because, however good the intentions of potential partners, if they cannot establish a relationship with partners with a similar business model that combines social and economic interests, collaboration may be impossible or ineffective (Ormiston et al., 2015). Thorgren et al. (2012) posit that partner fit is a requirement to unleash the potential synergies for collaborative entrepreneurship and that partner fit in relation to complementarity and compatibility can broaden knowledge on why organisations are motivated to collaborate. It is thus argued that, as SEs and IIs focus on creating social and economic impact, their compatibility in organisational mission, culture and practice in relation to complementarity of tangible and intangible resources is vital for a successful collaboration. Tangible resources comprise physical and quantitative resources available to organisations, e.g. cash, merchandise, marketable securities (as current resources), and office furniture, buildings and machinery (as fixed resources). Intangible resources include non-monetary resources with no physical substance, e.g. patent rights, intellectual property, shared values, trademarks and beliefs (Jawed & Siddiqui, 2019; Kamasak, 2017). Scholars (Yan & Gray, 2001; Zhang, 2017) affirm that capital and non-capital resources, which

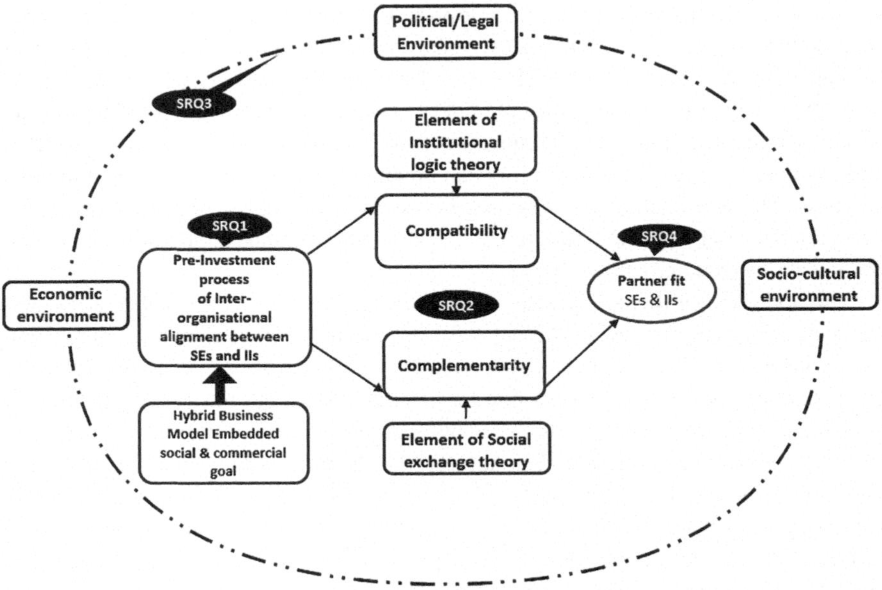

Fig. 2.5 Conceptual model of collaboration process between SEs and IIs. (Adapted and modified from Agrawal and Hockerts (2019a, p. 14))

"…range from financial resources to knowledge and reputation" (Sakarya et al., 2012: 1712), are critical success factors in any circumstances.

Compatibility refers to the resemblance between partners' organisational culture, management and operating style (Sarkar et al., 2001). Institutional scholars observe that motivated institutional entrepreneurs like SEs and IIs can build bridges by aligning or accommodating competing interests (Micelotta et al., 2017), which gives them the advantage for disrupting dominant logics to create, modify or transform society (DiMaggio, 1988; Greenwood & Suddaby, 2006; Hampel et al., 2017; Mair & Marti, 2009). It is thus argued that SEs and IIs can achieve their collective goals only by accommodating social and economic value propositions as part of their organisational strategy. This is the more so since cognitive effects from beliefs, behaviours, practices and attitudes of organisational actors are shaped by the macro environment they are embedded in (Sakarya et al., 2012), and they will likely align with compatible practices. For example, SEs with long-term experience in CSR (corporate social responsibility) practice can gain acceptance by IIs because of long-term reputation in delivering social impact, provided that their business model is also financially viable.

Similarly, complementarity occurs when partners leverage resources and complementary skills to jointly create additional value between them (Hamel, 1991; Hamel & Prahalad, 1993). A successful collaboration between SEs and IIs can only occur when both partners exchange different but valuable capabilities and resources. According to social business, an alliance can serve as a vehicle for innovative leveraging of resources and core competency exchange to create joint value between partners (Austin, 2000; Sakarya et al., 2012). In this connection, SEs may bring an innovative business model as a core competence which can be exchanged with financial investment from IIs. Social entrepreneurship literature has also acknowledged the imperative for "lone actors to pursue strategic partners that fill both such voids" (Montgomery et al., 2012: 377) and either "compensate for weakness" or "act as complementors" (VanSandt et al., 2009: 423). Child and Faulkner (1998) also argue that such types of alliance can provide strategic benefits, because organisations lacking resources or innovative ideas can connect to another with complementary resources.

To gain insight into how the SEs and IIs establish partner fit to collaborate in Nigeria, the present study asks the question: *In the process of collaboration, how do the SEs and IIs establish partner fit in pursuit of their social and economic interests in Nigeria?* Since the relationship between SEs and IIs is framed from the perspective of inter-organisational strategy akin to the acquisition of critical resources (Hallen & Eisenhardt, 2012; Navis & Glynn, 2010, 2011) between parties seeking and negotiating to maintain sustainable relationships (Jones, 2020), the study adopts the lens of social exchange theory to ascertain what micro-level factors influence how SEs and IIs collaborate in Nigeria. In particular, we are keen to explore how social dimensions of trust and mutual commitment influence the establishment of partner fit between SEs and IIs pursuing social and economic interests in Nigeria (Emerson, 1976; Homans, 1958; Prashant & Harbir, 2009). According to Liden et al. (2016: 155), "the term relationship is inherent in the dyadic relationship", and "the concept of mutuality seems critical for an accurate understanding of dyadic relationships".

Shared understanding between parties in dyadic relationship is a key component of social networks linked to the works of Blau (1964), Homans (1958), Emerson (1976) and Heider (2013). These proponents of social exchange theory thus posit that every social interaction has benefits that can be derived by the parties involved, and that, for a relationship to generate mutual benefits, trust, mutual commitment and reciprocities, they are inevitable (Blau, 2017; de Jesus et al., 2017). Trust in the context of this study is conceived as social capital that enables collaboration for mutual benefit between parties with compatible organisational logics interested in gaining complementary advantage. Social capital from the perspective of the OECD has a link to shared values and understanding between people in society, it enables groups of community to trust one another towards a common outcome (Menzies et al., 2020).

In search of organisation-level factors that could influence the relationship between investors and entrepreneurs (Agrawal & Hockerts, 2019b), the study asked the second sub-question: *At the micro-organisational level, what factors influence collaboration and partner selection between SEs and IIs in Nigeria?* Interestingly, institutional theorists (DiMaggio, 1988; Dacin et al., 2002) have also posited that dyadic relationships between organisations can be influenced by the relations they have with their distinct and unique macro environment. Notable findings have also revealed that macro-institutional factors can act either as support for or barriers to investment readiness of SEs (Davies et al., 2019; Glänzel & Scheuerle, 2016; Urban & Kujinga, 2017). This study aligns with Peattie and Morley's (2008: 94) assertion that "environmental context in terms of the political, economic, socio-cultural, and technological trends influence social enterprise and entrepreneurship". Indeed, the social, political and economic variables create a social entrepreneurial context (Bird, 1988; Shapero & Sokol, 1982). Our study seeks to identify the key factors in the context of Nigeria and their influence on how SEs and IIs establish partner fit to pursue their competing social and economic values. Burkett (2010) reveals that the concept of social enterprise as used in Nigeria may be different from that used in the UK, the US, Australia or any other country. Burkett and other scholars, therefore, contend that social enterprise needs to be contextualised, because there are specific political, social and economic drivers of the concept in every context (Battisti & Warren, 2016; Littlewood & Holt, 2015; Manolova et al., 2008; Urban, 2013). It is, therefore, critical to examine how country-specific environments enable or constrain the decision to collaborate, and in particular, the current study asks: *How does the Nigerian macro environment influence collaboration between SEs and IIs, and what factors enable or constrain the establishment of partner fit between them?*

Through the third question, the study seeks to ascertain the macro-level factors that are impacted positively or negatively from SEs' and IIs' collaboration experience and how they navigate them. It is contended that, in an enabling environment, where the socio-cultural, political and economic environment supports social entrepreneurship, SEs and IIs will gain trust and mutual commitment to accommodate social and economic interest for collective impact. The opportunity for trust and mutual commitment between SEs and IIs will be absent if the environment is disenabling. According to Johansen and Waldorff (2017: 21), "this idea confronts the institutional legacy, where organisations were at the mercy of external normative pressures", but exemplifies how inter-organisational resource exchange between parties with dyadic relations can disrupt the existing status quo to facilitate a new form of organising (Dorado, 2005; Garud et al., 2007; Greenwood et al., 2017).

According to Franco and Pessoa (2014), the learning experience of successful collaboration in terms of gained process knowledge is conceived as important lessons for future engagement of potential partners. Because successful collaboration experience between SEs and IIs in Nigeria is believed to increase trust and mutual commitment for future reciprocal exchange (Cropanzano et al., 2017), the study also asks: *What is the perceived learning experience from the collaboration and partner selection between SEs and IIs with dyadic relation in Nigeria?* The importance for examining the learning experience across the six dyad cases is to ascertain if mutual trust has played any role in achieving successful collaboration between SEs and IIs. This line of thinking stems from the example of studies that revealed inter-organisational collaboration between supplier and buyer characterised by reduced conflict as the outcome of trust (McEvily et al., 2017; Zaheer et al., 1998)—meaning that trust can play a critical role in ensuring tension-free interfirm collaboration such as this study envisages.

In the conceptual model above, collaboration begins with pre-investment process, where either SEs or IIs, classified as hybrid organisations, come together to pursue social and economic interests. Organisational alignment between SEs and IIs is then determined by their compatibility and complementarity, as indicated by the arrow. Compatibility and complementarity between SEs and IIs can also be ascertained from the elements of institutional logics and social exchange theories which guide collaboration at the organisational level. Established partner fit between SEs and IIs can potentially produce learning experience, a useful outcome that engenders trust for future collaboration. Because SEs and IIs do not operate in isolation from their contextual environment, the collaboration process can be constrained or enabled by political/legal, economic or socio-cultural environmental factors. As earlier stated, the central question is: How are SEs and IIs guided in determining their organisational compatibility and resource complementarity towards achieving partner fit in Nigeria? This question was elaborated into four sub-questions in Chap. 1 and revisited above in discussion.

2.25 Conclusion

The complexity characterising the social enterprise and impact investing theoretical stance has remained a source of academic debate. Hence our study integrates institutional logic and social exchange theories as the theoretical framework to guide it. Institutional logics theory is used to gain understanding of how SEs and IIs establish partner fit through compatibility of organisational logics. Social exchange theory is used to gain understanding of how SEs and IIs establish partner fit by leveraging on the strength of complementary resources. These theories combined explain the pre-investment process of establishing partner fit between SEs and IIs. The theories will be used to answer the research questions that cut across macro-institutional and behavioural aspects of hybrid organisations with dyadic relations in Nigeria. The next chapter provides an overview of social entrepreneurship in Nigeria.

References

Afonso, A., & Blanco-Arana, M. C. (2022). Financial and economic development in the context of the global 2008–09 financial crisis. *International Economics, 169*, 30–42.

Agrawal, A. (2018). Impact investing: Framework and future research avenues. *Social Business, 8*(3), 293–317.

Agrawal, A., & Hockerts, K. (2019a). Impact investing strategy: Managing conflicts between impact investor and investee social enterprise. *Sustainability, 11*(15), 4117.

Agrawal, A., & Hockerts, K. (2019b). Impact investing: Review and research agenda. *Journal of Small Business & Entrepreneurship, 33*(3), 1–29.

Ahokangas, P. (2014). The practice of creating and transforming a business model. *Journal of Business Models, 2*(1), 6–18.

Albert, H., Judd, R., Rivers, O., & Wagner, S. (2006). *Creating a winning E-Business*. 25 Thompson Pl., Course Technology Press.

Alter, S. K. (2006). Social enterprise models and their mission and money relationships. In *Social entrepreneurship: New models of sustainable social change* (pp. 205–232). Oxford University Press.

Amoako, I. O. (2019). Trust in interorganisational relationships. In *Trust, institutions and managing entrepreneurial relationships in Africa* (pp. 67–102). Springer.

Andresen, E., Lundberg, H., & Wincent, J. (2014). Processes in collaborative entrepreneurship: A longitudinal case study of how multiple actors exploit a radically new opportunity. *International Entrepreneurship and Management Journal, 10*(4), 713–726.

Au, K., Yuen, T., & Tam, J. (2016). Social enterprise development in Hong Kong: Legitimacy and institutional logics. In *Social entrepreneurship in the Greater China region* (pp. 51–61). Routledge.

Austin, J. E. (2000). Strategic collaboration between nonprofits and businesses. *Nonprofit and Voluntary Sector Quarterly, 29*(1_suppl), 69–97.

Austin, J., Stevenson, H., & Wei-Skillern, J. (2006). Social and commercial entrepreneurship: Same, different, or both? *Entrepreneurship Theory and Practice, 30*(1), 1–22.

Bacq, S., & Janssen, F. (2011). The multiple faces of social entrepreneurship: A review of definitional issues based on geographical and thematic criteria. *Entrepreneurship & Regional Development, 23*(5–6), 373–403.

Banks, J. (1972). Social movements and social change. In *The sociology of social movements* (pp. 41–56). Palgrave, Springer.

Battilana, J. (2018). Cracking the organizational challenge of pursuing joint social and financial goals: Social enterprise as a laboratory to understand hybrid organizing. *Management, 21*(4), 1278–1305.

Battilana, J., & Dorado, S. (2010). Building sustainable hybrid organizations: The case of commercial microfinance organizations. *Academy of Management Journal, 53*(6), 1419–1440.

Battilana, J., Leca, B., & Boxenbaum, E. (2009). How actors change institutions: Towards a theory of institutional entrepreneurship. *Academy of Management Annals, 3*(1), 65–107.

Battilana, J., Lee, M., Walker, J., & Dorsey, C. (2012). In search of the hybrid ideal. *Stanford Social Innovation Review, 10*(3), 51–55.

Battilana, J., Besharov, M., & Mitzinneck, B. (2017). On hybrids and hybrid organizing: A review and roadmap for future research. In R. Greenwood, C. Oliver, & T. B. Lawrence (Eds.), *The SAGE handbook of organizational institutionalism* (pp. 128–162). SAGE Publications Ltd.

Battisti, M., & Warren, L. (2016). *Early stage social enterprises in an accelerator environment.* Paper presented at the ICSB World Conference Proceedings, Dublin, London. Retrieved from https://icsb.org/wpcontent/uploads/2017/07/ICSB2014_CD_Proceedings.pdf

Bierly, P. E., III, & Gallagher, S. (2007). Explaining alliance partner selection: Fit, trust and strategic expediency. *Long Range Planning, 40*(2), 134–153.

Bird, B. (1988). Implementing entrepreneurial ideas: The case for intention. *Academy of Management Review, 13*(3), 442–453.

Blau, P. M. (1964). *Exchange and power in social life*. Transaction Publishers.

Blau, P. (2017). *Exchange and power in social life*. Routledge.

Bolton, E., & Savell, L. (2010). *Towards a new social economy: Blended value creation through social impact bonds*. Social Finance Ltd.

Bonini, S., & Emerson, J. (2005). *Maximizing blended value–Building beyond the blended value map to sustainable investing, philanthropy and organizations*. Retrieved from http://community-wealth.org

Bonnell, V. E., & Gold, T. B. (2015). The construction of a professional field: Resources, skills, and attributes of founders of the market research sector in Poland, 1989 to 1997. In *The new entrepreneurs of Europe and Asia* (pp. 128–153). Routledge.

Borzaga, C., & Defourny, J. (2001). Conclusions. Social enterprises in Europe: A diversity of initiatives and prospects. In *The emergence of social enterprise* (pp. 350–370). Routledge.

Boyd, N. G., & Vozikis, G. S. (1994). The influence of self-efficacy on the development of entrepreneurial intentions and actions. *Entrepreneurship Theory and Practice, 18*(4), 63–77.

Bradach, J. L. (2003). Going to scale: The challenge of replicating social programs. *Stanford Social Innovation Review*, 19–25. Retrieved from https://ssir.org/articles/entry/going_to_scale#

Brandstetter, L., & Lehner, O. M. (2015). Opening the market for impact investments: The need for adapted portfolio tools. *Entrepreneurship Research Journal, 5*(2), 87–107.

Brett, D. (2013). *Aavishkaar India micro venture capital fund*. Duke University Press.

British Council. (2016). *Social enterprise in a global context: The role of higher education institutions insight with Playmouth University*, Country Brief, California.

Bromberger, A. R. (2011). A new type of hybrid. *Stanford Social Innovation Review, 9*(2), 49–53.

Bromberger, A. R. (2013). Legal issues for social entrepreneurs. In R. Schultz (Ed.), *Creating good work*. Palgrave Macmillan.

Bruneel, J., Moray, N., Stevens, R., & Fassin, Y. (2016). Balancing competing logics in for-profit social enterprises: A need for hybrid governance. *Journal of Social Entrepreneurship, 7*(3), 263–288.

Bugg-Levine, A., & Emerson, J. (2011). Impact investing: Transforming how we make money while making a difference. *Innovations, 6*(3), 9–18.

Bugg-Levine, A., Kogut, B., & Kulatilaka, N. (2012). A new approach to funding social enterprises. *Harvard Business Review, 90*(1/2), 118–123.

Burand, D. (2012). *Globalizing social finance: How social impact bonds and social impact performance guarantees can scale development*. University of Michigan Law School.

Burkett, I. (2010). *Financing social enterprise: Understanding needs and realities*. Foresters Community Finance.

Cantillon, R. (1997). *Essai sur la nature du commerce en général*. Retrieved from https://www.ined.fr/fichier/s_rubrique/141/catalogue.editions.2020.21.fr.pdf

Carli Karlsson, S., & Nilsson, J. (2015). *The collaborative entrepreneurship process: A large firm perspective* (Master's thesis). Retrieved from http://uu.diva-portal.org/smash/get/diva2:824171/FULLTEXT01.pdf

Caseau, C., & Grolleau, G. (2020). Impact investing: Killing two birds with one stone? *Financial Analysts Journal, 76*(4), 40–52.

Castellas, E. I.-P., Ormiston, J., & Findlay, S. (2018). Financing social entrepreneurship: The role of impact investment in shaping social enterprise in Australia. *Social Enterprise Journal, 14*(2), 130–155.

Cetindamar, D., & Kozanoglu, H. (2014). *Fostering impact investment in developing countries*. Paper presented at the Proceedings of PICMET'14 Conference: Portland International Center for Management of Engineering and Technology; Infrastructure and Service Integration, Portland.

Chi, T., & Levitas, E. (2007). Resource complementarity, institutional compatibility, and some ensuing methodological issues in testing the resource-based view. *Research Methodology in Strategy and Management, 11*(4), 19–36.

Child, J., & Faulkner, D. (1998). *Strategies of cooperation: Managing alliances, networks, and joint ventures*. Oxford University Press.

Chong, P., & Kleemann, L. (2011). *The future of funding for social enterprises*. Retrieved from https://EconPapers.repec.org/RePEc:zbw:ifwkpb:34

Clark, S. (2015). *Social enterprise-business partnerships: Exploring the influence of institutional logics upon social enterprise partnership experiences and decision-making* (Doctoral dissertation). Retrieved from https://eprints.utas.edu.au/23155/1/Clark_whole_thesis.pdf

Clarkin, J. E., & Cangioni, C. (2016). Impact investing: A primer and review of the literature. *Entrepreneurship Research Journal, 6*(2), 135–173.

Corner, P. D., & Ho, M. (2010). How opportunities develop in social entrepreneurship. *Entrepreneurship Theory and Practice, 34*(4), 635–659.

Corrigan, P. (2011). *Social impact bonds. A new way to invest in better healthcare*. Social Finance Ltd.

Cropanzano, R., & Mitchell, M. S. (2005). Social exchange theory: An interdisciplinary review. *Journal of Management, 31*(6), 874–900.

Cropanzano, R., Anthony, E. L., Daniels, S. R., & Hall, A. V. (2017). Social exchange theory: A critical review with theoretical remedies. *Academy of Management Annals, 11*(1), 479–516.

Cumming, D. J., Johan, S. A., & Zhang, Y. (2019). The role of due diligence in crowdfunding platforms. *Journal of Banking & Finance, 108*, 105661. https://doi.org/10.1016/j.jbankfin.2019.105661

Curatolo, S., Addis, R., McCutchan, S., & Curatolo, S. (2017). *Impact investing: Submission to the Australian government on social impact investing discussion paper*. Impact Investing Australia.

Dacin, M. T., Goodstein, J., & Richard Scott, W. (2002). Institutional theory and institutional change: Introduction to the special research forum. *Academy of Management Journal, 45*(1), 45–56.

Dacin, M. T., Dacin, P. A., & Tracey, P. (2011). Social entrepreneurship: A critique and future directions. *Organization Science, 22*(5), 1203–1213.

Damayanthi, S., & Gooneratne, T. (2017). Institutional logics perspective in management control research: A review of extant literature and directions for future research. *Journal of Accounting & Organizational Change, 13*(4), 520–547. https://doi.org/10.1108/JAOC-01-2017-0002

Dart, R. (2004). The legitimacy of social enterprise. *Nonprofit Management and Leadership, 14*(4), 411–424.

Dato-on, M. C., & Kalakay, J. (2016). The winding road of social entrepreneurship definitions: A systematic literature review. *Social Enterprise Journal, 12*(2), 131–160.

Davies, I. A., & Chambers, L. (2018). Integrating hybridity and business model theory in sustainable entrepreneurship. *Journal of Cleaner Production, 177*, 378–386.

Davies, I. A., Haugh, H., & Chambers, L. (2019). Barriers to social enterprise growth. *Journal of Small Business Management, 57*(4), 1616–1636.

de Bruin, A., Shaw, E., & Lewis, K. V. (2017). The collaborative dynamic in social entrepreneurship. *Entrepreneurship & Regional Development, 29*(7/8), 575–585.

de Jesus, I. C., Bruni, A. L., Oliveira, S. R. G., & Araújo, E. A. C. (2017). *Dyadic relationships of trust and knowledge sharing in cooperation networks between micro and small enterprises for innovation* (Paper presentation). ICSB World Conference Proceedings, Washington.

Deeg, R., & Hardie, I. (2016). What is patient capital and who supplies it? *Socio-Economic Review, 14*(4), 627–645.

Defourny, J., & Borzaga, C. (2001). *From third sector to social enterprise*. Routledge.

Defourny, J., & Nyssens, M. (2010). Conceptions of social enterprise and social entrepreneurship in Europe and the United States: Convergences and divergences. *Journal of Social Entrepreneurship, 1*(1), 32–53.

Defourny, J., & Nyssens, M. (2014). The EMES approach of social enterprise in a comparative perspective. In *Social enterprise and the third sector* (pp. 58–81). Routledge.

Defourny, J., Nyssens, M., & Brolis, O. (2021). Testing social enterprise models across the world: Evidence from the "International Comparative Social Enterprise Models (ICSEM) project". *Nonprofit and Voluntary Sector Quarterly, 50*(2), 420–440.

Deiglmeier, K., & Greco, A. (2018). Why proven solutions struggle to scale up. *Stanford Social Innovation Review*. Retrieved from https://ssir.org/articles/entry/why_proven_solutions_struggle_to_scale_up

Demel, A. (2012). *Second thoughts on social impact bonds*. Retrieved from https://docplayer.net/17368050-Second-thoughts-on-social-impact-bonds.html

Dentoni, D., Bitzer, V., & Pascucci, S. (2016). Cross-sector partnerships and the co-creation of dynamic capabilities for stakeholder orientation. *Journal of Business Ethics, 135*(1), 35–53.

Deutsch, M. (1958). Trust and suspicion. *Journal of Conflict Resolution, 2*(4), 265–279.

Di Domenico, M., Tracey, P., & Haugh, H. (2009). The dialectic of social exchange: Theorizing corporate—Social enterprise collaboration. *Organization Studies, 30*(8), 887–907.

DiMaggio, P. (1988). Interest and agency in institutional theory. In L. G. Zucker (Ed.), *Research on institutional patterns: Environment and culture*. Ballinger Publishing Co.

Diouf, D. (2015). Exploring the barriers to impact investing in the sustainable energy area in West Africa. In *Decentralized solutions for developing economies* (pp. 177–183). Springer.

Dorado, S. (2005). Institutional entrepreneurship, partaking, and convening. *Organization Studies, 26*(3), 385–414.

Doz, Y., Hamel, G., & Prahalad, C. (1989). Collaborate with your competitors and win. *Harvard Business Review, 67*(1), 133–139.

Drexler, M., Noble, A., & Bryce, J. (2013). *From the margins to the mainstream: Assessment of the impact investment sector and opportunities to engage mainstream investors*. Retrieved from http://www3.weforum.org/docs/WEF_II_FromMarginsMainstream_Report_2013.pdf

Drnovšek, M., Franić, S., & Slavec, A. (2018). Exploring antecedents of business angels' intention to invest. *Zbornik radova Ekonomskog fakulteta u Rijeci: časopis za ekonomsku teoriju i praksu, 36*(2), 701–734.

Dyer, J. H., & Singh, H. (1998). The relational view: Cooperative strategy and sources of interorganizational competitive advantage. *Academy of Management Review, 23*(4), 660–679.

Dyer, J. H., Singh, H., & Hesterly, W. S. (2018). The relational view revisited: A dynamic perspective on value creation and value capture. *Strategic Management Journal, 39*(12), 3140–3162.

Ebrahim, A., Battilana, J., & Mair, J. (2014). The governance of social enterprises: Mission drift and accountability challenges in hybrid organizations. *Research in Organizational Behavior, 34*, 81–100.

Ekeh, P. P. (1974). *Social exchange theory: The two traditions*. Harvard University Press.

Emerson, R. M. (1976). Social exchange theory. *Annual Review of Sociology, 2*(1), 335–362. https://doi.org/10.1146/annurev.so.02.080176.002003

Emerson, J. (2003). The blended value proposition: Integrating social and financial returns. *California Management Review, 45*(4), 35–51.

Emerson, J. (2006). Moving ahead together: Implications of a blended value framework for the future of social entrepreneurship. In *Social entrepreneurship: New paradigms of sustainable social change* (pp. 391–406). Oxford University Press.

Engelmark, F., Mattsson, C., & Mannonen, T. (2015). *Social enterprises & impact investors-A complicated relationship* (Bachelor's thesis). Retrieved from https://lup.lub.lu.se/luur/download?func=downloadFile&recordOId=7373528&fileOId=7373538

Fase, A. (2016). *Achieving impact for impact investing–A roadmap for developed countries*. Retrieved from https://fa-se.de/static/fa_se_de/uploads/2018/05/Ashoka-FASE-McKinsey-Achieving-Impact-for-Impact-Investing-2016.pdf?x69731

Flatau, P. (2017). *The future of impact investing in Australia*. Retrieved from https://probonoaustralia.com.au/news/2017/07/future-impact-investing-australia/

Franco, M., & Pessoa, N. (2014). University sports partnerships as collaborative entrepreneurship: An exploratory case study. *Administration & Society, 46*(8), 885–907.

Friedland, R., & Alford, R. R. (1991). Bringing society back in: Symbols, practices, and institutional contradictions. In W. W. Powell & P. J. DiMaggio (Eds.), *The new institutionalism in organizational analysis* (pp. 232–267). University of Chicago Press.

Gaglio, C. M., & Katz, J. A. (2001). The psychological basis of opportunity identification: Entrepreneurial alertness. *Small Business Economics, 16*(2), 95–111.

Ganesh, U. (2017). Lessons from the Indian impact investing ecosystem. In *Principles and practice of impact investing: A catalytic revolution*. Routledge.

Garud, R., Hardy, C., & Maguire, S. (2007). *Institutional entrepreneurship as embedded agency: An introduction to the special issue*. Sage Publications.

George, G., Corbishley, C., Khayesi, J. N., Haas, M. R., & Tihanyi, L. (2016). Bringing Africa in: Promising directions for management research. *Academy of Management Journal, 59*(2), 377–393.

GIIN. (2015). *The landscape for impact investing in West Africa*. Retrieved from https://thegiin.org/knowledge/publication/westafricareport

GIIN. (2016). *Achieving the sustainable development goals: The role of impact investing*. Retrieved from https://thegiin.org/assets/GIIN_Impact%20InvestingSDGs_Finalprofiles_webfile.pdf

GIIN. (2022). *Sizing the impact investing market*. Retrieved from https://thegiin.org/assets/2022-Market%20Sizing%20Report-Final.pdf

Glänzel, G., & Scheuerle, T. (2016). Social impact investing in Germany: Current impediments from investors' and social entrepreneurs' perspectives. *Voluntas: International Journal of Voluntary and Nonprofit Organizations, 27*(4), 1638–1668.

Goldszmidt, R. G. B., Brito, L. A. L., & de Vasconcelos, F. C. (2011). Country effect on firm performance: A multilevel approach. *Journal of Business Research, 64*(3), 273–279.

Grafström, J., & Aasma, S. (2021). Breaking circular economy barriers. *Journal of Cleaner Production, 292*, 126002.

Grassl, W. (2012). Business models of social enterprise: A design approach to hybridity. *ACRN Journal of Entrepreneurship Perspectives, 1*(1), 37–60.

Greenwood, R., & Suddaby, R. (2006). Institutional entrepreneurship in mature fields: The big five accounting firms. *Academy of Management Journal, 49*(1), 27–48.

Greenwood, R., Díaz, A. M., Li, S. X., & Lorente, J. C. (2010). The multiplicity of institutional logics and the heterogeneity of organizational responses. *Organization Science, 21*(2), 521–539.

Greenwood, R., Raynard, M., Kodeih, F., Micelotta, E. R., & Lounsbury, M. (2011). Institutional complexity and organizational responses. *Academy of Management Annals, 5*(1), 317–371.

Greenwood, R., Oliver, C., Lawrence, T. B., & Meyer, R. E. (2017). *The Sage handbook of organizational institutionalism*. Sage Publications.

Grieco, C. (2015). Conceptualizing social entrepreneurship. In *Assessing social impact of social enterprises* (pp. 5–36). Springer.

Grimes, M. G., McMullen, J. S., Vogus, T. J., & Miller, T. L. (2013). Studying the origins of social entrepreneurship: Compassion and the role of embedded agency. *Academy of Management Review, 38*(3), 460–463. https://doi.org/10.5465/amr.2012.0429

Gupta, P., Chauhan, S., Paul, J., & Jaiswal, M. (2020). Social entrepreneurship research: A review and future research agenda. *Journal of Business Research, 113*(C), 209–229.

Haigh, N., Walker, J., Bacq, S., & Kickul, J. (2015). Hybrid organizations: Origins, strategies, impacts, and implications. *California Management Review, 57*(3), 5–12.

Hallen, B. L., & Eisenhardt, K. M. (2012). Catalyzing strategies and efficient tie formation: How entrepreneurial firms obtain investment ties. *Academy of Management Journal, 55*(1), 35–70.

Hamel, G. (1991). Competition for competence and interpartner learning within international strategic alliances. *Strategic Management Journal, 12*(S1), 83–103.

Hamel, G., & Prahalad, C. K. (1993). Strategy as stretch and leverage. *Harvard Business Review, 71*(2), 75–84.

Hampel, C., Lawrence, T., & Tracey, P. (2017). Institutional work: Taking stock and making it matter. In R. Greenwood, C. Oliver, & T. B. Lawrence (Eds.), *The SAGE handbook of organizational institutionalism* (pp. 558–590). SAGE Publications Ltd.

Hand, D., Ringel, B., & Danel, A. (2022). *Sizing the impact investing market: 2022*. The Global Impact Investing Network (GIIN).

Hart, G. (2016). *An assessment of the impact investing and social enterprise ecosystem in Virginia*. Retrieved from http://scholarscompass.vcu.edu/community_resources/68

Haugh, H. (2007). Community-led social venture creation. *Entrepreneurship Theory and Practice, 31*(2), 161–182.

Heider, F. (2013). *The psychology of interpersonal relations*. Psychology Press.

Henry, C. (2015). Doing well by doing good: Opportunity recognition and the social enterprise partnership. *Journal of Social Entrepreneurship, 6*(2), 137–160.

Ho, A. P.-Y., & Chan, K.-T. (2010). The social impact of work-integration social enterprise in Hong Kong. *International Social Work, 53*(1), 33–45.

Höchstädter, A. K., & Scheck, B. (2015). What's in a name: An analysis of impact investing understandings by academics and practitioners. *Journal of Business Ethics, 132*(2), 449–475.

Hoffman, A. J., Badiane, K. K., & Haigh, N. (2012). *Hybrid organizations as agents of positive social change: Bridging the for-profit and non-profit divide using a positive lens to explore social change and organizations* (pp. 152–174). Routledge.

Homans, G. C. (1958). Social behavior as exchange. *American Journal of Sociology, 63*(6), 597–606.

Huxham, C., & Vangen, S. (2013). *Managing to collaborate: The theory and practice of collaborative advantage*. Routledge.

Huybrechts, B., & Nicholls, A. (2013). The role of legitimacy in social enterprise-corporate collaboration. *Social Enterprise Journal, 9*(2), 130–146.

Hynes, B. (2009). Growing the social enterprise–issues and challenges. *Social Enterprise Journal, 5*(2), 114–125.

Ianes, A. (2020). Exploring the history of the first social enterprise type: Social co-operation in the Italian welfare system and its replication in Europe, 1970s to 2011. *Journal of Entrepreneurial and Organizational Diversity, 9*(1), 1–25.

Intellecap. (2017). *Taking social impact investing in Africa to the next level, workshop at 4th sankalp Africa summit, Nairobi, 2017.* Retrieved from https://idl-bnc-idrc.dspacedirect.org/bitstream/handle/10625/56834/IDL-56834.pdf

Jabłoński, A. (2016). Scalability of sustainable business models in hybrid organizations. *Sustainability, 8*(3), 194.

Jackson, E. T. (2013). Interrogating the theory of change: Evaluating impact investing where it matters most. *Journal of Sustainable Finance & Investment, 3*(2), 95–110.

Jackall, R. (1988). Moral mazes: The world of corporate managers. *International Journal of Politics, Culture, and Society, 1*, 598–614.

Jäger, U. P., & Schröer, A. (2014). Integrated organizational identity: A definition of hybrid organizations and a research agenda. *Voluntas: International Journal of Voluntary and Nonprofit Organizations, 25*(5), 1281–1306.

Jamali, D., Mohanna, N., Sherif, D. H., & El Sayeh, S. (2016). A comparative study of social enterprises: North vs. south perspectives. In R. Larattta (Ed.), *Social enterprise-context-dependent dynamics in a global perspective*. IntechOpen.

Janowicz-Panjaitan, M., & Krishnan, R. (2009). Measures for dealing with competence and integrity violations of interorganizational trust at the corporate and operating levels of organizational hierarchy. *Journal of Management Studies, 46*(2), 245–268.

Jap, S. D. (1999). Pie-expansion efforts: Collaboration processes in buyer–supplier relationships. *Journal of Marketing Research, 36*(4), 461–475.

Jawed, I., & Siddiqui, D. A. (2019). *What matters for firms' performance: Capabilities, tangible or intangible resources? Evidence from corporate sectors on Pakistan*. https://doi.org/10.2139/ssrn.3510562

Jay, J. (2013). Navigating paradox as a mechanism of change and innovation in hybrid organizations. *Academy of management journal, 56*(1), 137–159.

Johansen, C. B., & Waldorff, S. B. (2017). What are institutional logics – And where is the perspective taking us? In G. Krücken, C. Mazza, R. E. Meyer, & P. Walgenbach (Eds.), *New themes in institutional analysis: Topics and issues from European research* (pp. 51–76). Edward Elgar Publishing.

Jones, J. (2019). *The demand side of impact investing: Elevating the perspectives of local entrepreneurs in the impact sector*. Oxfam America. Retrieved from https://www.oxfamamerica.org/explore/research-publications/demand-side-impact-investing/

Jones, J. J. (2020). *How identity influences the investor entrepreneur relationship: The case of impact investing*. University of Colorado.

Jones, H. S., & Moncur, W. (2020). A mixed-methods approach to understanding funder trust and due diligence processes in online crowdfunding investment. *ACM Transactions on Social Computing, 3*(1), 1–29.

Kamasak, R. (2017). The contribution of tangible and intangible resources, and capabilities to a firm's profitability and market performance. *European Journal of Management and Business Economics, 26*(2), 252–275.

Kerlin, J. A. (2012). Defining social enterprise across different contexts: A conceptual framework based on institutional factors. In B. Gidron & Y. Hasenfeld (Eds.), *Social enterprises*. Palgrave Macmillan.

Kickul, J., & Lyons, T. S. (2016). *Understanding social entrepreneurship: The relentless pursuit of mission in an ever changing world*. Routledge.

Kickul, J., Janssen-Selvadurai, C., & Griffiths, M. D. (2012). A blended value framework for educating the next cadre of social entrepreneurs. *Academy of Management Learning & Education, 11*(3), 479–493.

Kiggundu, M. N. (1981). Task interdependence and the theory of job design. *Academy of Management Review, 6*(3), 499–508.
Kim, K. I., & Organ, D. W. (1982). Determinants of leader-subordinate exchange relationships. *Group & Organization Studies, 7*(1), 77–89.
Kirigia, J. M., Nganda, B. M., Mwikisa, C. N., & Cardoso, B. (2011). Effects of global financial crisis on funding for health development in nineteen countries of the WHO African region. *BMC International Health and Human Rights, 11*(1), 4.
Kirzner, I. (1973). *Competition and entrepreneurship*. University of Chicago Press.
Kirzner, I. M. (1979). *Perception, opportunity, and profit: Studies in the theory of entrepreneurship*. University of Chicago Press.
Knight, F. H. (1921). *Risk, uncertainty and profit*. Houghton Mifflin. Retrieved from https://oll.libertyfund.org/title/knight-risk-uncertainty-and-profit
Knoke, D. (2018). *Changing organizations: Business networks in the new political economy*. Routledge.
Kotz, D. M. (2009). The financial and economic crisis of 2008: A systemic crisis of neoliberal capitalism. *Review of Radical Political Economics, 41*(3), 305–317.
Krlev, G., Glänzel, G., & Mildenberger, G. (2013). *Capitalising social innovation. A short guide to the research for policy makers. A deliverable of the TEPSIE project*. European Commission, DG Research. Retrieved from https://www.academia.edu/25481887/Capitalising_Social_Innovation_A_short_guide_to_research_for_policy_makers
Langman, L. (2005). From virtual public spheres to global justice: A critical theory of internetworked social movements. *Sociological Theory, 23*(1), 42–74.
Lawrence, T. B., Hardy, C., & Phillips, N. (2002). Institutional effects of interorganizational collaboration: The emergence of proto-institutions. *Academy of Management Journal, 45*(1), 281–290.
Leach, E. (1961). General and ethnology: Social behavior: Its elementary forms. *American Anthropologist, 63*(6), 1339–1341.
Lehner, O. M. (2013). Crowdfunding social ventures: A model and research agenda. *Venture Capital, 15*(4), 289–311.
Lehner, O. M., & Nicholls, A. (2014). Social finance and crowdfunding for social enterprises: A public–private case study providing legitimacy and leverage. *Venture Capital, 16*(3), 271–286.
Liden, R. C., Anand, S., & Vidyarthi, P. (2016). Dyadic relationships. *Annual Review of Organizational Psychology and Organizational Behavior, 3*(1), 139–166.
Littlewood, D., & Holt, D. (2015). Social entrepreneurship in South Africa: Exploring the influence of environment. *Business & Society, 57*(3), 1–37.
Littlewood, D., & Holt, D. (2018). Social entrepreneurship in South Africa: Exploring the influence of environment. *Business & Society, 57*(3), 525–561.
Lounsbury, M. (2002). Institutional transformation and status mobility: The professionalization of the field of finance. *Academy of Management Journal, 45*(1), 255–266.
Lu, V. N., Plewa, C., & Ho, J. (2016). Managing governmental business relationships: The impact of organisational culture difference and compatibility. *Australasian Marketing Journal (AMJ), 24*(1), 93–100.
Lumineau, F., Eckerd, S., & Handley, S. (2015). Inter-organizational conflicts: Research overview, challenges, and opportunities. *Journal of Strategic Contracting and Negotiation, 1*(1), 42–64.
Mair, J., & Hehenberger, L. (2014). Front-stage and backstage convening: The transition from opposition to mutualistic coexistence in organizational philanthropy. *Academy of Management Journal, 57*(4), 1174–1200.
Mair, J., & Martí, I. (2006). Social entrepreneurship research: A source of explanation, prediction, and delight. *Journal of World Business, 41*(1), 36–44.
Mair, J., & Marti, I. (2009). Entrepreneurship in and around institutional voids: A case study from Bangladesh. *Journal of Business Venturing, 24*(5), 419–435.
Mair, J., Martí, I., & Ganly, K. (2007). *Institutional voids as spaces of opportunity*. Retrieved from https://hal.archives-ouvertes.fr/hal-02311879

Mair, J., Marti, I., & Ventresca, M. J. (2012). Building inclusive markets in rural Bangladesh: How intermediaries work institutional voids. *Academy of Management Journal, 55*(4), 819–850.
Majercakova, D., & Kocisova, L. (2016, September 1–2). *Impact investing–opportunity for creative investment.* Paper presented at the Cconomic and Social Development (Book of Proceedings), 16th International Scientific Conference on Economic and Social Development, Split.
Manolova, T. S., Eunni, R. V., & Gyoshev, B. S. (2008). Institutional environments for entrepreneurship: Evidence from emerging economies in Eastern Europe. *Entrepreneurship Theory and Practice, 32*(1), 203–218.
Martin, R., & Lohin, R. (2017). Impact investing: Tracking the adoption of a financial (and social) innovation. *Rotman Management*, 64–69.
Martin, R. L., & Osberg, S. (2007). Social entrepreneurship: The case for definition. *Stanford Social Innovation Review, 5*(2), 28–39.
Martin, R. L., & Osberg, S. (2015). *Getting beyond better: How social entrepreneurship works.* Harvard Business Review Press.
McEvily, B., Zaheer, A., & Kamal, D. K. F. (2017). Mutual and exclusive: Dyadic sources of trust in interorganizational exchange. *Organization Science, 28*(1), 74–92.
McGregor, D. (1989). The human side of enterprise. In *Readings in managerial psychology* (pp. 314–324). University of Chicago Press.
Mentzer, J. T., & Flint, D. J. (1997). Validity in logistics research. *Journal of Business Logistics, 18*(1), 199–216.
Menzies, J., Orr, S., & Paul, J. (2020). SME internationalisation: The relationship between social capital and entry mode. *Management International Review, 60*(4), 623–650.
Meyer, J. W., & Rowan, B. (1977). Institutionalized organizations: Formal structure as myth and ceremony. *American journal of sociology, 83*(2), 340–363.
Meyer, N. (2021). A theoretical analysis of social entrepreneurship: The case of Poland and South Africa. *Journal of Eastern European and Central Asian Research (JEECAR), 8*(1), 133–148.
Micelotta, E., Lounsbury, M., & Greenwood, R. (2017). Pathways of institutional change: An integrative review and research agenda. *Journal of Management, 43*(6), 1885–1910.
Michelson, G., Wailes, N., Van Der Laan, S., & Frost, G. (2004). Ethical investment processes and outcomes. *Journal of Business Ethics, 52*(1), 1–10.
Miles, R. E., Miles, G., & Snow, C. C. (2006). Collaborative entrepreneurship. *Organizational Dynamics, 1*(35), 1–11.
Miller, T. L., & Wesley, C. L. (2010). Assessing mission and resources for social change: An organizational identity perspective on social venture capitalists 'decision criteria. *Entrepreneurship Theory and Practice, 34*(4), 705–733.
Mindruta, D., Moeen, M., & Agarwal, R. (2016). A two-sided matching approach for partner selection and assessing complementarities in partners' attributes in inter-firm alliances. *Strategic Management Journal, 37*(1), 206–231.
Mitsuhashi, H., & Greve, H. R. (2009). A matching theory of alliance formation and organizational success: Complementarity and compatibility. *Academy of Management Journal, 52*(5), 975–995.
Mogapi, E. M., Sutherland, M. M., & Wilson-Prangley, A. (2019). Impact investing in South Africa: Managing tensions between financial returns and social impact. *European Business Review, 31*, 397–419.
Molm, L. D. (2006). The social exchange framework. In *Contemporary social psychological theories* (pp. 24–45). Stanford University Press.
Montgomery, A. W., Dacin, P. A., & Dacin, M. T. (2012). Collective social entrepreneurship: Collaboratively shaping social good. *Journal of Business Ethics, 111*(3), 375–388.
Moorman, C., Deshpande, R., & Zaltman, G. (1993). Factors affecting trust in market research relationships. *Journal of Marketing, 57*(1), 81–101.
Mulgan, G., Tucker, S., Ali, R., & Sanders, B. (2007). *Social innovation: What it is, why it matters and how it can be accelerated.* Basingsstoke Press.
Muthusamy, S. K., & White, M. A. (2005). Learning and knowledge transfer in strategic alliances: A social exchange view. *Organization Studies, 26*(3), 415–441.

Nair, S., & Blomquist, T. (2019). Failure prevention and management in business incubation: Practices towards a scalable business model. *Technology Analysis & Strategic Management, 31*(3), 266–278.

Navis, C., & Glynn, M. A. (2010). How new market categories emerge: Temporal dynamics of legitimacy, identity, and entrepreneurship in satellite radio, 1990–2005. *Administrative Science Quarterly, 55*(3), 439–471.

Navis, C., & Glynn, M. A. (2011). Legitimate distinctiveness and the entrepreneurial identity: Influence on investor judgments of new venture plausibility. *Academy of Management Review, 36*(3), 479–499.

Ngoasong, M., Paton, R., & Korda, A. (2015). *Impact investing and inclusive business development in Africa: A research agenda* (pp. 1–22). The Open University. Retrieved from https://oro.open.ac.uk/42157/1/ikd-working-paper-76.pdf

Nicholls, A. (2008). *Social entrepreneurship: New models of sustainable social change*. Oxford University Press.

Nicholls, A. (2010). The legitimacy of social entrepreneurship: Reflexive isomorphism in a pre-paradigmatic field. *Entrepreneurship Theory and Practice, 34*(4), 611–633.

Nicholls, A., & Daggers, J. (2016). *The landscape of social impact investment research: Trends and opportunities*. Retrieved from https://thegiin.org/research/publication/oxford-reviews-global-data,-literature-on-impact-investment-research

Nicholls, A., & Huybrechts, B. (2016). Sustaining inter-organizational relationships across institutional logics and power asymmetries: The case of fair trade. *Journal of Business Ethics, 135*(4), 699–714.

Nielsen, C., & Lund, M. (2015). *The concept of business model scalability*. https://doi.org/10.2139/ssrn.2575962

Nielsen, C., & Lund, M. (2018). Building scalable business models. *MIT Sloan Management Review, 59*(2), 65–69.

Noya, A., & Clarence, E. (2013). *Policy brief on social entrepreneurship: Entrepreneurial activities in Europe*. EUR-OP. Retrieved from https://www.oecd.org/cfe/leed/Social%20entrepreneurship%20policy%20brief%20EN_FINAL.pdf

O'Connor, G. C., & Rice, M. P. (2001). Opportunity recognition and breakthrough innovation in large established firms. *California Management Review, 43*(2), 95–116.

OECD. (1999). *Social enterprises*. OECD. Retrieved from https://www.oecd.org/cfe/leed/social-enterprises.htm

OECD. (2016). *The sustainable development goals as busines opportunities; Developement co-operation report 2016*. Retrieved from http://www.oecd.org/dac/development-co-operation-report-2016.htm

OECD. (2019). *Social impact investment: The impact imperative for sustainable development*. Retrieved from https://www.oecd.org/dac/financing-sustainable-development/development-finance-topics/Social-Impact-Investment-2019.pdf

Oh, C. H., Park, J.-H., & Ghauri, P. N. (2013). Doing right, investing right: Socially responsible investing and shareholder activism in the financial sector. *Business Horizons, 56*(6), 703–714.

Ormiston, J., Charlton, K., Donald, M. S., & Seymour, R. G. (2015). Overcoming the challenges of impact investing: Insights from leading investors. *Journal of Social Entrepreneurship, 6*(3), 352–378.

Osterwalder, A., & Pigneur, Y. (2010). Business model generation: a handbook for visionaries, game changers, and challengers: *John Wiley & Sons*.

Ozanne, L. K., Phipps, M., Weaver, T., Carrington, M., Luchs, M., Catlin, J., et al. (2016). Managing the tensions at the intersection of the triple bottom line: A paradox theory approach to sustainability management. *Journal of Public Policy & Marketing, 35*(2), 249–261.

Pache, A.-C., & Santos, F. (2010). When worlds collide: The internal dynamics of organizational responses to conflicting institutional demands. *Academy of Management Review, 35*(3), 455–476.

Pache, A.-C., & Santos, F. (2013). Inside the hybrid organization: Selective coupling as a response to competing institutional logics. *Academy of Management Journal, 56*(4), 972–1001.

Peattie, K., & Morley, A. (2008). Eight paradoxes of the social enterprise research agenda. *Social Enterprise Journal, 4*(2), 91–107.

Peredo, A. M., & McLean, M. (2006). Social entrepreneurship: A critical review of the concept. *Journal of World Business, 41*(1), 56–65.

Petrella, F., & Richez-Battesti, N. (2014). Social entrepreneur, social entrepreneurship and social enterprise: Semantics and controversies. *Journal of Innovation Economics, 14*(2), 143.

Pfeffer, J., & Salancik, G. R. (2003). *The external control of organizations: A resource dependence perspective*. Stanford University Press.

Phillips, S. D., & Johnson, B. (2019). Inching to impact: The demand side of social impact investing. *Journal of Business Ethics, 168*, 1–15.

Phillips, N., Lawrence, T. B., & Hardy, C. (2000). Inter-organizational collaboration and the dynamics of institutional fields. *Journal of Management Studies, 37*(1), 23–43.

Pirkey, M. (2016). *Being, doing, & creating community: Social exchange & the microfoundations of institutional logics* (Paper presentation). Academy of Management Proceedings. https://doi.org/10.5465/ambpp.2016.10979abstract

Podsakoff, P. M., MacKenzie, S. B., Paine, J. B., & Bachrach, D. G. (2000). Organizational citizenship behaviors: A critical review of the theoretical and empirical literature and suggestions for future research. *Journal of Management, 26*(3), 513–563.

Poon, D. (2011). The emergence and development of social enterprise sectors. In *Scholarly commons*. University of Pennsylvania. Retrieved from http://repository.upenn.edu/sire

Powell, W. W., & DiMaggio, P. J. (2012). *The new institutionalism in organizational analysis*. University of Chicago Press.

Powell, W. W., Koput, K. W., & Smith-Doerr, L. (1996). Interorganizational collaboration and the locus of innovation: Networks of learning in biotechnology. *Administrative Science Quarterly, 41*(1), 116–145.

Power, G., Wilson, B., Brandenburg, M., Melia-Teevan, K., Lai, J., & Gowda, R. (2012). *A framework for action: Social enterprise & impact investing*. United Nations Global Compact. Retrieved from http://www.unglobalcompact.org/docs/issues_doc/development/Framework_Social_Enterprise_Impact_Investing.pdf

Prashant, K., & Harbir, S. (2009). Managing strategic alliances: What do we know now, and where do we go from here? *Academy of Management Perspectives, 23*(3), 45–62.

Purdy, J. M., & Gray, B. (2009). Conflicting logics, mechanisms of diffusion, and multilevel dynamics in emerging institutional fields. *Academy of Management Journal, 52*(2), 355–380.

Reay, T., & Hinings, C. R. (2009). Managing the rivalry of competing institutional logics. *Organization Studies, 30*(6), 629–652.

Reeder, N., Jones, G. R., Loder, J., & Colantonio, A. (2014). *Measuring impact: Preliminary insights from interviews with impact investors*. LSE Cities, London School of Economics and Political Science. http://eprints.lse.ac.uk/id/eprint/59124

Reficco, E., & Márquez, P. (2012). Inclusive networks for building BOP markets. *Business & Society, 51*(3), 512–556.

Rivera-Santos, M., Holt, D., Littlewood, D., & Kolk, A. (2015). Social entrepreneurship in sub-Saharan Africa. *The Academy of Management Perspectives, 29*(1), 72–91.

Roberts, D., & Woods, C. (2005). Changing the world on a shoestring: The concept of social entrepreneurship. *University of Auckland Business Review, 7*(1), 45–51.

Ruebottom, T. (2013). The microstructures of rhetorical strategy in social entrepreneurship: Building legitimacy through heroes and villains. *Journal of Business Venturing, 28*(1), 98–116.

Ryan, A., & O'Malley, L. (2006). *Conceptualising dyadic inter-organisational relationships as complex adaptive systems* (Paper presentation). 22nd Imp Conference, Boconni University, Milan, San Diego, California. Retrieved from https://eprints.lancs.ac.uk/id/eprint/46867

Sakarya, S., Bodur, M., Yildirim-Öktem, Ö., & Selekler-Göksen, N. (2012). Social alliances: Business and social enterprise collaboration for social transformation. *Journal of Business Research, 65*(12), 1710–1720.

Saltuk, Y., & Idrissi, A. (2012). *A portfolio approach to impact investment: Global social finance research*. JP Morgan. Retrieved from https://thegiin.org/research/publication/a-portfolio-approach-to-impact-investment-a-practical-guide-to-building-analyz
Santi, E., & Sennett, L. (2016). Impact investing in Africa. In *Principles and practice of impact investing: A catalytic revolution*. Routledge.
Santos, F. M. (2012). A positive theory of social entrepreneurship. *Journal of Business Ethics, 111*(3), 335–351.
Santos, F., Pache, A.-C., & Birkholz, C. (2015). Making hybrids work: Aligning business models and organizational design for social enterprises. *California Management Review, 57*(3), 36–58.
Sarah, M. (2016). The rich history of impact investing: Funding social entrepreneruship moves more mainstream. *B Magazine*. Retrieved from http://www.dblpartners.vc/2016/11/the-rich-history-of-impact-investing-funding-social-entrepreneurship-moves-more-mainstream/
Sarason, S. B. (1972). *The creation of settings and the future societies*. Brookline Books. Retrieved from https://psycnet.apa.org/record/1989-97650-000
Sarkar, M. B., Echambadi, R., Cavusgil, S. T., & Aulakh, P. S. (2001). The influence of complementarity, compatibility, and relationship capital on alliance performance. *Journal of the Academy of Marketing Science, 29*(4), 358–373.
Saz-Carranza, A., & Longo, F. (2012). Managing competing institutional logics in public–private joint ventures. *Public Management Review, 14*(3), 331–357.
Scholtens, B. (2006). Finance as a driver of corporate social responsibility. *Journal of Business Ethics, 68*(1), 19–33.
Schumpeter, J. (1934). *The theory of economic development* (R. Opie, Trans.). *Harvard economic studies* (p. 40, 20). Harvard University Press.
Scott, W. R., Ruef, M., Mendel, P. J., & Caronna, C. A. (2000). *Institutional change and healthcare organizations: From professional dominance to managed care*. University of Chicago Press.
Seelos, C., Mair, J., Battilana, J., & Tina Dacin, M. (2011). The embeddedness of social entrepreneurship: Understanding variation across local communities. In *Communities and organizations* (pp. 333–363). Emerald Group Publishing Limited. Retrieved from http://www.iese.edu/research/pdfs/DI-0858-E.pdf
Seo, M.-G., & Creed, W. D. (2002). Institutional contradictions, praxis, and institutional change: A dialectical perspective. *Academy of Management Review, 27*(2), 222–247.
Serrano-Cinca, C., & Gutiérrez-Nieto, B. (2013). A decision support system for financial and social investment. *Applied Economics, 45*(28), 4060–4070.
Sesan, G. (2006). Social enterprise in Africa: An emerging concept in an emerging economy. *International NGO Journal, 1*(1), 004–008. https://academicjournals.org/INGOJ
Shams, R., Vrontis, D., Belyaeva, Z., Ferraris, A., & Czinkota, M. R. (2021). Strategic agility in international business: A conceptual framework for "agile" multinationals. *Journal of International Management, 27*(1), 100737.
Shane, S., & Venkataraman, S. (2000). The promise of entrepreneurship as a field of research. *Academy of Management Review, 25*(1), 217–226.
Shapero, A., & Sokol, L. (1982). The social dimensions of entrepreneurship. In *Encyclopedia of entrepreneurship* (pp. 72–90). Prentice-Hall.
Shaw, E., & de Bruin, A. (2013). Reconsidering capitalism: The promise of social innovation and social entrepreneurship? *International Small Business Journal, 31*(7), 737–746.
Short, J. C., Moss, T. W., & Lumpkin, G. T. (2009). Research in social entrepreneurship: Past contributions and future opportunities. *Strategic Entrepreneurship Journal, 3*(2), 161–194. https://doi.org/10.1002/sej.69
Šimić, M. (2015). Investment criteria set by venture capitalists. *Ekonomski Vjesnik/Econviews: Review of Contemporary Business, Entrepreneurship and Economic Issues, 28*(2), 457–479.
Singh, A. (2016). *The process of social value creation: A multiple-case study on social entrepreneurship in India*. Springer.
Smith, A. (1776/1976). In R. H. Campbell, & A. S. Skinner (Eds.), *An inquiry into the nature and causes of the wealth of nations*. Oxford University Press.

Smith, W. K., Gonin, M., & Besharov, M. L. (2013). Managing social-business tensions: A review and research agenda for social enterprise. *Business Ethics Quarterly, 23*(3), 407–442.

Sobotka, T., Skirbekk, V., & Philipov, D. (2011). Economic recession and fertility in the developed world. *Population and Development Review, 37*(2), 267–306.

Steiner, A., Farmer, J., & Bosworth, G. (2019). Rural social enterprise—Evidence to date, and a research agenda. *Journal of Rural Studies, 70*(01), 139–143.

Stephan, U., Uhlaner, L. M., & Stride, C. (2015). Institutions and social entrepreneurship: The role of institutional voids, institutional support, and institutional configurations. *Journal of International Business Studies, 46*(3), 308–331.

Suchman, M. C. (1995). Managing legitimacy: Strategic and institutional approaches. *Academy of Management Review, 20*(3), 571–610.

Suddaby, R., & Greenwood, R. (2005). Rhetorical strategies of legitimacy. *Administrative Science Quarterly, 50*(1), 35–67.

Sule, T. (2019). *What should Nigeria do to attract more impact investments?* Retrieved from https://businessday.ng/impact-investing/article/what-should-nigeria-do-to-attract-more-impact-investments/

Tansey, J., Svedova, J., & Cuyegkeng, A. (2017). The early days of impact investing: Market size, investment type and returns. In *Principles and practice of impact investing* (pp. 26–44). Routledge.

Tanskanen, K. (2015). Who wins in a complex buyer-supplier relationship? A social exchange theory based dyadic study. *International Journal of Operations & Production Management, 35*(4), 577–603.

Tapsell, P., & Woods, C. (2008). A spiral of innovation framework for social entrepreneurship: Social innovation at the generational divide in an indigenous context. *Emergence: Complexity and Organization, 10*(3), 25.

Tapsell, P., & Woods, C. (2010). Social entrepreneurship and innovation: Self-organization in an indigenous context. *Entrepreneurship and Regional Development, 22*(6), 535–556.

Taylor, J. B. (2009). *The financial crisis and the policy responses: An empirical analysis of what went wrong*. Retrieved from https://www.nber.org/papers/w14631

Terjesen, S. (2007). Building a better rat trap: Technological innovation, human capital, and the Irula. *Entrepreneurship Theory and Practice, 31*(6), 953–963.

Thomas, R., & Skinner, L. (2010). Total trust and trust asymmetry: Does trust need to be equally distributed in interfirm relationships? *Journal of Relationship Marketing, 9*(1), 43–53.

Thorgren, S., & Omorede, A. (2018). Passionate leaders in social entrepreneurship: Exploring an African context. *Business & Society, 57*(3), 481–524.

Thorgren, S., Wincent, J., & Örtqvist, D. (2012). Unleashing synergies in strategic networks of SMEs: The influence of partner fit on corporate entrepreneurship. *International Small Business Journal, 30*(5), 453–471.

Thornton, P. H. (2015). Culture and institutional logics. In *International encyclopedia of the social and behavioral sciences*. Elsevier.

Thornton, P., & Ocasio, W. (2008). Institutional logics. In R. Greenwood, C. Oliver, & R. Suddaby (Eds.), *The SAGE handbook of organizational institutionalism* (pp. 99–128). SAGE Publications Ltd.

Tina Dacin, M., Goodstein, J., & Richard Scott, W. (2002). Institutional theory and institutional change: Introduction to the special research forum. *Academy of management journal, 45*(1), 45–56.

Tjornbo, O., & Westley, F. R. (2012). Game changers: The big green challenge and the role of challenge grants in social innovation. *Journal of Social Entrepreneurship, 3*(2), 166–183.

Tomlinson, E. C., Dineen, B. R., & Lewicki, R. J. (2009). Trust congruence among integrative negotiators as a predictor of joint-behavioral outcomes. *International Journal of Conflict Management, 20*(2), 173–187.

Tough, H., Brinkhof, M. W., & Fekete, C. (2022). Untangling the role of social relationships in the association between caregiver burden and caregiver health: An observational study exploring three coping models of the stress process paradigm. *BMC Public Health, 22*(1), 1–14.

Tracey, P., & Jarvis, O. (2007). Toward a theory of social venture franchising. *Entrepreneurship theory and practice, 31*(5), 667–685.
Tracey, P., & Phillips, N. (2007). The distinctive challenge of educating social entrepreneurs: A postscript and rejoinder to the special issue on entrepreneurship education. *Academy of Management Learning & Education, 6*(2), 264–271.
Tracey, P., Phillips, N., & Jarvis, O. (2011). Bridging institutional entrepreneurship and the creation of new organizational forms: A multilevel model. *Organization Science, 22*(1), 60–80.
Trelstad, B. (2008). Simple measures for social enterprise. *Innovations: Technology, Governance, Globalization, 3*(3), 105–118.
Tuan, M. T. (2008). *Measuring and/or estimating social value creation: Insights into eight integrated cost approaches.* Bill & Melinda Gates Foundation. Retrieved from https://docs.gatesfoundation.org/documents/wwl-report-measuring-estimating-social-value-creation.pdf
Tzouvelekas, M. (2014). Social finance tools for cooperation and development: The cooperative banking sector as a potential pillar for impact investments in Greece. In *Proceedings of the EURICSE.*
UN. (2015). *Addis Ababa acction agenda of the third international conference on financing for development: Addis Ababa action agenda.* Retrieved from https://unctad.org/system/files/official-document/ares69d313_en.pdf
UNDP. (2015). *Impact investment in Africa, trends, constraints & opportunitites.* Retrieved from https://www.undp.org/sites/g/files/zskgke326/files/migration/africa/14aae1f27ec1834e6e96d4a6af4a75de5956e746f588c7accc93c84bde98d725.pdf
UNDP. (2016). *Impact investment: Financing solutions for sustainable development.* Retrieved from https://www.sdfinance.undp.org/content/sdfinance/en/home.html
Urban, B. (2013). Influence of the institutional environment on entrepreneurial intentions in an emerging economy. *The International Journal of Entrepreneurship and Innovation, 14*(3), 179–191.
Urban, B., & Kujinga, L. (2017). The institutional environment and social entrepreneurship intentions. *International Journal of Entrepreneurial Behavior & Research, 23*(4), 638–655.
Van de Ven, A. H. (1992). Suggestions for studying strategy process: A research note. *Strategic Management Journal, 13*(S1), 169–188.
Van de Ven, A. H., & Poole, M. S. (1995). Explaining development and change in organizations. *Academy of Management Review, 20*(3), 510–540.
Van Fenema, P. C., & Loebbecke, C. (2014). Towards a framework for managing strategic tensions in dyadic interorganizational relationships. *Scandinavian Journal of Management, 30*(4), 516–524.
VanSandt, C. V., Sud, M., & Marmé, C. (2009). Enabling the original intent: Catalysts for social entrepreneurship. *Journal of Business Ethics, 90*(3), 419–428.
Vaskelainen, T., & Münzel, K. (2018). The effect of institutional logics on business model development in the sharing economy: The case of German carsharing services. *Academy of Management Discoveries, 4*(3), 273–293.
Vissa, B. (2011). A matching theory of entrepreneurs' tie formation intentions and initiation of economic exchange. *Academy of Management Journal, 54*(1), 137–158.
Voltan, A., & De Fuentes, C. (2016). Managing multiple logics in partnerships for scaling social innovation. *European Journal of Innovation Management, 19*(4), 446–467.
Waddock, S. A., & Post, J. E. (1991). Social entrepreneurs and catalytic change. *Public Administration Review, 51*, 393–401.
Wageman, R., & Turner, M. (1999). *Groups at work: Advances in theory and research.* Retrieved from https://www.routledge.com/Groups-at-Work-Theory-and-Research/Turner/p/book/9780805820799
WEF. (2014). *From the margins to the mainstream investors can design visionary and practical impact investing strategies.* Retrieved from http://www3.weforum.org/docs/WEF_ImpactInvesting_Report_ChartingTheCourse.pdf

Welter, F. (2012). All you need is trust? A critical review of the trust and entrepreneurship literature. *International Small Business Journal, 30*(3), 193–212.

Williams, T. A., Gruber, D. A., Sutcliffe, K. M., Shepherd, D. A., & Zhao, E. Y. (2017). Organizational response to adversity: Fusing crisis management and resilience research streams. *Academy of Management Annals, 11*(2), 733–769.

Wong, M. C. S., & Yap, R. C. Y. (2019). Social impact investing for marginalized communities in Hong Kong: Cases and issues. *Sustainability, 11*(10), 2831.

Wood, D. (2012). *Impact at scale: Policy innovation for institutional investment with social and environmental benefit*. Insight at Pacific Community Ventures. Retrieved from https://hipinvestor.com/wp-content/uploads/ImpactReport_FINAL2.10.12-PCV.pdf

Wood, D., & Hagerman, L. (2010). Mission investing and the philanthropic toolbox. *Policy and Society, 29*(3), 257–268.

Wry, T., & York, J. G. (2017). An identity-based approach to social enterprise. *Academy of Management Review, 42*(3), 437–460.

Yan, A., & Gray, B. (2001). Antecedents and effects of parent control in international joint ventures. *Journal of Mmanagement Studies, 38*(3), 393–416.

Yap, R. C. Y. (2018). *Social impact investing in Hong Kong* (Doctoral dissertation), City University of Hong Kong. Retrieved from https://www.cb.cityu.edu.hk/dba/docs/research/thesis/Dr%20YAP%20Richard.pdf

Young, R. J. (1995). *Colonial desire: Hybridity in theory, culture and race*. Routledge.

Yunus, M. (2009). Creating a world without poverty: Social business and the future of capitalism. *Global Urband Development, 4*(2), 1–19. Retrieved from https://www.globalurban.org/GUDMag08Vol4Iss2/Yunus.pdf

Zaheer, A., McEvily, B., & Perrone, V. (1998). Does trust matter? Exploring the effects of interorganizational and interpersonal trust on performance. *Organization Science, 9*(2), 141–159.

Zahra, S. A., Gedajlovic, E., Neubaum, D. O., & Shulman, J. M. (2009). A typology of social entrepreneurs: Motives, search processes and ethical challenges. *Journal of Business Venturing, 24*(5), 519–532.

Zeyen, A., & Beckmann, M. (2011). Social entrepreneurship and institutional logics: How social entrepreneurs use a nonprofit-/for-profit organizational mix to deal with multiple institutional logics. In *EGOS conference*. Retrieved from http://fox.leuphana.de/portal/files/1110576/Zeyen_Beckmann_Social_Entrepreneurship_and_Institutional_Logics.pdf

Zhang, N. (2017). Relationship between intangible assets and financial performance of listed telecommunication firms in China, based on empirical analysis. *African Journal of Business Management, 11*(24), 751–757.

Zhao, E. Y., & Lounsbury, M. (2016). An institutional logics approach to social entrepreneurship: Market logic, religious diversity, and resource acquisition by microfinance organizations. *Journal of Business Venturing, 31*(6), 643–662.

Zucker, L. G. (1987). Institutional theories of organization. *Annual Review of Sociology, 13*(1), 443–464.

Chapter 3
Social Enterprises and Impact Investors in Nigeria

3.1 Introduction

This chapter explores the context of social entrepreneurship and impact investing emergence in Nigeria. It begins with an outline of the history, geographical location and the Nigerian people. It reviews studies on the emergence of non-profit social enterprises and for-profit and hybrid social enterprises, including the challenges they encounter in Nigeria. Second, it examines the need for impact investing finance in Nigeria and the current state of the country in this regard. It concludes with an overview of Nigeria's socio-cultural, political and economic environment vis-à-vis social entrepreneurship.

3.2 History, Geography and People

Modern Nigeria emerged when the British Protectorates of the North and South were amalgamated in 1914 and subsequently gained independence on 1 October 1960. Nigeria now comprises 36 semi-autonomous states and a Federal Capital Territory located around Abuja, the capital. Nigeria is located in the extreme inner part of the Gulf of Guinea in West Africa, sharing borders with Niger Republic to the North, Chad and Cameroon to the East, the Gulf of Guinea to the South and the Atlantic Ocean and Benin to the West. The country has a total landmass area of 923,768 square kilometres and is endowed with oil and gas reserves in the Southeast and rich agricultural farmland, predominantly in the Northern region. There are large deposits of other mineral resources, such as bitumen, coal, gold, iron ore, lead and zinc, salt and tin, spread across the South, West, the middle belt and parts of Northern Nigeria.

J. A. Emmanuel et al., *Social Enterprises and Impact Investors*, Advances in Theory and Practice of Emerging Markets,
https://doi.org/10.1007/978-3-031-59454-0_3

On a global level, Nigeria is the most populous black nation and makes up half the population of West Africa, with approximately 202 million people, also comprising the world's largest youthful population (World Bank, 2019). Rural and urban settlements in Nigeria are in the ratio of 48–52%, respectively (CIA, 2020), meaning almost half the population has been classified as rural communities. The rural population is generally defined as settlements with a small population size, mainly characterised by agricultural production (Madu, 2010). This rural population differs from other contexts due to its unique characteristics that are linked to poor access to infrastructure (Abdu, 2017; Ali-Akpajiak & Pyke, 2003; Amao et al., 2017). The country also has a culturally diverse population, with over 250 multi-ethnic groups and over 500 indigenous languages. English has remained the official language of communication and education, in addition to three major languages linked to three major regions: Yoruba in the West, Igbo in the East and Hausa in the North (CIA, 2020). The urban population is characterised as one that exceeds a threshold of 200,000 inhabitants in urban areas (Farrell, 2018), while many scholars (Madu, 2010; Mammud, 2019; Umebali & Akuibilo, 2006) highlight the lack of adequate infrastructure, a vicious cycle of poverty, high levels of illiteracy and high youth unemployment in rural areas. Rural youth migrate to urban areas for a better life as in many other developing countries in the world. Understanding these unique differences between rural and urban areas is important, because it provides the platform for the emergence of not-for-profit SEs in Nigeria.

3.3 Not-for-Profit Social Enterprises in Nigeria

Brown (1990) describes NGOs as non-profit-oriented organisations with self-governing bodies overseen by volunteers. Most NGOs operate outside the domain of government in terms of management, funding, process and the causes they pursue, which are geared towards the socio-economic and political transformation of a society. Scholars (Fernandez, 1987; Garilao, 1987; Kotler & Murray, 1975) argue that not-for-profit SEs as a voluntary sector are well-positioned to provide critical services in remote areas where the state and private sectors have failed. According to Adeyeye (2016), social entrepreneurship then becomes the vehicle for addressing the social needs of disadvantaged people through the activities of NGOs.

An empirical study by Ademola et al. (2019) observes the inability of both public and private sectors to meet the critical needs of the Nigerian populace, which impels passionate individuals and groups to create not-for-profit SEs. Ademola et al. further reveal that local conditions and intentional mindsets comprise the two key reasons why people engage in social entrepreneurial activities in Nigeria. Local conditions reflect the poor economic situation of people in relation to the characteristics of rural settlements as a key factor. Secondly, an intentional mindset relates to the belief that many Nigerians hold towards social causes with a conviction to act positively in the interests of the majority population. Owners of several NGOs or not-for-profit SEs in Nigeria are passionate people who believe in fighting for the cause of the less privileged. Rivera-Santos et al.'s work (2015) on social enterprises' emergence in Sub-Saharan Africa also affirms that contextual dimensions of issues of acute poverty and other unfavourable local conditions both engender and impede SE emergence in Africa.

Interviews with 37 leaders of NGOs classified as non-profit SEs in Nigeria by Thorgren and Omorede (2018) have validated the presence of passionate entrepreneurs in the non-profit sector. Thorgren and Omorede's study (2018: 511) emphatically reveals that "NGOs are not necessarily representative of social entrepreneurship: the partial overlap between social enterprises and NGOs in Nigeria may not be equally visible around the world, but in the African context, NGOs seem to have become a means for many purposes of which social entrepreneurship is only one". Their study complements Littlewood and Holt's (2018) study of for-profit and hybrid structure social enterprises in Africa. Our study, therefore, clearly differentiates between non-profit social enterprise by focusing on for-profit and hybrid social enterprises whose organisational philosophy and practice most likely align with an impact investing philosophy.

3.4 The Conception of Social Enterprise with Economic Impact

Historically, the concept of social development as a national strategy for economic development in Nigeria dates back to the late 1960s (Jinadu, 1985). This means the overarching feature of hybrid SEs has been conceived in Nigeria's development strategy since independence. A press release by the then-Federal Ministry of Social Development Youth & Sports (1977) states:

> Social development is now conceived as a comprehensive action programme designed to cater for the needs of all the people in the same way as economic development. In other word, social development should be complementary of economic development. (p. 7)

This clearly reveals Nigeria's political direction in relation to social and economic development, which provides a strong foundation to pursue the goals of social and economic investment. According to the OECD (2018), social enterprise has evolved from and within the context of the social economy sector, between the market and the state, and has often been associated with concepts such as the "third sector" and non-profit sector. Situating social enterprise between the social economic sectors further highlights the rationale for social entrepreneurship development, particularly as it hinges on social inclusion and service delivery (OECD, 2018). This explains why Nigeria's Economic Recovery & Growth Plan for 2017–2020 centred on social inclusion, with a focus on growing and developing small and medium enterprises (SMEs), to contribute to both economic and social goals (NIG, 2017). Although the Nigerian government believes that social enterprise should be one of the strategies for achieving national development, a concerted effort for developing the sector is yet to be seen (Adebayo & Kolawole, 2013; Agboli & Ukaegbu, 2006).

To consolidate social and economic benefits, the Nigerian government established the Small and Medium Enterprise Development Agency (SMEDAN) in 2003 to facilitate the development of SMEs. It is argued that SMEs constitute the economy's engine room for meeting both economic and social obligations, such as poverty reduction, jobs and wealth creation and provision of goods and services to the marginalized and under-served population (NIG, 2017). These issues (that the Nigerian government aims to address) align with the goals of impact investing across international markets. Nigeria also falls in the category of countries with weaker institutions and is prone to developmental challenges. Therefore, institutional voids and societal challenges in Nigeria, as in other developing countries, have presented the country as an attractive setting and opportunity for investors seeking profound social impact together with financial returns (Mersland et al., 2020).

A survey by GIIN reveals that the concept of social entrepreneurship in Nigeria is still in the infant stage and not very popular (Wilson et al., 2015); this identified commercial SMEs with embedded social impact as a large target for impact investing. The important role of SMEs in economic growth and social and environmental impact has set them apart as hybrid social enterprises within the context of Nigeria (Ebitu et al., 2016). Rivera-Santos et al. (2015: 81) affirm this:

> Recognising that social entrepreneurs may not self-identify as social entrepreneurs in some context, despite their having all the characteristics of social entrepreneurs in the literature, has implications for data collection strategies, as it has become relatively common for researchers to rely on self-perception to identify social entrepreneurs.

GIIN (2015), therefore, targets over 72,838 SMEs in Nigeria as potential recipients of impact capital, given their role in employment creation and provision of goods and services to under-served populations. Further, part of Nigeria's Economic Recovery & Growth Plan (2017–2020) for bridging SMEs' funding gaps hinges on "partnering with the International Development Banks and the GIIN to promote and facilitate impact investment for SMEs in Nigeria" (NIG, 2017: 85). Therefore, for the purposes of this study, we must highlight here that commercial SMEs and social enterprises in Nigeria mean the same thing. Johnson and Lee (2013) also reveal it is in the interest of IIs to differentiate SEs that meet their investment goals through the IIs' decision framework, which guides investors in building impact investing portfolios within the context of long-term investment pools through complete examination of an organisation's situation, risk and governance issues (Bugg-Levine & Emerson, 2011; Diouf, 2015).

More recent surveys further reveal that Nigeria has remained Africa's most populous nation, with a population of over 196 million as of 2019 and set to grow to 377 million by 2050 (Statista, 2022). Hence the nation holds a great potential to harness its human capital for productive deployment and utilisation of impact investment opportunities. Unfortunately, there is currently considerable scepticism concerning impact investing due to lack of awareness of its potential and real objectives (Ademola et al., 2019; IIF, 2019). The community of impact investors in Nigeria is considered small compared to the size of the market, which means there are no more

IIs because only a few investable SEs exist in Nigeria. Currently, 30 IIs have a physical presence in Nigeria, as against eight investors' presence in 2015, while about 32 impact investors operate from overseas, as against 20 that initially operated from the United States and Europe in 2015 (GIIN, 2015; IIF, 2019). The impact investor type comprises development finance institutions (DFIs) and non-development finance (non-DFIs). DFIs play a critical role in financing private enterprise investing in Africa as an important complement to overseas aid (Dickinson, 2008). Examples of DFIs are multilateral and bilateral DFIs, including domestic government DFIs. Non-DFIs are private IIs who may also partner with DFIs in providing needed expertise and funding to social enterprises. Figure 3.1 below provides a clear description of DFIs and non-DFIs in Nigeria and their location. Dickinson (2008) argues that SE partnerships with DFIs in project financing are a rich potential source of development externalities. Positive externalities are derivable benefits of social entrepreneurship that impact third-party individuals who are not directly involved in the process.

Although studies reveal that IIs are interested in developing countries characterised by weaker institutions, whose by-products include inequality, deprivation, poverty, poor healthcare and corruption, it is also notable that some investors avoid contact with high-risk factors that could diminish their expectations of a higher return on investment (Mersland et al., 2020). Despite many challenges, Nigeria still presents tremendous opportunities and prospects for impact investing. Some perceived opportunities to deploy capital include microfinance and other financial services, agriculture, infrastructure and energy in the country. Therefore, this study has chosen to explore the potential of impact investing as a sustainable source of funding in growing SEs in Nigeria. The focus on Nigeria hinges on it being the largest economy in West Africa, with a growing number of both DFIs and a non-DFI impact

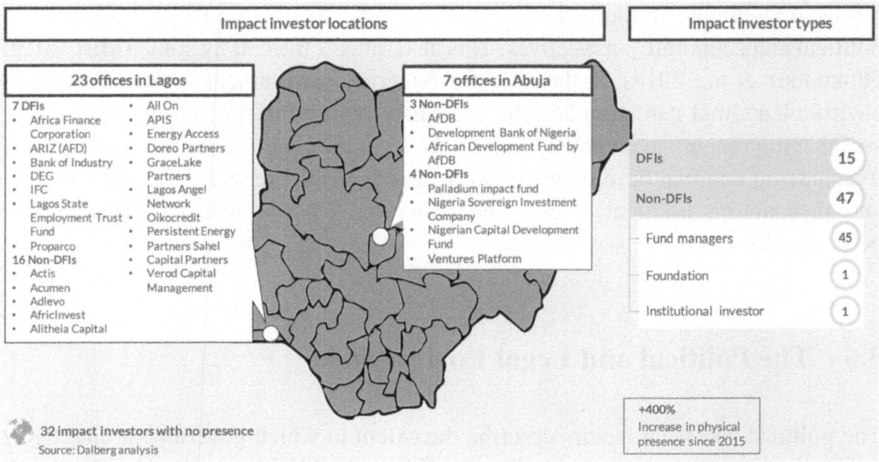

Fig. 3.1 Impact investors in Nigeria—types and location. (Source: IIF, 2019, p. 47)

investing community (GIIN, 2015; Hurst, 2015; IIF, 2019). The next section provides an overview of the Nigeria macro-environment for investment.

3.5 The Nigerian Macro-environment

Among real drivers of investment across the world is the external environment, which contributes a greater share in either enabling or disenabling investment opportunities. Hence, our study seeks to explore factors that have impeded or enabled collaboration between SEs and IIs with dyadic relationships. Mersland et al. (2020) reveal that international market selection of organisations for impact capital is mainly driven by market competition and economic, social and political factors. Examination of the context of the Nigerian environment is supported by the role that the macro-institutional environment plays in determining the barriers, enablers and drivers of SE activities (Littlewood & Holt, 2015). Classification of the macro-environment is contextually determined, as different factors manifest differently across contexts. In this study, conceptualization of the institutional environment in Nigeria follows the scholarly approaches of Du (2018) and Griffiths, Gundry and Kickul (2013) and Urban and Kujinga's (2017) classification of the institutional environment into economic, social and legal/political environments. In Nigeria, too, the influence of the institutional environment on businesses cuts across formal and informal contexts, based on Scott's (2008) characterisation of that environment.

The informal context relates to norms, practices and conventions that determine the behaviour of social enterprises in a specific social environment. Miri (2019) observes that social factors influencing the activities of social enterprises differ from one context to another and also determine the ability of entrepreneurs to give effect to their intentions. The influence of the formal context in Nigeria relates to laws and regulatory frameworks that guide the operation of social enterprises from political and economic perspectives. This also reflects the call by some (Miri, 2019; Olokundun et al., 2018) on the need for Nigeria's government to create enabling environments that can stimulate the growth of highly innovative and enthusiastic social entrepreneurs to creatively find solutions to the socio-economic impediments to achieving national development. Our research, therefore, examines the enabling and disenabling political, social and economic environment for collaboration between SEs and IIs.

3.6 The Political and Legal Environment

The political and legal factors describe the extent to which government directly or indirectly influences businesses. Ogunro (2014) highlights issues related to such factors in Nigeria that include labour law, tax policy, environmental law, tariffs, incentives, trade restrictions and political stability. In relation to stability, some scholars notice that there has been a decrease in political confidence in Nigerian governance in regard to transparency and accountability in the fight against corruption, which now undermines social relations and trust (Egharevba & Chiazor, 2013; Obadare, 2005). Indeed, the deepening crisis of trust in the political leadership of Nigeria has created a dearth of trust in social intercourse between ordinary citizens and the Nigerian political leadership. Consequently, the unfavourable tax and trade policies, labour law and business incentives are a manifestation of unfavourable policies from a "sick" political leadership. Despite the political setbacks, according to Doing Business (2020), Nigeria has made some remarkable progress, rising 15 places to rank 131 from 146 in the previous year of the World Bank global index of ease of doing business. Twenty-nine states in Nigeria have also implemented 43 reforms across four strategic areas that are benchmarked, making it easier for local entrepreneurs to start and operate a new business. This development followed the establishment of the Presidential Enabling Business Environment Council (PEBEC) in 2016 (Salaudeen, 2019). Recently, the Nigerian government has introduced a new Companies and Allied Matters Act (CAMA), which replaces the Companies and Allied Matters Act 1990. The new Act provides impetus for a robust reform of legal, regulatory and administrative bottlenecks that have over three decades impeded investment in micro, small and medium enterprises (MSMEs) (Toyin et al., 2020). Despite this development, there is not yet a regulatory legal and institutional status for hybrid social enterprises in Nigeria (Miri, 2019) which is comparable to the robust legal forms adopted by European countries (Defourny & Nyssens, 2010). Ogunro (2014) notes that insecurity, particularly in the northern part of Nigeria connected to "Boko-Haram", has closed down the operation of several businesses in the region.

3.7 The Economic Environment

A World Bank (2019) report categorised Nigeria among middle-income countries with a mixed economy and emerging market of fast-growing telecommunications, financial services and entertainment sectors. These sectors were initially not captured in the Gross Domestic Product (GDP). After rebasing of the economy by the National Bureau of Statistics (NBS) in April 2014, from about USD 270 billion to USD 510 billion, Nigeria emerged as the largest economy in Africa and 26th in the world (World Bank, 2014). The economy has been primarily driven by oil, accounting for about 65% of government revenues and 88% of Nigeria's foreign exchange earnings (KPMG, 2019). This explains why fluctuation in global oil prices has drastically affected Nigeria's budget and other domestic policies. Therefore, it is believed that opportunities abound for Nigeria to harness impact-investing opportunities by driving other sectors of the economy into the country's mainstream revenue sources.

Studies also reveal that several economic indicators influence the rate of investment in Nigeria, including interest rates, exchanges and the rate of inflation (Abdu, 2017; Adamu, 2009). The interplay between these indicators has helped define whether a nation's economy is experiencing growth or development, since these mean different things. Economic growth primarily focuses on a quantifiable metric such as gross national product (GNP) or aggregate income. Economic development focuses on tangible outcomes such as infrastructure, education, poverty levels and public health (Feldman & Storper, 2018). Sen (1990) provides a balanced definition of economic development as one that entails capacity development with potential for expanding economic actors' capabilities. Scholars assert that the economic environment is the great driver of domestic and foreign direct investment (FDI) into Nigeria, and this also determines growth and development (As, 2011; Wafure & Nurudeen, 2010). Wafure and Nurudeen (2010) have identified exchange rates as a key determinant of FDI.

Since the introduction of Structural Adjustment Programmes (SAP) in 1986, Nigeria's exchange rate policy has remained the lifeline in transforming the economy (Anyanwu et al., 2017). The premise for SAP was to achieve a favourable balance of payment from SMEs' import and export transactions, with the ultimate goal of making the economic environment more attractive for domestic and foreign investors (Akyuz, 2019). The introduction of SAP marked the beginning of the depreciation of the local currency (the *naira*) against the US dollar, which has not been regained to date. At the inception of SAP, the naira to dollar rate surged from N3.32 in 1986 to N755 dollars currently (Fasanya & Akinwale, 2022; Anyanwu et al., 2017). The unfavourable exchange rate underpins the challenges of Nigeria's economy today. Osabuohien et al. (2018) attribute the instability in the economy to exchange rate fluctuations brought about by the depreciation of the naira in the foreign exchange market. The effect has been evidenced in the poor performance of the economy, with the unemployment rate, as of 2020, rising to 27%, which has also been impacted by COVID-19 (Statista, 2020).

Irrespective of the state of the current economic indices, through Vision 20:2020, Nigeria was predicted to become among the first 20 global economies by 2020. The vision was coined following the assessment of the rich human and material resources believed to engender robust growth and development if well deployed and managed, based on realistic economic projections. What constitute challenges in Nigeria's economic environment today also present as opportunities. Several studies reveal that IIs are motivated to direct impact funds to regions with greater social impact opportunities (Kipfer, 2019; Ormiston et al., 2015; Roundy et al., 2017).

3.8 Socio-cultural Environment

According to Ogunro (2014), social factors in the Nigeria business environment also include the cultural aspect of the country's population. Kareem et al. (2020: 499) argue that "the socio-cultural environment consists of the components that make up the social systems and the way of life of the people in a particular environment". If deconstructed, the social aspect comprises the population growth rate and age distribution, attitude and safety nets. The social aspect of the environment determines the demand for an organisation's products and how it operates (Ogunro, 2014). The social environment of every business constitutes that segment of the society that determines the level of human interaction with the social world. In the cultural orientation and technological advancement of a country, it is critical to determine the level of interaction and engagement with the business world. It is worth noting that the influence of the socio-cultural aspect of the environment on enterprise development has remained under-explored (Thornton et al., 2011). From Scott's dimensions of the environment, the cultural cognitive and normative pillars represent the constituents of the socio-cultural environment (Scott, 2013). Informal arrangements often fall within norms, practices and conventions that determine how organisations operate in any context. Addressing Nigeria's social environment dimension will provide a better understanding of how the social environment shapes the entrepreneurial decision-making process between SEs and IIs.

Kareem et al. (2020) undertook an empirical study to ascertain the socio-cultural factors affecting the development of small-scale agro-allied manufacturing enterprises in Nigeria. Participant responses reveal the following percentages: religious belief (20/1%), corruption (14.6%), ostentatious lifestyle (11.0%), nepotism (8.7%), spirituality (9.8%), illiteracy (10.7%), extended family (8.9%) and commitment to wealth (8.9%). These findings show the significant roles of religious beliefs, lifestyle, literacy and corruption in Nigeria's socio-cultural environment. These factors at different points have impacted on the social institutions and organisations within the social system. The findings from Kareem et al. validate several arguments that socio-cultural factors that cut across beliefs, norms, values, corruption and people's attitudes have a significant influence on organisational development.

The next section explores for-profit and hybrid SEs' operation across Nigeria's social, political and economic environment.

3.9 For-Profit and Hybrid Social Enterprises in Nigeria

Our study empirically examines how SEs with blended motives achieve social impact while also making profit from their activities in Nigeria. The nature of social enterprise examined in Nigeria aligns with the OECD (1999: 3) definition as "any private activity conducted in the public interest organised with entrepreneurial strategy, but whose main purpose is not the maximization of profit but the attainment of certain economic and social goals, and which has the capacity for bringing innovative solutions to the problems of social exclusion and unemployment". In Nigeria, examples of for-profit or hybrid SEs working in line with impact investing motives fall into the category of microfinance institutions (Ogbo et al., 2019). Several microfinance providers operate dual objectives of reaching many poor clients that are mostly SMEs in urban or rural areas seeking financial sustainability to meet the needs of the poor population. The key distinguishing feature of these enterprises in Nigeria is their mission which prioritises social benefits above financial returns. When profit is generated from their activities, it is reinvested into the business to further the social mission instead of distributing it to shareholders.

It is important to note, however, that SEs that operate as for-profit or hybrid structures are not common in Nigeria. While financing options open to these categories of social enterprise that focus on social propositions, but with financial returns, abound, findings from an empirical study by Ademola et al. (2019) reveal that several SEs (mostly NGOs) largely depend on traditional finance options of grants, donations and sponsorship from foundations, government support, etc. This is first because some non-profit SEs cannot qualify for bank loans due to stringent institutional requirements and conditionality attached to such funds. The second reason is that innovative financing options of impact investing and social bonds are alien to most SEs operating as non-profit organisations in Nigeria. The study reveals that 77.5% and 79.8% disagree and strongly disagree, respectively, to use impact investing and social bonds as a source of finance; 14.45% and 10.25% were undecided—apparently due to ignorance of either impact investing or social bonds. Ademola et al. (2019) thus reveal lack of awareness about impact investing finance options. The findings also validate the direction of the current study to provide empirical examples of how some few SEs are indeed benefiting from impact investing funds and to demonstrate how they qualify for such funding, in order to inspire others.

3.10 The Need for Impact Investing in Nigeria

Over-dependence on public funds from oil revenue has slowed development in Nigeria, giving rise to the recent economic recession (Benjamin, 2017; Onyele Ko, 2016). The COVID-19 pandemic, which has crippled economies around the world, has also necessitated innovation, seeking a more sustainable solution for dealing with the health and financial crises in Nigeria. Impact investing, a business-like and well-being approach to financing SEs, is believed capable of engendering a robust change in the social and environmental challenges in Nigeria (UNDP, 2015). The premise of impact investing is that it will stimulate the process of diversifying the Nigerian economy, which currently depends on 95% of revenue from oil to fund the national budget, so that diversification of the economy for sustained growth remains crucial (Onyele Ko, 2016; UNDP, 2015). JPMorgan and GIIN observe that growing the impact investing industry in Nigeria has been impeded by lack of viable SEs with good track records and relevant characteristics that could attract impact investors (Clarkin & Cangioni, 2016). Mersland et al. (2020) find that international market selection of SEs is contingent upon their hybridity. These overarching features distinguish them from other types of organisations. This again justifies the focus of this study on hybrid SEs. Roundy et al. (2017) observe that some IIs have selected

SEs on the strength of their management team or the venture's scalability potential. Examples of those few that have met the investment appetites of IIs, presented in subsequent chapters of this study, will, we hope, inspire the emergence of more hybrid SEs.

3.11 Conclusion

Because social entrepreneurship is a contextually driven phenomenon, this chapter explored the emergence of social enterprise and impact investing, including the influence of the socio-cultural, political and economic environment on social entrepreneurship in Nigeria. The chapter concluded with a discussion on the need for impact investing opportunities in Nigeria in relation to her current challenges in diversifying the economy, given the strong reliance on crude oil. Chap. 4 explores the research design and methodology which guide data collection and analysis in addressing the identified research opportunities in Nigeria.

References

Abdu, M. (2017). Human development index: A paradox for the Nigerian economy. *International Journal of Advanced Studies in Business Strategies and Management, 5*(2), 1–14.

Adamu, A. (2009). The effects of global financial crisis on Nigerian economy. *International Journal of Investment and Finance, 1*(1&2), 11–21.

Adebayo, O., & Kolawole, J. A. (2013). The historical background of entrepreneurial development in Nigeria: Its gains, shortcomings and needful. *Journal of Emerging Trends in Economics and Management Sciences, 4*(5), 493.

Ademola, A. H., Olajide, O. P., Ayodele, A. Y., & Olusola, A. J. (2019). An examination of financing practices of social entrepreneurs in Nigeria: A study of selected non-governmental organisations. *Academy of Entrepreneurship Journal, 25*(2), 1–17.

Adeyeye, M. M. (2016). Non-governmental organisations and social entrepreneurship growth in Niger State of Nigeria. *Journal of African Political Economy and Development, 1*(1), 56–75.

Agboli, M., & Ukaegbu, C. C. (2006). Business environment and entrepreneurial activity in Nigeria: Implications for industrial development. *Journal of Modern African Studies, 44*(1), 1–30.

Akyuz, M. (2019). Effect of structural adjustment programme on the performance of small and medium scale enterprises in Nigeria. *International Journal of Social Science and Humanities Invention, 6*(8), 5565–5570.

Ali-Akpajiak, S. C., & Pyke, T. (2003). *Measuring poverty in Nigeria*. Oxfam GB.

Amao, J. O., Ayantoye, K., & Fanifosi, G. E. (2017). An analysis of multidimensional poverty and its determinants in rural Nigeria. *Journal of Development and Agricultural Economics, 9*(11), 303–311.

Anyanwu, F., Ananwude, A., & Okoye, N. (2017). Exchange rate policy and Nigeria's economic growth: A granger causality impact assessment. *International Journal of Applied Economics, Finance and Accounting, 1*(1), 1–13.

As, B. (2011). The determinants of private domestic investment in Nigeria. *Far East Journal of Psychology and Business, 4*(3), 27–37.

Benjamin, S. S.-I. (2017). Economic recession in Nigeria: A case for government intervention. *International Journal of Economics and Management Studies, 4*(6), 48–51.

Brown, G. (1990). *Role of NGO in development cooperatives*. Research Paper UNDP/Yale Collaborative Programs, Olera Publications, Maslyukivska, New Heaven.

Bugg-Levine, A., & Emerson, J. (2011). Impact investing: Transforming how we make money while making a difference. *Innovations, 6*(3), 9–18.

CIA. (2020). *The world fact book*, Nigeria. Retrieved from https://www.cia.gov/library/publications/the-world-factbook/geos/ni.html

Clarkin, J. E., & Cangioni, C. (2016). Impact investing: A primer and review of the literature. *Entrepreneurship Research Journal, 6*(2), 135–173.

Defourny, J., & Nyssens, M. (2010). Conceptions of social enterprise and social entrepreneurship in Europe and the United States: Convergences and divergences. *Journal of Social Entrepreneurship, 1*(1), 32–53.

Dickinson, T. (2008). *Development finance institutions: Profitability promoting development*. Retrieved from http://www.oecd.org/dev/41302068.pdf

Diouf, D. (2015). Exploring the barriers to impact investing in the sustainable energy area in West Africa. In *Decentralized solutions for developing economies* (pp. 177–183). Springer.

Doing Business. (2020). *Comparing business in 190 economies: Region profile Sub-Saharan Africa*. Retrieved from https://www.doingbusiness.org/content/dam/doingBusiness/media/Profiles/Regional/DB2020/SSA.pdf

Du, Z. (2018). A literature review on institutional environment and technological innovation. *American Journal of Industrial and Business Management, 8*(9), 1941–1950.

Ebitu, E. T., Glory, B., & Alfred, U. J. (2016). An appraisal of Nigeria's micro, small and medium enterprises (MSMEs): Growth, challenges and prospects. *British Journal of Marketing Studies, 4*(5), 21–36.

Egharevba, M., & Chiazor, A. I. (2013). Political corruption and national development in Nigeria. *International Journal of Social Sciences and Humanities Review, 4*(1), 14–23.

Farrell, K. (2018). An inquiry into the nature and causes of Nigeria's rapid urban transition. *Urban Forum, 29*(3), 277–298.

Fasanya, I. O., & Akinwale, O. A. (2022). Exchange rate shocks and sectoral stock returns in Nigeria: Do asymmetry and structural breaks matter? *Cogent Economics & Finance, 10*(1), 2045719.

Federal Ministry of Social Development Youth & Sports. (1977). Introduction to the social development division, Press release.

Feldman, M., & Storper, M. (2018). Economic growth and economic development: Geographical dimensions, definition, and disparities. In *The new Oxford handbook of economic geography* (Vol. 143). Oxford University Press.

Fernandez, A. P. (1987). NGOs in South Asia: People's participation and partnership. *World Development, 15*(suppl 1), 39–49.

Garilao, E. D. (1987). Indigenous NGOs as strategic institutions: Managing the relationship with government and resource agencies. *World Development, 15*, 113–120.

GIIN. (2015). *The landscape for impact investing in West Africa*. Retrieved from https://thegiin.org/knowledge/publication/westafricareport

Griffiths, M. D., Gundry, L. K., & Kickul, J. R. (2013). The socio-political, economic, and cultural determinants of social entrepreneurship activity: An empirical examination. *Journal of Small Business and Enterprise Development, 20*(2), 341–357.

Hurst, G. (2015). *Impact investing powers up east African economies*. Institutional Investor. Retrieved from https://www.institutionalinvestor.com/article/b14z9w8yhzj3b6/impact-investing-powers-up-east-african-economies

IIF. (2019). *Nigeria and Ghana Impact investing and policy landscape*. Retrieved from https://thegiin.org/assets/IIF%20Study%20on%20Impact%20Investing%20Full%20Report.pdf

Jinadu, G. M. (1985). Social development in Nigeria: A case analysis. *The Journal of Sociology & Social Welfare, 12*(4), 850–877.

Johnson, K., & Lee, H. (2013). *Impact investing: A framework for decision making*. Cambridge Associates LLC.

Kareem, A. O., Jiboye, T. F., Adejumo, O. O., & Akinyosoye, M. O. (2020). Socio-cultural factors and performance of small-scale enterprise in agro-allied manufacturing firms in Nigeria. In *The Palgrave handbook of agricultural and rural development in Africa* (pp. 495–512). Springer International Publishing.

Kipfer, R. (2019). *What drives impact investors?: A comparison between a developed and a developing country*. Retrieved from https://www.sitra.fi/en/blogs/what-drives-impact-investors/

Kotler, P., & Murray, M. (1975). Third sector management-The role of marketing. *Public Administration Review, 35*(5), 467–472.

KPMG. (2019). *Nigerian iil and gas update*. Retrieved from https://assets.kpmg/content/dam/kpmg/ng/pdf/tax/Nigerian-Oil-and-Gas-Update.pdf

Littlewood, D., & Holt, D. (2015). Social entrepreneurship in South Africa: Exploring the influence of environment. *Business & Society, 57*(3), 1–37.

Littlewood, D., & Holt, D. (2018). Social entrepreneurship in South Africa: Exploring the influence of environment. *Business & Society, 57*(3), 525–561.

Madu, I. A. (2010). The structure and pattern of rurality in Nigeria. *GeoJournal, 75*(2), 175–184.

Mammud, V. E. (2019). Rural development in Nigeria: Concept, approaches, challenges and prospects. *Global Scientific Journals, 7*(5), 2320–9186.

Mersland, R., Nyarko, S. A., & Sirisena, A. B. (2020). A hybrid approach to international market selection: The case of impact investing organizations. *International Business Review, 29*(1), 101624.

Miri, D. F. (2019). *Influence of institutional environment and the development of social enterprises in Nigeria* (Doctoral thesis), University of Huddersfield. Retrieved from http://eprints.hud.ac.uk/id/eprint/34957

NIG. (2017). *Nigeria economic recovery & growth plan 2017 – 2020*, Abuja. https://statehouse.gov.ng/policy/economy/economic-recovery-and-growth-plan/

Obadare, E. (2005). A crisis of trust: History, politics, religion and the polio controversy in Northern Nigeria. *Patterns of Prejudice, 39*(3), 265–284.

OECD. (1999). *Social enterprises*. OECD. Retrieved from https://www.oecd.org/cfe/leed/social-enterprises.htm

OECD. (2018). *Social enterprise sector: A conceptual framework*. OECD. Retrieved from https://www.oecd.org/cfe/leed/37753595.pdf

Ogbo, A., Igwe, A., Ezeobi, J., Modebe, N., & Kalu, E. U. (2019). The impact of social entrepreneurship on the sustainability of selected small and medium enterprises in Nigeria. *Advances in Research, 19*, 1–15.

Ogunro, V. O. (2014). Nigeria's business environment: Issues challenges and prospects. *International Journal of Academic Research in Business and Social Sciences, 4*(4), 132–138.

Olokundun, A. M., Moses, C., Falola, H. O., Ibidunni, A. S., Salau, O. P., & Oluremi, O. A. (2018). The role of social entrepreneurship and the state in propelling national development in Nigeria: A conceptual approach. *International Journal of Entrepreneurship, 22*(1), 1–6.

Onyele Ko, N. E. (2016). Sources of public funds and economic prosperity: The Nigerian case. *Journal of Business & Financial Affairs, 5*(4), 1–11.

Ormiston, J., Charlton, K., Donald, M. S., & Seymour, R. G. (2015). Overcoming the challenges of impact investing: Insights from leading investors. *Journal of Social Entrepreneurship, 6*(3), 352–378.

Osabuohien, E., Obiekwe, E., Urhie, E. S., & Osabohien, R. (2018). Inflation rate, exchange rate volatility and exchange rate passthrough nexus: The Nigerian experience. *Journal of Applied Economic Sciences, 2*(56), 574–585. Retrieved from http://eprints.covenantuniversity.edu.ng/id/eprint/12229

Rivera-Santos, M., Holt, D., Littlewood, D., & Kolk, A. (2015). Social entrepreneurship in sub-Saharan Africa. *The Academy of Management Perspectives, 29*(1), 72–91.

Roundy, P., Holzhauer, H., & Dai, Y. (2017). Finance or philanthropy? Exploring the motivations and criteria of impact investors. *Social Responsibility Journal, 13*(3), 491–512.

Salaudeen, A. (2019). Nigeria improves in World Bank ease of doing business ranking, but is it easier to do business there? *CNN*. Retrieved from https://edition.cnn.com/2019/10/24/africa/nigeria-improves-in-world-bank-ranking/index.html#:~:text=Doing%20business%20in%20Nigeria&text=Nigeria's%2015%2Dplace%20rise%20on,Top%2070%20position%20by%20 2023

Scott, W. R. (2008). *Institutions and organizations: Ideas and interests*. Standford University, Sage Publications, Inc..

Scott, W. R. (2013). *Institutions and organizations: Ideas, interests, and identities*. Sage Publications.

Sen, A. (1990). Development as capability expansion. In *The community development reader* (pp. 41–58). Oxford University Press.

Statista. (2020). *Unemployment rate in Nigeria 2019*. Retrieved from https://www.statista.com/statistics/812300/youth-unemployment-rate-in-nigeria/

Statista. (2022). *Population forecast in Nigeria in selected years between 2025 and 2050 access via*. https://www.statista.com/statistics

Thorgren, S., & Omorede, A. (2018). Passionate leaders in social entrepreneurship: Exploring an African context. *Business & Society, 57*(3), 481–524.

Thornton, P. H., Ribeiro-Soriano, D., & Urbano, D. (2011). Socio-cultural factors and entrepreneurial activity: An overview. *International Small Business Journal, 29*(2), 105–118.

Toyin, S., Tosin, O., & Banwo, E. (2020). *CAMA 2020: Reforming provisions that impact the Nigerian business community*. Retrieved from https://www.proshareng.com/news/Taxes%20&%20Tariffs/CAMA-ACT-2020%2D%2DReforming-Provisions-that-Impact-the-Nigerian-Business-Community/52707#

Umebali, E. E., & Akuibilo, C. (2006). Readings in cooperative economics and management. In *Rural resources farm business management and rural development*. Computer Edge Publishers.

UNDP. (2015). *Impact investment in Africa, trends, constraints & opportunitites*. Retrieved from https://www.undp.org/sites/g/files/zskgke326/files/migration/africa/14aae1f27ec1834e6e96d4a6af4a75de5956e746f588c7accc93c84bde98d725.pdf

Urban, B., & Kujinga, L. (2017). The institutional environment and social entrepreneurship intentions. *International Journal of Entrepreneurial Behavior & Research, 23*(4), 638–655.

Wafure, O. G., & Nurudeen, A. (2010). Determinants of foreign direct investment in Nigeria: An empirical analysis. *Global Journal of Human Social Science, 10*(1), 26–34.

Wilson, K. E., Silva, F., & Ricardson, D. (2015). *Social impact investment: Building the evidence base*. Retrieved from https://sites.duke.edu/casei3/files/2013/03/OECD-social-impact-investment.pdf

World Bank. (2014). *Nigeria economic report*. Retrieved from. https://www.worldbank.org/en/country/nigeria/publication/nigeria-economic-report-improved-economic-outlook-in-2014-and-prospects-for-continued-growth-look-good

World Bank. (2019). *The World Bank in Nigeria: Overview*. Retrieved from https://www.worldbank.org/en/country/nigeria/overview#1

Chapter 4
Exploring the Dynamics Involved in Dyadic Partnerships

4.1 Chapter Objectives

> All social life is essentially practical. All mysteries which led theory to mysticism find their rational solution in human practice and in the comprehension of this practice. Bottomore et al. (1991: 325)

This chapter presents the philosophical assumptions underpinning the study and introduces the research design and empirical techniques adopted to answer the research questions. As discussed in Chap. 2, four research sub-questions were developed to explore how SEs and IIs establish partner fit to pursue their social and economic interests in Nigeria. These research questions investigate what factors in the micro- and macro-environments influence their collaborative process and what is learned from their experience. This chapter is organised firstly with an overview of philosophical assumptions grounded in critical realism (CR), then the presentation of research design, sample selection (purposive sampling), data collection strategy (primary and secondary data) and data analysis.

4.2 Philosophical Assumption: Critical Realism

> Critical realism provides philosophical principles upon which dynamical non-linear characteristics can be understood… These principles allow knowledge that is socially constructed, and therefore fallible, that represents an understanding of the world in which real mechanisms exist, but which can only be sensed by their effects. For example, the appearance of novel structures and patterns can be explained by a conception of contingent or latent powers inherent in the inter-relationships, rather than by the external imposition of order. (Fuller & Moran, 2001: 49)

J. A. Emmanuel et al., *Social Enterprises and Impact Investors*, Advances in Theory and Practice of Emerging Markets,
https://doi.org/10.1007/978-3-031-59454-0_4

Critical realism as a qualitative research philosophy in this study is based on the premise that any study centred on exploring human experiences should focus on human cultural norms, symbols, values and social processes observed from a subjective perspective (Bhaskar, 1998). CR views society as inseparable from human components, since society's existence depends largely on the activities of humans (Archer et al., 2013; Archer, 1995). Central to CR is the explanation of social phenomena through an in-depth understanding of human behaviour and experiences by uncovering the mechanism that produces them (Archer et al., 2013). According to Bhaskar (1978), the philosophy of reality should begin with the theory "of being" (ontology) as distinct from the theory "of knowledge" (epistemology). Simply put, ontology refers to what actually exists in nature, that is, the assumption about the nature of reality that researchers investigate. Epistemology, in contrast, refers to how researchers acquire knowledge of what exists. The distinct characteristic of CR lies in its delineation between ontology and epistemology. In this sense, CR combines realist ontology, which believes in the existence of a real-world independent of our beliefs and construction, with constructivist epistemology, which holds that our knowledge of the world is inevitably our construction and that it is impossible to achieve a completely "objective" account independent of other specific perspectives (Maxwell, 2012). The implication of this viewpoint for our study is that the researcher cannot capture the reality of SEs' and IIs' collaboration in the macro- and micro-environment without immersion in their experience in the real world.

Ryan et al. (2012) contend there is a gap in the application of ontology in mainstream business relationship research, but believe the application of CR philosophy in business relationship research can help in overcoming the challenges. Our study draws upon CR as an appropriate vehicle for social science and entrepreneurship research (Bergene, 2007; Blundel, 2007; Gerrits & Verweij, 2013) to understand and explain the pattern of collaboration between dyadic partners (Ryan & O'Malley, 2006). Dyadic partners in this present study comprise SEs and IIs with dyadic relations in Nigeria.

The first justification for applying CR philosophy is that CR is widely acknowledged as being particularly apposite in relationship studies (Easton, 1995, 2003, 2010; Ryan et al., 2012), and can add great value in explaining the development of dyadic relationships (Ryan & O'Malley, 2006). The second justification is rooted in Blundel's (2007: 9) description of CR as a suitable vehicle for entrepreneurial research under three themes: first, "CR can provide the much-needed contextualisation of entrepreneurial phenomena in research studies", such as contextualising SEs and IIs collaboration experience in Nigerian; second, "CR can facilitate greater theoretical integration between disciplines and across multiple levels of analysis", such as the integration of social exchange and institutional logic frameworks in the current study; and third, "CR can enhance the explanatory potential of existing qualitative research techniques", such as explaining the pattern of collaborative relationship between SEs and IIs. Scott (2005) argues that studies that are responsive to investigation using CR philosophy often focus on the relationship between structure and agency: hence the search for structural conditions from the entrepreneurial environment and generative mechanisms to explain the challenging complexity and nature of social and business relationship (Ryan & O'Malley, 2006; Ryan et al., 2012), because dyadic-level research is concerned with exploring how relationships are initiated, developed and maintained (Wilson, 1995). It is important to note that our study focuses on the pre-investment aspect of the SE and II relationship.

We use CR to facilitate a more nuanced integration of competing theories in management studies (Wynn Jr & Williams, 2012): Social exchange and institutional logic theories are combined to understand contextual entrepreneurial patterns of behaviour between SEs and IIs. The SET link to CR hinges on its explanatory power of the relationship between agency and structure as a mechanistic process (Ryan et al., 2012; Vincent, 2008). SET offers a lens to examine the micro pattern of complementary exchange behaviours between SEs and IIs from the perspective of determining factors for mutuality between dyad partners, while CR provides the philosophical perspective for explaining the mechanism through which inter-organisational dyadic relationships and networks are developed (Ryan et al., 2012). This perspective aligns with Vincent's (2008: 877) argument that "CR offers an ontology and meta-theory that has various implications for how we approach ideas about social structures, agencies and processes".

From an institutional logic perspective, Leca and Naccache (2006) contend that institutional entrepreneurs can collaboratively use a hybrid organisational form as a structure shaped by contextual factors to create or modify existing logics. The principal motivation for using CR is thus that: (1) SE and II hybrid organisational form underlies the emergence of any institution and is situated in the real domain; (2) since institutions are "self-reproducing recurrent patterns of behaviour" identifiable by researchers, they fall within the actual domain; and (3) institutions can be observed in the empirical domain. Hence, CR's role in the study helps in explaining the micro-level patterns of social change through the collaboration influence by both structure and agency (Bhaskar, 1998; Danermark et al., 2005; Hu, 2018).

CR argues that agency has causal powers that cannot be reduced to deterministic conditions (Vincent, 2008), as seen in institutional theory. Blundel (2007) further states that CR can provide the basis for contextualising entrepreneurial phenomena. Sayer (2004) adds that we should aim to know beyond the strategies behind the move of actors, but what is unique about the context that enabled them to be successful. In other words, we do not just need to know how SEs and IIs collaborate in Nigeria; more importantly, we need to know what contextual factors account for their success or failure. Scott (2005) asserts that studies that are responsive to investigation using a CR approach often focus on the relationship between structure and agency.

Our study contends that while SET and Institutional logic enable our understanding of structural properties and inter-organisational relations (Vincent, 2008), they have been criticised for being deterministic and lacking consideration of the influence of the environment on social patterns of relationships. They both pose limitations for the potential of agency in engendering social change. CR philosophy can help conceptualize inter-organisational dyadic business relationships as real socially constructed entities or structures, because they are governed by institutionalised beliefs and practices (Bhaskar, 1998). According to Ryan et al. (2012), business inter-organisational dyadic relationship-related activities happen when the mechanisms of these entities or structures become activated and exercised. These mechanisms are explained in social exchange theory (SET) as exchange processes that encompass human actions, perceptions and decisions of actors and their consequences for their relationship in a given context, including the learning experience. SEs' and IIs' decisions before establishing partner fit from resource complementarity and organisational compatibility are critical to investment success.

4.3 Research Design

A research design connotes the master plan or framework of a study that sheds light on how the investigation is to be executed. Our study uses an inductive approach to qualitative research as the suitable method in view of the nascent stage of impact investing and social enterprise organisations. The qualitative research method provides the right platform to explore the subjective perspective of SEs and IIs about the real world, and facilitates dialogue between the researcher and participants (Wahyuni, 2012). It also features sample selection, measurement tools and strategy for data collection to address the research questions. According to Mouton (1996: 175), the research design serves to "plan, structure and execute" the study to maximise the "validity of the findings". It provides a compass for the study through the lens of the underlying philosophical assumptions. The overarching role of the dyadic design adopted in this study is to answer the research question by drawing on a data set from social enterprises and impact investors with dyadic relations in Nigeria.

The research design here explores the perspective of entrepreneurial-oriented relationships between firms in a dyadic relation. That approach aligns with Manning and Kunkel's (2015) view that a relationship-oriented topic can benefit immensely from dyadic analysis. Actors in dyads were analysed to uncover the pattern through which such relationships developed by capturing individual narratives and experience. Stemming from qualitative research philosophy, the study seeks to understand the meaning and experiential dimension of people's lives from interaction with the social world (Fossey et al., 2002). The study is akin to understanding the pattern of a relationship that evolves into an established partner fit between a social enterprise and an impact investor in a dyad. The study uses a qualitative dyadic design with an emphasis on "thinking with theory" beyond the conventional qualitative mechanistic coding, thematic analysis and composing transparent narratives (Jackson & Mazzei, 2011). These approaches are utilised, but "thinking with theory" further stretches research data and theory to the limit of producing knowledge differently (Jackson & Mazzei, 2013). The approach is aligned with CR philosophy in searching for deeper reality of a participant's experience of a phenomenon.

4.4 Unit of Analysis

Scholars have acknowledged that dyadic research design is connected to data that comprise interactions between actors in which the unit of analysis is usually the dyad (Cranmer & Desmarais, 2016). Using SEs and IIs with dyadic relations in this study implies that the components of the study are examined at the dyadic level. According to Thompson and Walker (1982), each level of the research process involving the dyad as the unit of analysis must have a relationship with mutually patterned action or attributes of the two entities as the object of the study. Interactions between these entities can take different formats of networks and inter-organisational alliances or collaboration, as framed in the current study. Social and behavioural scientists have recognised the relevance of both inter-organisational (Amoako, 2019; Ojukwu et al., 2007) and interpersonal trust from the context of dyadic relations (Lu et al., 2017; Vanneste, 2016; Wang et al., 2018). For example, some studies have examined the effect of social motives (Olekalns et al., 2002; Srivastava & Chakravarti, 2009) and friendship (Luvison & Cummings, 2017; Olk & Elvira, 2001) on the perception of trust in the context of negotiation. Similarly, this study argues that inter-organisational trust between collaborating partners can be developed through the exchange of complementary resources and alignment of organisational beliefs to enhance mutual commitment. The analysis, therefore, aims to reveal the determinants of trust at the micro-organisational level from the context of inter-organisational collaboration between social enterprises and impact investors. This line of reasoning will contribute to knowledge of the determining factors of trust in dyadic negotiation (Lu et al., 2017).

Alluding to the importance of dyadic relationships in business-to-business and social settings as framed in this study, researchers strongly suggest the need to direct substantial attention to the embedded context where dyadic business relationships emerge (Anderson et al., 1994). For example, since this study examines economic and social interests as the motive for collaboration between SEs and IIs, the analysis will provide greater insight into dyadic relationships when social and economic interests are involved. The analysis is framed from the context of social and commercial activities across hybrid social enterprises in Nigeria (Fig. 4.1).

4.5 Methods

In dyadic research, the unit of analysis is the dyadic partners (Maguire, 1999). This study uses qualitative research tools such as interviews, coding and thematic analysis to explore how collaboration in the six dyad cases evolves. The study adopts an affective mode of dyadic analysis to examine the pattern of relationship across the dyad cases. Patterns of relationships within dyads in this study have been conceptualized from the research problem down to the methods and interpretation (Eisikovits & Koren, 2010). Thompson and Walker (1982) suggest five characteristics

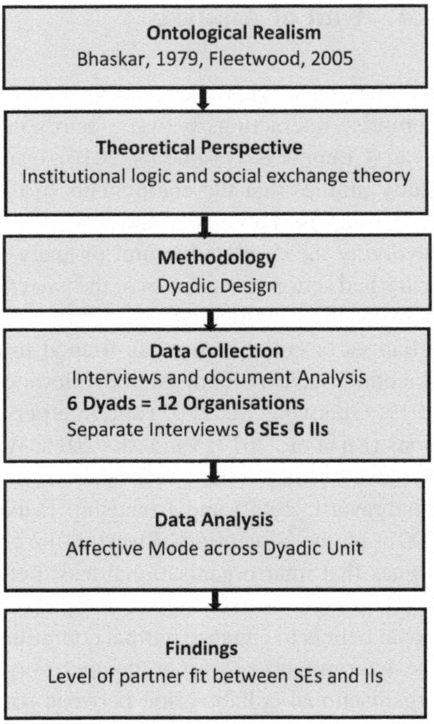

Fig. 4.1 Research design

associated with a dyadic research method. (1) The problem is conceptualized at the level of the relationship—the pattern between two people or organisation as in the current research. (2) The sample of participants is contingent upon involvement in representative relationships, although one or both members may be chosen as informants. In the case of the current study, two collaborating organisations are labelled as SEs and IIs and selected as dyads. (3) In regard to measurement, one or both members of a relationship may be assessed on self, other and/or the relationship. The current study measures the relationship between two organisations to ascertain how they collaborate to pursue their unique social and economic interest. (4) The analysis is interpersonal or inter-dyadic, providing information about the pattern between individuals or between relationships. The current study's analysis is based on the dyadic inter-organisational relationship (Ryan & O'Malley, 2006). Inter-dyadic in the context of this study connotes a pair of SEs and IIs coming together to form inter-dyadic relations. It is inter-dyadic because the relationship is from an inter-organisational perspective. (5) Interpretations of the data and implications refer to the relationship between two people. In the current study, data are interpreted from the implication of micro and macro influence on collaboration between two organisations.

Dyadic researchers have observed that studying dyadic phenomena from one dyad member (i.e., the use of nonreciprocal data) tends towards theoretical deficiency (Krasikova & LeBreton, 2012). Theoretical deficiency occurs when there is a misalignment of theory by neglecting the dyads' appropriate-level theory and conceptual characteristics (Tse & Ashkanasy, 2015). For example, a study involving interpersonal negotiation with the potential for conflict will require data collection from more than one party. Otherwise, there will be conceptual deficiency because of the methodological frame relying on a single source of data, which may create an imbalance in the problem under investigation.

4.6 Sample Selection

Every study is carried out within a defined population. Sampling in research refers to a specific population from which the sample will be selected as representative, and second, it ensures that every person from this predefined population is given a chance of inclusion that is greater than zero and can also be measured (Emmel, 2013). A study population is referred to as the totality of the target population from which cases may be legitimately sampled for interview (Robinson, 2014). The study population here comprises SEs and IIs with dyadic relationships in Nigeria.

The study draws on a geographic sample population to align with the contextual knowledge gap on the application of institutional theory in social entrepreneurship research (Armstrong et al., 2016; George et al., 2016; Lawrence et al., 2002; Rivera-Santos et al., 2015). Nigeria, as earlier mentioned, was chosen because of its large population and great market opportunity for impact investment in the Sub-Saharan Africa region. Secondly, the researcher has extensive work experience across a range of stakeholders in both public and private sectors, with fluid opportunity to navigate data collection. The search for meaning and not number in qualitative studies is believed to draw great insight from the Nigerian context as the largest economy in Africa (Emmel, 2013).

The population sampling also considered Nigeria's rich history, narratives, experiences and language to capture a true picture of the reality of the emerging concept of social enterprise and impact investing (Emmel, 2013; Robinson, 2014). There are many lessons to be learned from Nigeria about how SEs and IIs collaborate to establish partner fit, with generalisation potential across Africa. Achieving this goal requires the researcher to be immersed with participants to establish an ongoing fruitful relationship while reflecting on the study's theoretical underpinning to address the research questions (Crouch & McKenzie, 2006).

The next section examines how specific groups of SEs and IIs were purposively selected. This has enabled the study to capture the right information necessary for understanding the mechanistic pattern of collaboration between actors and how institutional factors affect SE and II behaviour in Nigeria.

4.7 Purposive Sampling and Selection of the Sample

Purposive sampling is "the strategic selection of where, when, and from whom data will be collected, based on the objectives of the study" (Maxwell, 2012: 94). This is to guide the researcher in selecting information-rich cases that best provide insight into the research questions and are capable of convincing the audience about the research approach (Emmel, 2013). According to the dyadic sampling approach, a dyad can be distinguished in a study based on empirical meaningful roles (Kashy et al., 2008). Several factors can be used to determine the roles of dyads (Wittenborn et al., 2013): for example, age, gender and roles have been used to distinguish between dyads in family research. However, the distinguishing factors between dyad partners in the current study are their roles in the collaboration, that is, impact investors as fund providers and social enterprises as recipients of investment funds. Specific categories of SEs benefiting from impact investment funds from IIs in Nigeria were selected for interview to explore how their dyadic relationship evolved. The principal researcher carried out a prior search to ascertain IIs and SEs that already had a relationship. According to Patton (1990), a pragmatic approach to purposive sampling means that a construct can only be sampled in so far as they are real-world examples, which refers to sampling that emanates from the participants' lived stories and experiences in a given investigation. The phenomena of impact investing are still new in Nigeria, as in any other emerging economy. It was difficult to identify SEs that identified as hybrid or commercial enterprises in line with IIs' collaboration motives of social impact with financial return. The sample selection was made based on their ability to provide rich and diverse information from their real experience in the Nigerian context (Patton, 1990). The criterion for selecting either an impact investor or social enterprise for interview took into consideration that the SE and II had a prior relationship. In other words, SEs selected must have benefited from impact investors' funds in any part of Nigeria, and IIs selected most have invested equity into SEs operating in Nigeria.

Six dyads comprising six SEs and six IIs were designated for interview in Nigeria. These were selected because of their information-rich cases capable of providing greater insight into the process of their collaboration. The validity of our findings largely depends on the richness and experience of the sample. Similarities and contrasts between each dyad's experience provide greater insight about micro and macro factors influencing their collaboration (Patton, 2015). The study focuses on finding impact investors connected to social enterprises operating in Nigeria. The authors achieved this by using the Google search engine to identify impact investing firms partnering with social enterprises in Nigeria. The approach focused on impact investors with an online presence since globalisation has enabled local and overseas investors to operate through an online presence.

One might ask, why interview a specific number of organisations as a small sample size for the study? As Boddy (2016) argues, sample size in qualitative research is contextual and partially dependent on the scientific paradigm of an investigation. For example, positivist-oriented research will require a large sample population compared to constructivist research, such as this study. Thus, a small sample size denotes a small number of participants, but any sample size with fewer than 20 participants is appropriate for qualitative studies (Boddy, 2016; Marshall et al., 2013). In qualitative research, respondents are not drawn from target populations; rather sample sizes are selected based on unique "cases" with evidence of meaningful experience (Crouch & McKenzie, 2006).

The sampling in line with dyadic design has considered that there could be distinguishing factors in the roles of SEs and IIs, with implications for theoretical importance to the research questions (Wittenborn et al., 2013). For example, the determining factors of trust from the SEs' and IIs' perspective will provide insight into the determinants of trust in the dyadic relationship. The researcher was able to determine the sample population of SEs connected with IIs through online documentation of IIs' antecedents of impact funds supply to SEs. Six SEs connected to IIs were eventually found prior to interview. In some circumstances, informants provided referrals to dyadic partners benefiting from previous and existing relationships. The interviews with the six dyads in the study seek to provide answers to our research questions. A summary of dyad cases is provided in Table 4.1, highlighting their unique characteristics in line with the objectives of the study.

4.8 Description of Dyadic Cases

Case One: II1 and SE1

II1 is a fund manager that invests in private businesses solving economic and social problems across regions of the world, particularly in South Africa, Ghana and Nigeria. The organisation's birth was in Nigeria in 2008 with a mission to create wealth and transform lives by driving SME growth in Nigeria and providing risk capital to commercially viable businesses with solid financial return and proven social impact (Onukwue, 2020). II1's fund management strategy focuses on businesses that address social problems through business solutions, with operational head offices in Nigeria and South Africa. The organisation's target is a $100 million investment in SMEs, with the potential to scale beyond their countries of origin to create a social outcome of 5000 jobs for women and provide over 100,000 women with access to essential services (Onukwue, 2020). It also partners with Goodwell Investment, a Netherlands-based, early-stage investment firm focusing on India and Africa's financial service and tech companies. For example, through Goodwell's funds, II1 has invested in organisations such as Paga, MAX.ng and Lidya, resulting in expanding operations to Poland and Lithuania in 2019.

SE1 is a software company founded in 2012 to promote Nigeria's financial inclusion through cloud-based technology services to microfinance banks (MFBs) in rural areas. This technology-driven company draws investment from II1, which has enabled it to drive financial inclusion services in microfinance institutions operating

Table 4.1 Summary cases of social enterprises and impact investors

	Social enterprise information						Impact Investors information					
SEs	Office location (SEs)	Mission statement (SEs)	Sector (SEs)	Years in operation	Customers/employee (SEs)	Years of dyadic relation (SEs & IIs)	Investment locations (IIs)	Country of origin (HQ)	Sector (11s)	Years in operation (IIs)	Mission statement (IIs)	IIs
SE1	Nigeria, Lagos	Financial inclusion in Nigeria through cloud-based technology services to Microfinance	Technology	6	25 (Nig. & West Africa)	2	Nigeria, Ghana, South Africa, Kenya & Netherlands	Nigeria, Lagos & South Africa (Regional)	Technology, micro-finance	10	Creating Wealth and transforming lives	II1
SE2	Nigeria, Lagos	Provide web-based printing platform on-demand to businesses across Nigeria	Printing	6	45	5	Sub-Saharan Africa, North America	Nigeria, Lagos (Regional)	Technology-driven enterprise	6	Financing and cross-pollinating viable technology companies in Sub-Saharan Africa	II2

SE3	Nigeria, Lagos	To promote financial inclusion through microfinance services to economically poor	Micro-finance	6	3636	2	Nigeria, Ghana, Cote d'Ivoire, Togo and Benin Republic	Nigeria. Lagos (Local)	Health, agriculture, affordable housing, education climate, finance	5	Investing in high-growth companies in West Africa that promote social impact projects, while making strong financial return to their investors	II3
SE4	Nigeria, Lagos	To reduce insecurity by making smallholder farmer members more money	Agric sector	7	407/21,000	2	80 Countries	Netherlands (Foreign)	High-risk and early-stage social enterprise.	12	Financial inclusion for micro-entrepreneurs and medium-sized enterprise	II4

(continued)

Table 4.1 (continued)

	Social enterprise information						Impact Investors information					
SEs	Office location (SEs)	Mission statement (SEs)	Sector (SEs)	Years in operation	Customers/ employee (SEs)	Years of dyadic relation (SEs & IIs)	Investment locations (IIs)	Country of origin (HQ)	Sector (11s)	Years in operation (IIs)	Mission statement (IIs)	IIs
SE5	Nigeria, Lagos	Providing quality, certified and affordable healthcare products to consumers & reduce the mortality rate in West Africa	Health	23	100	3	Lagos, Port Harcourt, Abuja & Kaduna (14 countries)	Mauritius (Foreign)	Health, Education, "manufacturing", agric. & ICT	12	To help entrepreneurs succeed by providing them with business loans and business support	II5
SE6	Nigeria, Kwara State	To boost local meat production through agricultural chicken farming	Agric sector	3	230	3	Nigeria, Ghana, Mali, Senegal and Asian countries	Nigeria, Lagos (Local)	Agriculture	6	To unlock the great potential of agriculture and nutrition landscape in West Africa	II6

in rural communities of Lagos. SE1 operates in eight countries and has recently extended its services to DEC (Development Exchange Centre), an organisation working in Bauchi State, Nigeria, to serve mainly women organisations' business finance needs, particularly in Northern states. II1 and SE1 have had an ongoing dyadic relation for over 2 years.

Case Two: II2 and SE2

II2 is an experienced early-stage and growth venture-capital organisation established in 2013 with the mission to finance and cross-pollinate viable technology companies in Sub-Saharan Africa. Its investment size ranges from $50,000 to $20 million, subject to the growth stage, opportunity and capital requirements of the business. The social impact focus of the organisation centres around under-served entrepreneurs and geographical location. It incubates local high-potential growth enterprises and also provides mentorship opportunities, including local networks. Examples of growth-stage enterprises II2 has invested in Sub-Saharan Africa, in partnership with TPG Growth and The Rise Fund, include Gro Intelligence, SystemOne, Mines.io, etc. Some investments were also made into seed- and early-stage enterprises such as Lifebank, Kukua, WorldCover, Lori Systems, and Shopex. Although the organisation invests in social impact businesses, it prefers not to brand itself an impact investor: It does not invest in companies with deliberate intentions of social impact; it is a profit-first-driven investor. Yet II2 invested in a tech-enabled organisation providing access to life-saving blood to hospitals, which indirectly demonstrates social impact. The researcher could not interview LifeBank but interviewed SE2, another tech-enabled social enterprise located in Lagos and currently in a dyadic relationship with II2.

SE2 was established in 2013 with a mission to provide web-based, on-demand printing platforms to businesses across Nigeria. Its social impact comes through providing easy access to printing services to organisations through online order and delivery across Nigeria without a physical presence. Its activities have resulted in the creation of job opportunities for youth in the technology-driven services industry. Products include greeting cards, posters, stickers, envelopes, letterhead, banners, etc. II2 and SE2 have been in a dyadic relationship for over five years.

Case Three: II3 and SE3

II3 is an impact investment and fund management organisation incorporated in 2013 with headquarters in Lagos. The organisation has a mission to invest in high-growth companies in West Africa that promote social impact projects, while making strong financial returns for its investors by supporting companies that contribute to a better world. II3 is a USD 75 million closed-end fund domiciled in Mauritius and invests in growth/expansion stage companies with funding needs ranging from $500,000 to $6,000,000. The organisation aims to fill an estimated SME funding gap of $60 billion annually across the West African market, focusing on Nigeria, Ghana, Cote d'Ivoire Togo and Benin Republic. II3 has intentional triple-bottom-line investment motives, targeting sectors ranging across agriculture, healthcare, affordable housing, education and climate finance. Apart from direct impact investment, it leverages on its extensive network to facilitate impact investment opportunities for companies that may not fall within its investment portfolio or interests. It has invested in several microfinance institutions and SMEs.

SE3 is an example of a microfinance institution that II3 facilitates through impact investing, with headquarters in Lagos and several branches across Nigeria. SE3 was established in 2006 with the mandate to promote financial inclusion through microfinance services to an economically poor population actively engaged in small trading and micro-productive activities in various parts of Nigeria. It provides micro-loan services to customers with a triple-bottom-line impact motive. Its strong drive for sustainable livelihood extends to other emerging countries in Africa. Promoters of the organisation draw inspiration from their experience in the United Nations, where they have served in various capacities.

SE3 has partnered with the International Finance Corporation (IFC) World Bank Group, Nordic Micro Finance Initiative (NMI), Blue Orchard Impact Investment Manager, etc. It is ranked among the highest-rated microfinance institutions worldwide for both institutional and social performance by MicroRate. It has been in a dyadic relationship with N-IIFG for over 2 years.

Case Four: II4 and SE4

II4 is a foreign financial inclusive fund set up in 2006 and managed on behalf of the Dutch Ministry of Foreign Affairs. It has been investing in Nigeria since the 1970s but began investment in financial inclusion enterprises, that is, microfinance institutions, in 2013. It is active in about 80 countries globally, particularly low-income, but operates from the head office in the Netherlands. Its mission is to enhance financial inclusion for micro-entrepreneurs and medium-sized enterprises (MSMEs) that are negatively affected by the lack of access to financial services. Through its €545 million portfolio, II4 supports 7,600,786 microloans and 112,300 (M)SME loans, including 61% of women-owned and 67% of rural MSMEs. The fund aims to support intermediaries that reach out to MSMEs in fragile and low-income countries, such as Nigeria. MSMEs in rural areas are mainly those dependent on agriculture, women-and-youth-owned MSMEs, and intermediaries providing access to productive goods and services for under-served individuals in the poorest socio-economic segments. II4 targets high-risk and early-stage social enterprises. Its overwhelming interest in creating a sustainable impact on people at the "bottom of the pyramid" informs the type of organisations it selects for impact investment.

II4 invested in SE4, a social enterprise established in 2012 to be financially sustainable and scalable agricultural enterprise co-owned by its farmers. SE4's mission is to end insecurity by making smallholder farmer members more money. It operates mainly in northern Nigeria, where the terrorist group Boko-Haram (which prohibits Western education) has operated for over 10 years. That group has claimed several lives, but creating new jobs for idle youth in the region in the agricultural sector is believed to be a remedy for an increasing crisis. SE4 utilizes a model that includes financial service through cost-effective capital to finance smallholder farmers, agricultural input services at highly competitive prices, training and development for technical competence and marketing services towards good warehousing practices and access to goods markets for increased profitability. It also works with other institutional and individual investors, including the Nigerian government, to finance its smallholder farmers. It has been in a dyadic relationship with II4 for over 2 years.

Case Five: II5 and SE5

II5 is a foreign impact investor established in 2004 with administrative headquarters in Mauritius, and operational headquarters, established in 2002, in South Africa. It has a vast network of local offices spread across 15 countries in Africa and the Middle East. II5 came to Nigeria in 2007 and currently has two offices, in Lagos and Port Harcourt. Its mission is to help entrepreneurs succeed by providing them with business loans and business support in terms of expert advice and continuous guidance to grow their enterprise. It believes that a growing SME sector which creates sustainable jobs is the most powerful driver of social and economic development that truly changes people's lives. It is supported by 34 international finance institutions, development organisations and private funders that have committed nearly $535 million in capital to its funds. Since its inception, it has invested in over 735 SMEs, targeting social and economic impact in the range of $100 k to $1.5 m, focusing on education, health and manufacturing. It also offers technical and formal advice in financial management and accounting, human resources, marketing, and operations to SEs. It assists enterprises in areas such as formalising their business structure and succession planning.

SE5 is a commercial enterprise established in 1995 and specialises in manufacturing a range of ethical consumer healthcare pharmaceutical brands. It has a mission to be a leading provider of quality, certified and affordable healthcare products to consumers and to reduce the mortality rate in West Africa. The innovative and ethical brands of products manufactured by SE5 fit into the investment appetite of II5, and it has had a dyadic relationship with II5 for over a year. Besides the innovative and ethical impact of its products, SE5 has created over 100 employment opportunities across Nigeria, while helping curb the mortality rate in West Africa with its products.

Case Six: II6 and SE6

The II6 fund manager was established in late 2013 as a private equity business with a passion for unlocking the great potential of the agriculture and nutrition landscape in West Africa by creating strong agricultural sector-driven economic growth. The headquarters is in Lagos. It manages investment funds from the African Development Bank (ADB), CDC (an investment arm of the United Kingdom) and the Nigerian government. CDC is a Development Finance Institution (DFI). In 2017, II6 closed its maiden fund at $65.9 million with added capital raised from AfDB, CDC Group, Dutch Good Growth Fund (DGGF) and the Nigerian Sovereign Investment Authority (NSIA). The organisation carries out impact investment in Burkina Faso, Liberia, Ghana, Mali Senegal, Nigeria and some Asian countries. It has invested in several organisations across states in Nigeria.

This study interviewed SE6, among many organisations with whom II6 has established dyadic relations within the last 3 years. SE6 is a social enterprise established in 2014 to boost local meat production through agricultural chicken farming. It is located in Kwara state, in the Northcentral region. In recent years, it has impacted positively in its areas of operation by creating over 250 jobs while meeting the increasing livestock demand across Nigeria. SE6 has continued to make social impact through job creation for a variety of academics and professionals with backgrounds in finance, engineering, science, technology and the humanities.

4.9 Data Collection

The unique advantage of qualitative research has been described as allowing a detailed exploration of a research topic of interest in which the researcher collects rich information through interviews, case studies, ethnographic works and other means (Harwell, 2011). Data collected in the current study were further classified into secondary and primary data. "Primary data are data that are collected afresh and for the first time and thus happen to be original in character" (Kothari, 2004: 95). The originality of primary data is rooted in the fact that they are raw, either as text or audio-recorded. Secondary data are information which has already been collected by researchers and has already undergone statistical processing (Kothari, 2004). Ghauri and Grønhaug (2005) and Lowing (2011) highlight the strategic importance of both primary and secondary data in research such as the current study in providing an in-depth view of SEs' and IIs' experience and current organisational practice in the Nigerian environment.

4.10 Interviews

Primary data were obtained through interviews to explore the relationship between empirical data and theoretical framing of social enterprise and impact investing. Smith and Elger (2014) argue that the central attraction of interviews as a form of research inquiry hinges on the fact that they offer the researcher direct access to key points of view of interviewees, in terms of attitudes they hold and accounts of their experiences. Interviews were chosen because of their great potential to provide in-depth information concerning the opinions, perceptions and lived experience and histories of SEs and IIs that may not be achieved through quantitative data collection techniques (Creswell & Poth, 2017). Although this study holds great promise when combined with quantitative strands of insight on social entrepreneurship in developed and emerging markets, time for the study was limited.

In this study, strategic primary data collection occurred in Nigeria between December 2018 and January 2019 through semi-structured interviews with six impact investing and social enterprise organisations in dyadic relationships (Maxwell 2012). The selection of the six cases was based on their real-life experience in addressing the research questions, in line with the underlying CR philosophy of the research (Emmel 2013; Martin & Wilson, 2016). Most interviews were conducted face-to-face. However, some were carried out through Skype and telephone, especially for participants whose business schedules and accessibility were unfavourable.

Most informants interviewed were CEOs, founders and co-founders and investment managers, fund managers, etc. The interview guide covered the theoretical underpinning of dyadic inter-organisational collaboration and institutional framing. In line with the semi-structured format, the interviewer asks probing questions to ascertain a deeper reality of participants' experiences. In most instances, organisations in dyads provided referrals to their dyad partner who were subsequently interviewed (snowballing). Most interviews lasted for 60 min and a minimum of 20 min. All interviews were conducted in English and audio-recorded with prior permission. In the case of the Skype interview, the researcher further audio-recorded the conversation using a voice tracer to forestall the loss of recorded conversation. A few informants requested not to be audio-recorded, and the researcher then took notes. Twelve in-depth interviews were transcribed verbatim. The audio recording and notes were transcribed into Microsoft Word and files for analysis with the aid of NVivo software. Table 4.2 provides an overview of the participants.

The entire study is anchored on an overarching question: "How are social enterprises and impact investors guided to determine their compatibility in organisational logics and complementarity of resources prior to establishing partner fit in pursuit of their social and economic interests in a Nigerian environment?" Four research sub-questions (Creswell & Clark, 2007) were developed to explore how SEs and IIs collaborate, the influence of micro and macro context and the perceived learning experience. Two interview guides were developed to explore each dyad's perception

Table 4.2 Participant profiles

IIs	Participant Position (IIs)	Gender (IIs)	Office location (IIs)	Office location (SEs)	Gender (SEs)	Participant position (SEs)	SEs
II1	Social impact/ ESG manager	Female	Nigeria, Lagos	Nigeria, Lagos	Male	CEO	SE1
II2	Snr corporate council	Female	Nigeria, Lagos	Nigeria, Lagos	Male	Chief growth/ BD & partnerships	SE2
	Principal investment officer	Female					
II3	Communication & legal officer	Female	Nigeria, Lagos	Nigeria, Lagos	Male	Head of executive support & strategy unit	SE3
	Admin officer	Male					
II4	Fund manager	Male	Netherland (Oversees)	Nigeria, Lagos	Female	Principal corporate finance officer	SE4
II5	Country manager	Male	Nigeria, Lagos (Headquarters Mauritius)	Nigeria, Lagos	Male	Sales & marketing director	SE5
II6	Vice president Operations/ESG	Male	Lagos	Nigeria, Kwara Sate	Male	General manager	SE6

and experience of the relationship in an individual interview, that is, separate interviews for SE and IIs.

Questions 1–4, section 1 (see Appendix 8, 9) of the interview guide, seek to answer RQ1, which focused on how dyadic SEs and IIs in Nigeria are guided to determine partner fit from organisational compatibility and resources complementarity in pursuit of social and economic interests. The questions draw on insight around institutional beliefs and literature on reciprocity power in building mutual trust within dyads.

Questions 7–10 focus on RQ2, which seeks to ascertain the micro-level factors that influence the type of resources determining power dynamics and trust level for collaboration between the dyad partners. The questions draw on insight into the dimension of trust in social exchange relationship to ascertain the determining factors of trust, because the sustainability of productive value of network of relationship is high when trust and reciprocity become a norm for moral obligation for efficient engagement between SEs and IIs (Hald, 2005). Van de Ven (1976) further argues that companies will only engage in dyadic inter-organisational collaboration when the parties involved in the exchange that follows expect to achieve valuable returns.

Questions 11 and 12 across the dyads focus on RQ3 to ascertain what macro factors in the Nigerian environment constrain or enable collaboration between SEs and IIs. The questions draw on insight from the literature on the macro-institutional environment in entrepreneurial research.

Questions 1–7, section 2 from the interview guide, focus on RQ4 to likewise ascertain the learning experience from the collaboration process. They specifically draw on the lens of trust in social exchange theory to ascertain the influence of trust factors in determining sustainable collaboration between SEs and IIs, including future prospects for collaboration.

4.11 Secondary Data

Stewart and Kamins (1993: 1) observe that secondary sources of information usually offer "quick and inexpensive answers" and are "almost always the point of departure for primary research". Secondary data can be retrieved from a variety of sources and come in different forms, while the largest and most frequently sought source of data used has been the library. Examples of secondary data used in this study include practitioners' reports, newspapers, archives, government and private sector reports and organisation websites accessible via the Monash University library and online learning tools were consulted with a view to eliciting insight into context-specific issues related to social enterprise and impact investing across regions.

Before and during the study, documentary data of SEs and IIs were retrieved and studied via organisation websites and annual reports. Such data provided insight into the type of enterprise operating in Nigeria and the impact investing organisations that were investing equity in them. Relevant data were retrieved and stored for contact through emails and telephone calls. The use of secondary data sources complements primary data, bearing in mind the challenges surrounding primary data collection (Cowton, 1998). The use of secondary data not only saved cost but also enabled the researcher to obtain information that could have been difficult to obtain with the accuracy required.

4.12 Data Analysis

Data analysis is the interplay between the researcher and the data (Strauss & Corbin, 1998: 13). Data analysis in this study utilises a qualitative approach, which involves a review, synthesis and interpretation of dyadic data to describe and explain SEs' and IIs' perceptions to generate new meaning (Fossey et al., 2002; Stake, 2006). The study also uses qualitative analysis, because of limited knowledge of theories and methods for exploring social enterprise and impact investing phenomena (Creswell & Poth, 2017). The study applies a complex process of qualitative data analysis underpinned by CR philosophy that understands business relationships as "real" affect such that their properties are legitimate objects of analysis (Ryan et al., 2012). The CR conception of relationships and networks as real aligns with affective modes in dyad analysis in social network research (Ferris et al., 2009). To aid with analysing the large data set collected, the qualitative data software package QSR NVivo 12 plus was utilised to safely store and analyse transcribed data. This software was chosen because of its features, which have the ability to code various data sources, perform queries, and create different matrices and visual diagrams capable of explaining the relationships between data.

4.13 Conclusion

The methodology chapter of this book provides guidance on how social enterprise and impact investors establish partner fit in pursuit of social and economic interest in Nigeria. A qualitative phenomenological approach underpinned by CR philosophy was appropriate because it explained dyadic relationships based on contextual realities (Easton, 2010). A dyadic affective mode of analysis was utilised to capture participants' experiences and behavioural patterns. The philosophical assumptions of the study very much align with the method of analysis and the theoretical lens. This now provides the basis to apply this method to answer the four research sub-questions to ascertain the research findings.

References

Amoako, I. O. (2019). Trust in interorganisational relationships. In *Trust, institutions and managing entrepreneurial relationships in Africa* (pp. 67–102). Springer.

Anderson, J. C., Håkansson, H., & Johanson, J. (1994). Dyadic business relationships within a business network context. *Journal of Marketing, 58*(4), 1–15.

Archer, M. S. (1995). *Realist social theory: The morphogenetic approach.* Cambridge University Press.

Archer, M., Bhaskar, R., Collier, A., Lawson, T., & Norrie, A. (2013). *Critical realism: Essential readings* (1st ed.). Routledge.

Armstrong, F., Armstrong, D., & Barton, L. (2016). *Inclusive education: Policy, contexts and comparative perspectives*. Routledge.

Bergene, A. (2007). Towards a critical realist comparative methodology: Context-sensitive theoretical comparison. *Journal of Critical Realism, 6*(1), 5–27.

Bhaskar, R. (1978). *A realist theory of science*. Routledge.

Bhaskar, R. (1998). Philosophy and scientific realism. In *Critical realism: Essential readings* (1st ed., pp. 16–47). Routledge.

Blundel, R. (2007). Critical realism: A suitable vehicle for entrepreneurship research? In H. Neergaard & J. P. Ulhoi (Eds.), *Handbook of qualitative research methods in entrepreneurship* (pp. 49–74). Edward Elgar.

Boddy, C. R. (2016). Sample size for qualitative research. *Qualitative Market Research: An International Journal, 19*(4), 426–432.

Bottomore, T., Harris, L., Kiernan, V. G., & Miliband, R. (1991). *The Marxist thought*. Blackwell Publishers Ltd..

Cowton, C. J. (1998). The use of secondary data in business ethics research. *Journal of Business Ethics, 17*(4), 423–434.

Cranmer, S. J., & Desmarais, B. A. (2016). A critique of dyadic design. *International Studies Quarterly, 60*(2), 355–362.
Creswell, J. W., & Clark, V. L. P. (2007). *Designing and conducting mixed methods research*. University of Cincinnati, Sage Publications.
Creswell, J. W., & Poth, C. N. (2017). *Qualitative inquiry and research design: Choosing among five approaches* (4th ed.). University of Michigan, Sage Publications.
Crouch, M., & McKenzie, H. (2006). The logic of small samples in interview-based qualitative research. *Social Science Information, 45*(4), 483–499.
Danermark, B., Ekstrom, M., & Jakobsen, L. (2005). *Explaining society: An introduction to critical realism in the social science*. Routledge.
Easton, G. (1995). *Case research as a methodology for industrial networks: A realist apologia*. Paper presented at the IMP Conference (11th), Manchester. Retrieved from https://www.escholar.manchester.ac.uk/uk-ac-man-scw:2n485
Easton, G. (2003). Case research as a method for industrial networks: A realist apologia. In *Realist perspectives on management and organisations* (pp. 221–235). Routledge.
Easton, G. (2010). Critical realism in case study research. *Industrial Marketing Management, 39*(1), 118–128.
Eisikovits, Z., & Koren, C. (2010). Approaches to and outcomes of dyadic interview analysis. *Qualitative Health Research, 20*(12), 1642–1655.
Emmel, N. (2013). *Sampling and choosing cases in qualitative research: A realist approach*. Sage.
Ferris, G. R., Liden, R. C., Munyon, T. P., Summers, J. K., Basik, K. J., & Buckley, M. R. (2009). Relationships at work: Toward a multidimensional conceptualization of dyadic work relationships. *Journal of Management, 35*(6), 1379–1403.
Fossey, E., Harvey, C., McDermott, F., & Davidson, L. (2002). Understanding and evaluating qualitative research. *Australian & New Zealand Journal of Psychiatry, 36*(6), 717–732.
Fuller, T., & Moran, P. (2001). Small enterprises as complex adaptive systems: A methodological question? *Entrepreneurship & Regional Development, 13*(1), 47–63.
George, G., Corbishley, C., Khayesi, J. N., Haas, M. R., & Tihanyi, L. (2016). Bringing Africa in: Promising directions for management research. *Academy of Management Journal, 59*(2), 377–393.
Gerrits, L., & Verweij, S. (2013). Critical realism as a meta-framework for understanding the relationships between complexity and qualitative comparative analysis. *Journal of Critical Realism, 12*(2), 166–182.
Ghauri, P., & Grønhaug, K. (2005). *Research methods in business studies*. FT, Prentice Hall.
Hald, K. S. (2005). *Managing inter-organizational relationships: Using the force of partner attraction*. Copenhagen Business School. Retrieved from https://research-api.cbs.dk/ws/portalfiles/portal/58880103/4.pdf
Harwell, M. R. (2011). Research design in qualitative/quantitative/mixed methods. In *The SAGE handbook for research in education: Pursuing ideas as the keystone of exemplary inquiry* (pp. 147–164). SAGE Publications, Inc..
Hu, X. (2018). Methodological implications of critical realism for entrepreneurship research. *Journal of Critical Realism, 17*(2), 118–139.
Jackson, A. Y., & Mazzei, L. (2011). *Thinking with theory in qualitative research: Viewing data across multiple perspectives*. Routledge.
Jackson, A. Y., & Mazzei, L. A. (2013). Plugging one text into another: Thinking with theory in qualitative research. *Qualitative Inquiry, 19*(4), 261–271.
Kashy, D. A., Donnellan, M. B., Burt, S. A., & McGue, M. (2008). Growth curve models for indistinguishable dyads using multilevel modeling and structural equation modeling: The case of adolescent twins' conflict with their mothers. *Developmental Psychology, 44*(2), 316–329.
Kothari, C. R. (2004). Research methodology: Methods and techniques (2nd ed.): New Delhi: New Age International Publishers.
Krasikova, D. V., & LeBreton, J. M. (2012). Just the two of us: Misalignment of theory and methods in examining dyadic phenomena. *Journal of Applied Psychology, 97*(4), 739–757.

Lawrence, T. B., Hardy, C., & Phillips, N. (2002). Institutional effects of interorganizational collaboration: The emergence of proto-institutions. *Academy of Management Journal, 45*(1), 281–290.

Leca, B., & Naccache, P. (2006). A critical realist approach to institutional entrepreneurship. *Organization, 13*(5), 627–651.

Lowing, K. (2011). Educational research and inquiry: Qualitative and quantitative approaches, edited by D. Hartas. *British Journal of Educational Studies, 59*(3), 350–351.

Lu, S. C., Kong, D. T., Ferrin, D. L., & Dirks, K. T. (2017). What are the determinants of interpersonal trust in dyadic negotiations? Meta-analytic evidence and implications for future research. *Journal of Trust Research, 7*(1), 22–50.

Luvison, D., & Cummings, J. L. (2017). Decisions at the boundary: Role choice and alliance manager behaviors. *Group & Organization Management, 42*(2), 279–309.

Maguire, M. C. (1999). Treating the dyad as the unit of analysis: A primer on three analytic approaches. *Journal of Marriage and the Family, 16*(1), 213–223.

Manning, J., & Kunkel, A. (2015). Qualitative approaches to dyadic data analyses in family communication research: An invited essay. *Journal of Family Communication, 15*(3), 185–192.

Marshall, B., Cardon, P., Poddar, A., & Fontenot, R. (2013). Does sample size matter in qualitative research? A review of qualitative interviews in IS research. *Journal of Computer Information Systems, 54*(1), 11–22.

Martin, L., & Wilson, N. (2016). Opportunity, discovery and creativity: A critical realist perspective. *International Small Business Journal, 34*(3), 261–275.

Maxwell, J. A. (2012). *A realist approach for qualitative research.* Sage Publications.

Mouton, J. (1996). *Understanding social research.* Van Schaik Publishers.

Ojukwu, D., Georgiadou, E., & House, R. (2007). *Towards improving inter-organisational trust amongst SMEs: A case-study from developing countries.* Paper presented at the Proceedings of the 9th IFIP International conference on the social implications of computers in developing countries. Retrieved from http://www.ifipwg94.org.br/fullpapers/R0096-1.pdf

Olekalns, M., Lau, F., & Smith, P. (2002). *Spirals of trust: Identifying the factors that shape and sustain trust in negotiation.* Paper presented at the IACM 15th Annual Conference.

Olk, P., & Elvira, M. (2001). Friends and strategic agents: The role of friendship and discretion in negotiating strategic alliances. *Group & Organization Management, 26*(2), 124–164.

Onukwue, A. O. (2020). Africa's Next Decade of Public Policy Development Is Being Led by Technology Innovators. *Africa Policy Journal*, 16–19.

Patton, M. Q. (1990). *Qualitative evaluation and research methods* (2nd ed.). SAGE Publications, Inc.

Patton, M. Q. (2015). *Qualitative research & evaluation methods: Integrating theory and practice* (p. 255, 286). SAGE Publications, Kindle Edition.

Rivera-Santos, M., Holt, D., Littlewood, D., & Kolk, A. (2015). Social entrepreneurship in sub-Saharan Africa. *The Academy of Management Perspectives, 29*(1), 72–91.

Robinson, O. C. (2014). Sampling in interview-based qualitative research: A theoretical and practical guide. *Qualitative Research in Psychology, 11*(1), 25–41.

Ryan, A., & O'Malley, L. (2006). *Conceptualising dyadic inter-organisational relationships as complex adaptive systems* (Paper presentation). 22nd Imp Conference, Boconni University, Milan, San Diego, California. Retrieved from https://eprints.lancs.ac.uk/id/eprint/46867

Ryan, A., Tähtinen, J., Vanharanta, M., & Mainela, T. (2012). Putting critical realism to work in the study of business relationship processes. *Industrial Marketing Management, 41*(2), 300–311.

Sayer, A. (2004). Why critical realism. In *Critical realist applications in organisation and management studies* (Vol. 11, No. 6). Routledge.

Scott, W. R. (2005). Institutional theory: Contributing to a theoretical research program. In *Great minds in management: The process of theory development* (Vol. 37, No. 2, pp. 460–484). Oxford University Press.

Smith, C., & Elger, T. (2014). Critical realism and interviewing subjects. In P. Edwards, J. O'Mahoney, & S. Vincent (Eds.), *Studying organizations using critical realism: A practical guide* (pp. 109–131). Oxford University Press.

Srivastava, J., & Chakravarti, D. (2009). Channel negotiations with information asymmetries: Contingent influences of communication and trustworthiness reputations. *Journal of Marketing Research, 46*(4), 557–572.

Stake, R. E. (2006). Multiple case study analysis. New York, NY. Guilford Press. Strain, PS, & Bovey, EH (2011). Randomized controlled trial of the LEAP model of early intervention for young children with Autism Spectrum Disorders. *Topics in Early Childhood Special Education, 31*, 133–154.

Stewart, D. W., & Kamins, M. A. (1993). *Secondary research: Information sources and methods* (Vol. 4). Sage.

Strauss, A., & Corbin, J. (1998). *Basics of qualitative research techniques*. Sage Publications.

Thompson, L., & Walker, A. J. (1982). The dyad as the unit of analysis: Conceptual and methodological issues. *Journal of Marriage and the Family, 44*(4), 889–900.

Tse, H. H., & Ashkanasy, N. M. (2015). The dyadic level of conceptualization and analysis: A missing link in multilevel OB research? *Journal of Organizational Behavior, 36*(8), 1176–1180.

Van de Ven, A. H. (1976). On the nature, formation, and maintenance of relations among organizations. *Academy of Management Review, 1*(4), 24–36.

Vanneste, B. S. (2016). From interpersonal to interorganisational trust: The role of indirect reciprocity. *Journal of Trust Research, 6*(1), 7–36.

Vincent, S. (2008). A transmutation theory of inter-organizational exchange relations and networks: Applying critical realism to analysis of collective agency. *Human Relations, 61*(6), 875–899.

Wahyuni, D. (2012). The research design maze: Understanding paradigms, cases, methods and methodologies. *Journal of Applied Management Accounting Research, 10*(1), 69–80.

Wang, B., Kang, Y., Childerhouse, P., & Huo, B. (2018). Interpersonal and inter-organizational relationship drivers of supply chain integration. *Industrial Management & Data Systems, 118*(1), 1170–1191.

Wilson, D. T. (1995). An integrated model of buyer-seller relationships. *Journal of the Academy of Marketing Science, 23*(4), 335–345.

Wittenborn, A. K., Dolbin-MacNab, M. L., & Keiley, M. K. (2013). Dyadic research in marriage and family therapy: Methodological considerations. *Journal of Marital and Family Therapy, 39*(1), 5–16.

Wynn, D., Jr., & Williams, C. K. (2012). Principles for conducting critical realist case study research in information systems. *MIS Quarterly, 36*, 787–810.

Chapter 5
Partner Fit Between Social Enterprises and Impact Investors

5.1 Introduction

This chapter applies a qualitative method to analyse the dyadic data and present the key findings. Our focus is on how organisational compatibility and resource complementarity have been applied to establish partner fit between SEs and IIs. Semi-structured interview responses from six SEs and IIs with dyadic relations were initially analysed through a coding process, and organised into themes. The empirical indicators generated were further subjected to what Jackson and Mazzei (2011) describe as after coding "thinking with theory", which pushes researchers to further analyse empirical indicators alongside theoretical underpinning to generate dyadic themes.

The study drew on scholarly work (Dhurkari & Nandakumar, 2015; Sarkar et al., 2001; Solesvik & Encheva, 2010) to gain understanding about how organisations select partners to increase inter-firm collaboration. Some researchers in this area focus on alliances between buyer and supplier relationships, and on innovation from the perspective of organisational compatibility and resource complementarity (Manotungvorapun & Gerdsri, 2016). This present approach fills the knowledge gap on how IIs select their social enterprises, the type of resources that determine the power dynamic between them and macro-institutional influences on their innovative strategy for solving difficult social problems. The approach also sheds theoretical light on the Nigerian environment's influence on social entrepreneurship literature.

J. A. Emmanuel et al., *Social Enterprises and Impact Investors*, Advances in Theory and Practice of Emerging Markets,
https://doi.org/10.1007/978-3-031-59454-0_5

5.2 Thematic Analysis of Interview Data

Interviews across the six dyad cases were at the individual level. The analysis brings together findings from all dyads to explore how each had established partner fit. Partner fit matches investor and investee with compatible, complementary potential to collectively pursue social and economic interests. Separate interview guides were used (Appendices 8 and 9) to answer sub-RQ1: *In the process of collaboration, how do SEs and IIs establish partner fit in pursuit of their social and economic interests in Nigeria?* Interview questions 1–5, relating to how similarities in firm goals are aligned with differences in resource type, aim to capture compatible organisational logics and complementary resources that motivate actors to establish partner fit. Several scholars have argued that the institutional logics of social enterprises and their potential business partners greatly influence how they form partnerships and the process involved (Di Domenico et al., 2009; Thornton & Ocasio, 1999). Consequently, a social enterprise's collaboration goal will strongly align with the organisational objectives of impact investors whose contribution holds valuable and potential impact. The analysis noted various contrasting, overlapping and similar features in participants' responses in the course of their unique narratives (Manning & Kunkel, 2015; Thompson & Walker, 1982).

The coding process involved an iterative process of identifying and refining relevant concepts. Initial coding searched for empirical labels linked to each sub-research question. For the first sub-research question, this generated a cluster of empirical labels describing how actors establish partner fit. Figure 5.1 reveals several descriptive similarities of firms' missions and criteria, as well as differences in resource type, across the six dyad cases. The constructs under similarities of the

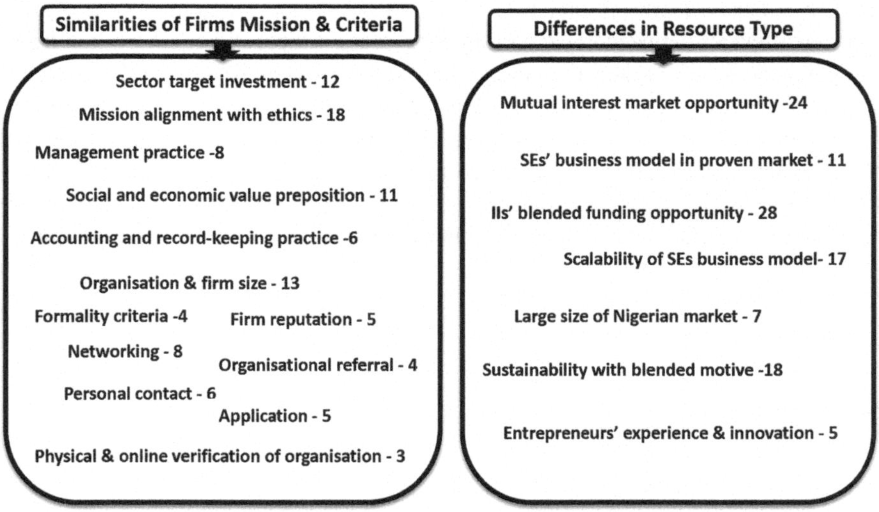

Fig. 5.1 Empirical labels linked to similarities and differences

firm's mission and criteria show how IIs align compatibility with SEs by looking at the mission statements of SEs and using certain criteria to determine II compatibility with particular SEs. There has been a high-level rejection of business proposals by equity investors for reasons directly related to proposals that do not align with investment criteria (Mason & Kwok, 2010a, b; Mason & Stark, 2004). Besides mission statements, IIs have selection criteria which include the profile of the management team, business strategy, business operational practices, products/services, market potential, financial records, skills set, integrity and industry experience (Mason & Kwok, 2010b; Mason & Stark, 2004). These criteria vary across industry and impact investors.

With the aid of NVivo software, the coding process across the six cases generated common and different themes linked to similarities in firms' missions and criteria, which illustrated organisational compatibility, and differences in resource type, which illustrated resource complementarity.

5.3 Second Stage Data Analysis

The second stage analysis explores specific themes emerging from individual dyads linked to their similarities in the firm's mission/criteria and differences between tangible and intangible resources. The process across the six cases aims to capture differences in resource type (complementarity) and similarities (compatibility) in their mission and criteria to determine how these concepts applied in each dyad to establish partner fit. Similarities are ascertained by aligning the mission of SEs and how IIs envision the type of organisation to which to direct impact funds, including criteria SEs are expected to meet. Differences in tangible and intangible resources are ascertained by examining the key attracting types of resources that motivate IIs' engagement with SEs and SEs' primary motives for seeking collaboration with IIs and how they both align their motivations.

II1's interest in a range of social and economic impact SEs using technology to drive financial inclusion across West Africa is a goal that aligns with the mission of SE1, a commercial enterprise which also aims to provide access to cloud-based technology for microfinance institutions operating in rural areas of Nigeria. Comparing the two organisations' missions, their similarity is notable in terms of organisational mission centres on addressing technology setbacks in microfinance institutions across rural areas. Their compatibility in organisational logic brought them together and established partner fit, with over 2 years' dyadic relations.

The interview guide asked questions related to how IIs ascertain the type of organisation that fit into their investment motivations, and the criteria SE1 needed to achieve II1 compatibility with SE1. Similarly, it asked SE1 about its mission statement, including the criteria it needed to be met to attract collaboration with II1 and demonstrate SE1 compatibility. (This principle has been applied across the six cases analysed in this chapter.)

Analysis of dyadic empirical themes from Case 1 reveals deeper narratives and the reality of how they established partner fit. Examples of themes that captured their compatibility from their mission statement and investment criteria include SE1 mission focus on software solutions to servicing microfinance in rural areas, aligned with II1's funds targeting SEs with a mission around technology-sector-driven social impact. The two organisations also have a shared motive to pursue social impact through a financially inclusive model that targets Nigeria's poorest people. Blended motives and a financially inclusive model represent an organisational strategy to pursue social and economic interests as a goal. The analysis finds II1's interest in financing an inclusive model focusing on technological-driven impact aligns with SE1's logics for building communication software to service microfinance software challenges in rural areas—that is, a compatible and valuable mission for II1's investment interest. Each member of the dyad described how compatible organisational logics applied to their situation:

> We also have a financial product and company called SE1, they are a software service, they provide core banking solutions for micro-finance institutions. (II1)
>
> We are a technology company servicing microfinance institution that is also involved in social enterprise… Other technology providers are targeting, commercial institutions or credit delivery providers that are mostly located in city centres. But our organisation built a system to provide the same level of service for institutions that are operating in hard-to-reach environments like rural communities. (SE1)

These statements suggest how organisational compatibility influenced collaboration in pursuit of social and economic objectives. Alignment of similar missions showed the mobilisation of the two organisations' compatible identity to satisfy blended motives. From SE1's collaboration experience with II1, it is clear how SE1 expressed its identity in the area of a technology-driven mission to attract II1 to an impact investing opportunity. The alignment of their missions presents a typical example of how organisations symbolically endorse certain practices prescribed by one logic, and often one that is more aligned with their organisational goals (Pache & Santos, 2013).

Besides the compatibility in firm mission, it is also clear that their compatibility has been determined from the perspective of management practice. SE1 had a good management team, an established reputation, and experience similar to II1's investment criteria (and ascertained through due diligence checks): SE1's reputation and experience in social and economic impact met II1's criteria for impact investing. Both organisations testified that managerial practices as criteria have been used to determine their compatibility:

> We provide both capital and value for up-scaling our business. Companies that we invest in are companies whose growth rate meet our mandate with excellent management and proven market. (II1)
>
> All that is information [that is] actually being managed by our investment arm, [but] I do not have those details. I think in your interaction with II1, they should be able to provide those details. (SE1)

Although SE1 did not provide specific information about management practice, it affirmed that information given by II1 regarding management criteria could be relied upon. The management practice similarity seemed to be a driving force in their collaboration experience. It is not unlikely that such similarity sparked mutual trust and commitment between them to build reliable partnerships. The analysis also finds shared empirical themes relating to the type of resources that captured their complementarity. The resources cut across tangible and intangible resources that motivated collaboration between SE1 and II1 and revealed the power dynamics between them.

When asked about different types of resources that motivate collaboration between SE1 and II1 to determine partner fit, the emerging themes that captured complementary resources cut across tangible and intangible resources and ranged from access to capital, viable business models to technical support. A viable business model in the context of SE and II collaboration is likened to businesses that generate both social impact and financial returns: a viable business model is a social business model that has been proven to generate financial return on investment with measurable social impact. SE1's desire to collaborate with II1 stems from the need to access financial capital (tangible resources) and innovative skills different from its possession of a viable and scalable business model (intangible resources). II1 found the SE1 social business model was a viable pipeline and appropriate to achieving its blended motives of social and financial returns. Each member of the dyad described how possession of different types of resources by each partner enabled the establishment of partner fit:

> Typically, we provide capital for growth, where a business is looking to expand its reach. That means the business should have been in operation, at least two or three years with a proven business model, and market and just looking to make returns from scale... We believe in a profit with a purpose and we are commercial investors, but we understand the need is fundamentally social. (II1)
>
> II1 saw the need to invest in our organisation—they liked what we were doing, providing a scalable technology for microfinance institutions to directly impact on the different clients they are providing services, somewhere along the line we got connected to them, and they ended up investing in SE1. (SE1)

The evidence from the collaboration experience revealed a positive impact of different types of resources that motivated their collaboration. Empirical evidence capturing different types of resources shows mutual commitment to pursuing collective, interest which comes from the possession of different types of tangible and intangible resources. Successful collaboration is feasible in any area when a firm cooperates with partners in possession of complementary resources, regardless of whether they are strong or weak. The power dynamic in the collaborations can be determined from the strength and weakness in resources contributed to the partnership. In this analysis, II1 possessed stronger tangible resources, which included financial capital and technical capability. II1 was able to determine if SE1's social business model was viable for generating both social and financial returns. In this case, SE1 successfully established partner fit with II1, because it also possessed a social business model, viable for generating financial returns on investment as perceived by II1. This implies that the two parties brought different but complementary resources that could generate mutual benefit. II1 also ascertained that the number of assets owned by SE1 was potential beneficial capital for the partnership. As SE1 righty stated, "providing scalable technology for microfinance..." implies the products hold great potential to deliver expected returns on investment as well as social impact. Since II1 and SE1 in the dyad stand to benefit from the relationship, it is no longer debatable that each partner's different type of resources captured some element of mutual reciprocal behaviour. They brought to the table such resources so that the combination of viable business models from SE1 and financial and technical support on innovation from II1 could create greater economic and social value.

II2 is an indigenous technology and early start-up investor that invested in SE2, a printing technology sector SE with a 5-year relationship. The two organisations established partner fit by aligning similar missions in social and economic goals. Dyadic empirical themes that emerged from these dyads' narratives provide further details on the similarity of mission/criteria and types of resources that determined their compatibility and complementarity to establish partner fit. After aligning similarities between the organisational mission of SE2 with the impact investment appetite of II2 and its criteria, the analysis found that II2's investment philosophy on tech-enabled organisation aligned with SE2's technology-enabled printing service mission aimed at solving African technology problems.

It is also notable that SE2 is an early-stage SE, which suits II2's targeting investment in early-stage social enterprises. Aligning II2's investment target with SE2's mission illustrates a form of compatibility in the two firms' belief in technology in Africa. Both demonstrated how organisational practices and beliefs determined their compatibility and its influence on their collaboration experience:

> We invest in SE2, who are tech-enabled businesses. But I think the other thing is that we don't only invest in Nigeria; we invest across Africa. So, if there are a couple of portfolio companies that are not necessarily African but are solving African problems... The core thing that runs through all our investments is that they must be solving African problems, African pinpoints. (II2)
>
> So, we wanted to build a company that would order prints from anywhere, either homes, office or any part of the country, whether in Niger or Sokoto state...When discussing, it was obvious that [II2] ...was like a perfect match, and it was just a matter of time they got themselves there, and three months later we had another meeting and they were, like, just three months... It was a done deal, our interaction with them. (SE2)

II2's and SE2's collaboration experience was facilitated by aligning organisational similarities in mission and investment goals. They both have similar organisational logic to use technology and address social and economic problems within the African region and Nigeria. Their collaboration centre's rallying point is the similarity of the logic to harness market opportunity through tech-enabled business with a focus on early-stage businesses.

Besides aligning similar missions, II2 and SE2 affirmed their collaboration experience has also been determined by the fulfilment of certain managerial practices, linked to good leadership. Having a strong leadership team appeared a criterion II2 looked for before investing in SE2. Meeting the leadership criteria by SE2 positively influenced the collaboration. II2 revealed the importance of having a good leadership team which was agreed upon by SE2:

> We look at the founders; the founder has to be committed to the problem they are solving, because we are not going to run the company for you, that is not our model. (II2)
>
> It will also make sense to have experienced managers on your team, because it would be very funny if you are building as a pioneer and you don't have an experienced team, it will speak down about your team, but if your team is the pioneer, and you have a very solid team, and not just a solid team, a solid advisory team you can look up to, because the team helps you to shape your direction. (SE2)

Their statements demonstrate how organisational leadership and team commitment determine organisational compatibility and the subsequent establishment of partner fit. As II2 said, "We are not going to run the company for you". This comment points to the role of a good leadership profile that SEs hold in determining collaboration between dyad partners.

From the dimension of different types of resources, dyadic empirical themes between II2 and SE2 also demonstrate how possession of different tangible and intangible resources determines partner fit. In the analysis, II2 found SE2 to be an innovative enterprise, operating in a location with strong opportunities. These opportunities motivated II2 and it was willing to commit financial resources to SE2's viable social business model because of the potential for financial return on investment. SE2 revealed that accessing financial capital from II2 to scale its innovative business model across Nigeria is the different type of resource it needs to achieve the desired social and economic impact. II2, importantly, perceives the scalability potential of SE2's business idea as an intangible type of resource with a positive indicator of financial return on investment. Scalability means that SE2's social business model can replicate across several locations. The greater the scalability potential of SEs' business model, the faster and greater the return on investment with profitability. II2 described how SE2's different types of resources, defined as viable and innovative business opportunity in the technology sector, motivated complementary access to Nigerian impact opportunity:

> We look at the product: are you solving a problem or is it just a nice to have, is it a fancy product that looks nice but it doesn't really solve anything? How well has the product been developed, how well has it been thought through? If somebody else comes into the market, will you still have a good chance of competing with them…? We believe that technology can allow us to leap forward to all the steps that other developed markets have had to go through and so that's why we are focused here [on SE2]. (II2)

SE2 also explained how access to financial resources from II2 represented a different type of resources that motivated them to seek collaboration:

> Mr O. was running the business daily with his funds, along the lines we discussed, how we want to get to the next level. We had plans and strategy to move on, but we definitely will need investment, and we need to show reasons why we need financing from II2.

II2 and SE2 described how they mutually leverage on different types of, but complementary, resources to pursue their social and economic interests. A combination of financial capital and deployment of innovative research discovery in the use of technology are such types that align for these dyads. Besides the provision of financial resources, SE2's search for the capacity to innovate and scale its enterprise further demonstrates the value of II2's possession of technical capability that it hopes to bring into the partnership with SE2:

> We decided, if we're able to access all these resources, all these financial resources, then we need to deploy them here and help solve existing problems that we have experienced while living here and while growing up here. (II2)

SE2 agreed:

> Internal growth knowledge: we call it economics. Everything you do in the day-to-day operation can be captured, how you record actively the number of people who use the platform, everything about the business, the number of staff, everything has to be captured, because what investors are looking at is what is the number of potentials, is it capturing a large market?

The comments showed that they both possess differing types of complementary resources and point to how these resources determine the establishment of partner fit. II2's comment underlines its possession of financial resources and technical experience for navigating the challenges that SE2 is trying to solve. This experience may be different from the existing internal growth strategy knowledge that SE2 possesses, but, when joined together, it can capture potential market opportunity, as SE2 explained. Combinations of expert knowledge are proven to support innovation in emerging markets such as Nigeria, where investment opportunities abound.

II3 is an impact investor in a range of sectors that address social inclusion challenges across West Africa. The investor has had dyadic relations with SE3 for more than two years. SE3 is well-established in promoting financial inclusion through microloans for the economically poor in Nigeria. Analysis of themes revealed how the organisations established partner fit by aligning similar organisational missions and different types of resources. Analysis revealed some similarities in SE3's mission with the investment motives of II3 and demonstrated just how they established partner fit. II3 observed that the mission focus of SE3 in providing microloans targeting the "bottom of the pyramid" or BoP aligned with their investment target to provide microloans for small enterprises. The dyad also has a blended investment motive that focuses on pursuing social and economic interests in Nigeria. Thus, aligning similar missions and investment motives for social inclusion through microloans has positively guided and determined collaboration:

> II3 is an impact investment management firm that focuses on three major areas. We make impact investment in specific sectors: agriculture, healthcare, affordable housing, education, basic finance and weather effects—everything that we do is built around these sectors. We previously had a $US25 million fund for SMEs looking at small businesses. So, we looked at microloans, not really microloans beyond $5000. But now we're kind of shifting focus to slightly bigger ones that are bigger than what the microloans will support, but maybe not big enough for the mainstream banks. (II3)

SE3 corroborated how aligning their mission with II3's investment motive influenced the collaboration:

> SE3 was incorporated as a trust to provide microfinance services to its members, who are typically the economically active poor in Nigerian society; it is a business enterprise with a

> strong social mission. SE3 was set up to bridge the gap for those who are excluded from the conventional financial system in Nigeria. (II3)

The description of the type of organisation and sectors that II3 invests in from the themes provides evidence on how its similarity in mission aligns with SE3's organisational mission. Consequently, the interest in II3's addressing SMEs' funding challenges aligned with SE3's mission to meet the funding challenges for people at the "bottom of the pyramid". II3 commented that meeting the criteria of having a good management team by SE3 positively determined and influenced collaboration between them:

> We also look at the management of the organisation and target our investment using a triple bottom line approach. There's profit, people and planet. Whatever it is that we're doing, we want to make money of course, for ourselves, for our investors, and the investees… Our model is sort of, we don't only provide the fund, we make sure the fund will actually help the investees to achieve the impact. (II3)

SE3 also revealed how having an audited financial record history served as a determinant which met II3's investment criteria:

> …keeping good financial records at least three years of audited financial statement and objective external audit, what we call the microfinance institutional rating, which is done by several rating institutions in the space.

Corroborating empirical evidence from this dyad, a combination of a good management team and sound financial records, set as criteria by II3, were key determining criteria that SE3 met and determined the organisations' compatibility for collaboration. The analysis also means that, besides similarity in organisational missions and goals, SE3's possession of a good financial history and leadership capability had impacted positively on collaboration.

From different types of resources, themes between SE3 and II3 also demonstrate how complementarity of resources determined the establishment of partner fit. II3 revealed themes connected to how impact funding and technical support on risk management to SE3 motivated collaboration. It was also notable that SE3 presented a scalable business model with a huge potential for financial and social impact as different types of intangible resources, which was perceived by II3 as motivation and engendered mutual commitment to achieve complementary goals. Evidence from II3 sheds better light on how the capital needs of SE3 demonstrate a financial type of resources that positively influenced their partner fit:

> We situated our impact investment management firm in this part of the world, because the West African market is probably in most need of impact investment… We could have done a purely commercial [deal] and still be successful, but the truth is, you want to make financial returns, yes, but you also want to trickle down to those at the bottom of the pyramid… We want to grow the businesses; we provide technical assistance for the business and render services to SMEs in these sectors… We don't want to give you one-off funding and be okay at that level. Can you scale? Can this idea be replicated in another environment? SE3 has been around for quite a while in this space… (II3)

SE3 corroborated how access to funding and technical assistance from II3 motivated their collaboration and would be reciprocated with a scalable business model with a potential for both social and financial returns to II3:

> As at the time, access to credit was a big tropical issue in terms of developmental goals across the world, [SE2] was set up to bridge that gap for those who are excluded from the conventional financial system in Nigeria… We've pulled in technical assistance: specifically, we had technical assistance in the area of risk management, in the area of rural development and it is always good to exchange knowledge. (SE3)

The evidence from II3 and SE3 corroborates how potentially different types of resources, i.e., capital and technical support by II3 and a scalable business model by SE3, determined partner fit. There is no doubt that there are differences in the type of resources contributed by each partner, as II3 tends to commit more resources to the partnership than SE3. This also demonstrates the power dynamic connected to the type and volume of resources contributed by each partner. However, the fact that SE3 follows a business model with the potential to generate social impact and financial return to II3 validates the argument that the relationship will result in mutual benefit, although the type of resources contributed by each partner may not be the same.

II4 is a foreign impact investor active in over 80 countries with interest in high-risk and early-stage SEs addressing critical problems affecting people at the bottom of the pyramid. The organisation has had an ongoing dyadic relation with SE4 for over 2 years. II4's interest in SE4 stems from its commitment to addressing the insecurity challenges in the Northern part of Nigeria, through job creation for unemployed youth in agricultural farming. Analysis of II4 and SE4 revealed how they established partner fit by aligning similar organisational mission and investment criteria. Empirical themes helped us ascertain their goals by matching SE4's mission and II4's investment motives and criteria. Emerging themes from II4 showed investment motivation as targeting social enterprises in the early stage or start-ups. II4's investment goal also targets SEs with inclusive business models. "Inclusive" in this context means SEs operating in areas that focus on helping the poorest in the community.

From the perspective of SE4, its mission was to impact on smallholder farmers in rural areas through its inclusive business model, which aligned with II4's investment motive. Comparing II4's investment target with the inclusive SE model and SE4's mission to smallholder farmers in rural areas, it is evident that they both have compatible organisational missions to deliver inclusive social impact. Evidence from II4 demonstrates how SE4's mission fit into the investment motive of II4, and presents a key determinant in the collaboration experience between them:

> Since its inception in 2006, II4 has been extending risk capital, medium- and long-term debt in local (LCY) and hard (HCY) currency to financial intermediaries in developing countries to enhance financial inclusion… [SE4] utilises a farmer-service model that provides end-to-end services to a network of farmer groups in Nigeria. These institutions, in turn, serve their end-beneficiaries: micro entrepreneurs, small- and medium-sized enterprises (MSMEs), and lower-income households. (II4)

SE4 likewise affirmed how the similarity of its mission with II4's investment motives determined established partner fit:

> It's because our goals are quite closely aligned, so [II4] are focused not just on making the organisation profitable but it's really on the impact they are making on the lives of these individuals.

Besides the similarity in organisational goals, two themes relating to management style also determined how partner fit was established. Analysis shows corporate governance and good financial record practice emerged as management practices that also influenced collaboration. The similarity of organisational mission and meeting specific criteria joined with the maintenance of good governance and financial records by SE4. These attributes played key roles in determining SE4 suitability for II4. II4 explained how SE4's ability to meet good governance and financial record practice played a key determining role in their collaborative experience:

> Our criteria for investment in SE4 centred around the II4 strategy, which considers the activities of SE4, business model, corporate governance and their investment needs.

SE4 also affirmed that meeting certain criteria, particularly with respect to financial record keeping, had determined its compatibility to establish partner fit with II4:

> I think your track record is very important. Really, what we have been able to do with the funding that we have received so far. A lot of the conversation was around what impact we have had so far, and they were very interested in speaking to the farmers, really connecting, just to make sure that this is a model that has worked in the past and it's scalable.

On the dimension of the different types of resources, themes also revealed how they established partner fit from their different but complementary resources. These are linked to different types of tangible and intangible resources that both perceived would mutually benefit the partnership. For example, SE4 holds resources in the form of a scalable and innovative business model in agricultural farming, whereas II4 holds tangible and intangible resources in the form of financial capital and technical expertise in agricultural farming, which SE4 requires to pursue its social and economic interests. Comments from both partners revealed how their relationship from the outset evolved from perceived differences in resource type:

> We invest in Lapo microfinance bank that provides funding to several SMEs in Nigeria and SE4 as well… SE4 utilises a farmer service model that provides end-to-end services to a network of farmer groups in Nigeria… Scalability is necessary to expand SE4's franchise model and reach at least 50,000 additional smallholder farmers by 2019, as part of increasing the food security of 1 million smallholder farmers living in Nigeria by 2025. (II4)

SE4 reiterated how collaboration was determined by perceived differences in resource type whereby its business model offered a promising financial return to II4:

> …I think it's really about the returns you are giving to your investors. But it is important for us to be a sustainable business, so it's not just about receiving handouts from [II4]. It was important to set up the business as for-profit rather than a non-profit to ensure that the business model itself works. It just goes to show that it's a sustainable business model as well as social impact.

Evidence from these organisations demonstrates how collaboration was motivated and made possible due to the differences in resource type they brought to the partnership. These resources offered great potential to achieve mutual benefits while pursuing collective interests. The benefits came from the provision of finance as capital by II4, since SE4's business model had been shown to generate the desired financial returns that II4 envisaged. The financial returns were judged sufficient to pay back the initial investment in the blended business model of SE4 with a potential to achieve measurable social impact. Thus, despite differences in resource type in this dyad, they both could derive mutual benefit from the relationship.

II5 is a foreign impact investor in SEs focusing on specific sectors with promising impact on people at the BoP. The organisation has had dyadic relations with SE5 for over a year. II5 invested in SE5 as a social enterprise producing innovative healthcare products accessible to people in remote or rural areas in Nigeria. Analysis provides further insight into how IIs and SEs establish partner fit from firms' compatibility and a combination of different complementary types of resources.

The analysis reveals similarities in their missions and investment criteria. For example, SE5's mission to address social challenges in health sectors through accessible healthcare products aligns with the investment appetite of II5 to pursue social impact with financial returns through impact investment in the health sector: The parties established partner fit based on the resemblance in their mission and goals to address social challenges in the sector. II5 revealed how similarity in their mission with SE5 was determined prior to establishing partner fit:

> I told you that we do what banks do, but we also do what banks don't do, and what banks don't do is the social investment part… When I joined II5, the first assignment I did was to develop what they call a strategy paper. In the strategy paper, you're expected to outline the sectors you're interested in, and I picked five sectors… the other one is health… Our focus is on SMEs… but our definition of SMEs is slightly different from the definition you'll find in the literature. For us, there are three things that we distinguish: two out of the three will distinguish our target market. We say an SME must be a client whose total asset base is less than $6 million. It must be an entrepreneur who employs less than 150 people.

SE5 also described how the similarity of its mission and firm size fit into II5's investment motive in determining collaboration:

> We have over a hundred staff at SE5, a health-care product limited-liability company registered with CAC… Somebody introduced us to [II5], and we found out they were in our complex. We never knew what they were doing, but somebody introduced them [II5] to us, and we connected.

Evidence from the dyad revealed that the two organisations established partner fit based on the compatibility of their mandate to address social issues in the health sector. There is a matching compatibility between SE5's mission with II5's investment goals targeting SEs in the health sector. It is also clear that meeting other criteria, such as legitimisation through formal registration with legal bodies in Nigeria (e.g., the CAC), had influenced the establishment of partner fit.

Some evidence also shows that partner fit has been motivated by a combination of different types of resources. The would-be partners brought tangible and intangible resources they hoped would mutually benefit the relationship. II5 found SE5's business model an innovative solution to healthcare challenges in Nigeria: It could impact socially disadvantaged people but also provide the investor with profit; SE5 saw capital access from II5 as a resource needed to scale its innovative health product in the market with both social impact and financial returns. These differences determined and guided collaboration:

> II5 was established through studies conducted by Shell Foundation, and two bodies conducted the study where the idea was to find out why SMEs fail. Part of which is that they are not formalised, they don't have access to finance. When they go to conventional financial institutions to access funds the conditions given to them are difficult to meet… II5 says it is not important, what's important is the viability of the business, once the business is viable, we'll avail you of funding, believing out of that viability, you'll return the principal given to you with the premium added… Down the line, by 2009, II5 realised it was the biggest mistake. First of all, the moment you do that, the average SME player believes that is part of the national cake. They wouldn't be in a hurry to return that money, II5 shifted and said, yes, viability is important, but there has to be an investment on your part. What do you have in the deal? At least let us see that you have an office, you have paid your rent. You must have a minimum of 30% of the amount you're asking for invested already in the deal. (II5)

More succinctly:

> We had the issue of funding: bringing in our innovative product they gave us fund that has really impacted positively on our business. (SE5)

These remarks are further evidence how II5's provision of financial capital and SE5's innovative healthcare business model describe complementary resources for establishing partner fit. For II5, SE5's business model was an intangible resource through which an initial investment would generate financial returns and social impact. SE5 also contributed tangible resources to the partnership in the form of over 30% of valuable assets. The dyad also established partner fit from a combination of relatively strong resources from each partner—a model and capital from SE5 and finance and technical contributions from II5. Such mutual commitment of tangible and intangible resources met collective interests.

II6 is a foreign impact investor with strong local presence in Nigeria. Its investment focus is agricultural impact-driven social enterprises. It has had an ongoing dyadic relation with SE6 for over three years. SE6 is a social enterprise established to create employment opportunities in Nigeria through poultry farming. Similar organisational missions and criteria, including differences in resource type, again determined the establishment of partner fit: II6's organisational compatibility linked to SE6's focus on the agricultural sector, including its low-risk status, suited II6's investment criteria and SE6's low-risk status meant that, after due diligence, II6 found the risk for investing in SE6 to be at a minimal level. The compatibility between II6 and SE6 stems from their interest to create jobs through agricultural farming:

> We also have our poultry project that is SE6, where we encourage women and the youth to rear chicken. We then buy from them and train them on the best practices to rear these chickens… It all begins like the process of getting married, looking for social enterprises that can fit into your investment appetite… These are companies we try to help for the

> people around them, that is, women, youth, and the main players within the supply chain, and how we can help empower them, develop whatever they are doing to a better scale. (II6)
>
> We are involved in the poultry or algae section here and essentially in the production of on or before day-old chicks. But right now, our focus is on broiler production, swollen chicken. We are trying to carve a niche in the broiler market because we are about a year old in that section now. (SE6)

Compatible organisational interest in agricultural poultry farming motivated collaboration to address social and economic hardship. It was also notable that II6's organisational compatibility with SE6 was determined by aligning managerial practice with II6 criteria and firm size. II6 provided evidence in relation to firm size:

> Looking at the size of the company, have you ever carried out an environmental assessment? Are you conducting subsequent audits, and complying with the requirements of the regulatory agencies, do you have a human resource policy and procedures? How do you conduct your recruitment, what are your employee policies…? (II6)

SE6 likewise revealed partner fit with II6 was determined from financial record keeping as an example of managerial practice:

> II6 looked at the cash flow of the organisation, looking at the assets and liability. And then the equity. I think when they were satisfied with all those things, they decided to come in with their funds.

In terms of resource complementarity, analysis revealed themes relating to how resource differences guided the establishment of partner fit. The themes showed they possessed different types of resources that could be of mutual benefit. For example, II6's finance and technical support on business management skills exemplified a combination of tangible and intangible resources. SE6's financially viable business model for poultry farming was an intangible resource. Since II6 expected financial returns from the SE6 business model, this constituted a different type of resource with value, as II6 explained:

> First, we see how financially viable are these companies; then, the two key things are to look at the environmental and social impact. A project that will have a huge environmental impact we will not invest in. We are guided by the Nigerian regulation through the Federal Ministry of Environment, which grades projects in 1, 2, 3, one being the highest which has environmental impact, two has a reversible environmental impact, three has no adverse impact. We focus more on two and three and not doing one. A company that has a huge environmental impact and negative social impact, even if the company is doing well financially, we will not go on to work with that company because of reputational damage.

SE6 also revealed the role of II6 funding:

> II6 came in, as I said, about two years ago; we are in the third year running now. That was at a time we were looking for funds to expand the scope and coverage of the farm. Before then, we were into only breeder management, commercial table egg production, both lay and broiler day-old. But at this time, we were looking for how to go into real broiler fattening; they virtually controlled houses at the same time to establish a processed food plant called an abattoir and get other logistics like cold vans for delivering of finished products. The fund required then we could not generate internally, and, through the chairman, we made [links] with investors, and other things followed.

The organisations established partner fit based on differences in resources, which also engendered mutual commitment to create social and economic impact. It is important to note that II6 has a strong intention to generate social impact; however, that intention will not trade off risk of financial loss in the process, since profitability is key for repayment of investment made into the business. Although a trade-off is a key characteristic of SE and II relations, it is relative: SE6 showed that it already secured a viable market where the potential to meet a profit margin or investment appetite for II6 was in place—that is, the relationship is not parasitic but symbiotic, judging from each partner's contribution of different type of resources.

5.4 Establishment of Partner Fit Between SEs and IIs

Analysis across the six dyadic cases generated several individual themes, which revealed each dyad's distinct experience on how they established partner fit. The narratives revealed how similarity of firm mission and II investment criteria are aligned to determine compatible organisational logics. Simultaneously, differences in tangible and intangible resources revealed the type of complementary resources that motivate actors' collaboration. A summary of themes describing compatible organisational logics and complementary type of resources is presented in Tables 5.1 and 5.2. Differences in the tables explain each partner's perception about how they established partner fit from the similarity of firms' mission/criteria and resource differences. Themes around compatibility revealed different determining organisational-related logics. Themes around complementarity revealed differences in resources they both leverage to establish partner fit. It is important to note there could be differences in resource type between some dyads, but this did not prevent

Table 5.1 Empirical themes of compatible logics within dyads

S/N	IIs	Dyadic empirical themes	Dyadic empirical themes	SEs
1.	II1	Impact via tech business	Logic of technology	SE1
		Reputation on impact	Intentionality for impact	
2.	II2	Investing across Africa	Focus on African issues	SE2
		Technology in printing	Technology focus	
3.	II3	Impact with profit	Blended motive	SE3
		Good financial records	Management team	
4.	II4	Smallholder farmers	Early-stage start-up	SE4
		Experience & good record	Good governance	
5.	II5	Health care service	Focus on health	SE5
		Formalised	Registered with CAC	
			150 minimum employee	
6.	II6	Agrotech farming	Investment focus on agriculture	SE6
		Environmental ethics	Firm size and records	
			Minimal risk level	

Table 5.2 Empirical themes of complementary resources between dyad partners

S/N	IIs	Dyadic empirical themes	Dyadic empirical themes	SEs
1.	II1	Access to capital	Inclusive model	SE1
		Technical skills	Scalability	
			Market opportunity	
2.	II2	Access to capital	Innovative model	SE2
		Capacity for growth	Good experience	
			Scalability	
3.	II3	Technical skills	Scalability	SE3
		Access to capital	Business strategy	
4.	II4	Finance for blended impact	Scalability	SE4
		Innovation and skills	Viable business model	
5.	II5	Finance for scalability	Innovative model	SE5
			Blended impact	
			Investment asset	
6.	II6	Finance to scale	Blended impact model	SE6
		Managerial support		

their collaboration: resource differences instead determine the power dynamic in the relationship between mutual and asymmetrical levels.

Table 5.1 shows how similar organisational mission and investment criteria across dyads are aligned to strongly determine the compatibility of SEs and IIs. For example, columns 3 and 4 demonstrate shared compatible organisational beliefs, mission and managerial practice. Table 5.2 likewise reveals different types of resources that motivate each dyad to establish partner fit. For example, column 3 demonstrates resources that IIs found to be complementary, while column 4 demonstrates resources that SEs found to be complementary. Each dyad was motivated to align these resource types to establish partner fit for mutual benefit. It is important to note that the type of resources contributed in dyads determines the power dynamic between them: when IIs provide more resources, such as finance and technical assistance/managerial expertise, and SEs provide only viable models, such a relationship may imply asymmetry, for example, in Case 6. Yet the imbalance in resource type did not prevent collaboration in this study, because profit maximisation is not the ultimate goal for the partnership, for example, see Case 3.

From the literature, it was established that complementarity of resources from inter-organisational alliances occurs when organisations seek partnerships to gain complementary resources and capabilities to overcome internal resource limitations and in order to unleash mutual benefits (Kwon, 2008; Manotungvorapun & Gerdsri, 2016). Examples of themes emerging from previous studies on the dimensions of complementarity of resources include technical capability, technical assets, applicability of research discoveries, organisational capital and human capital (Dhurkari &

Nandakumar, 2015; Manotungvorapun & Gerdsri, 2016). Compatibility of organisations in partner fit indicates stability from organisational harmonisation of strategic alliances that can generate mutual trust and commitment (Kwon, 2008). This line of thinking supports research showing where dissimilarities in institutional models overcome potential conflict through goal alignment towards mutually beneficial collaboration (Mair & Hehenberger, 2014; van Fenema & Loebbecke, 2014).

It contrasts with a common view that competing institutional logics impede cooperation between actors (Mair & Hehenberger, 2014; Shields & Watermeyer, 2020). Some studies focus on examining the relationship between two or more organisations pursuing competing interests to ascertain the stability of such relationships and the likely trade-offs. Our study, however, focuses on the pre-investment strategies of engagement between SEs and IIs and not necessarily what happens during the relationship period (Agrawal & Hockerts, 2019), but rather the experience from the inter-organisational engagement process. This aligns with scholarly categorisation of non-technical compatibility as collaboration with heterogeneous partners requiring congruence of goals and cooperation (Brouthers et al., 1995; Spekman, 1988). According to Chesbrough and Schwartz (2007), compatibility entails the alignment of business goals, objectives and models. Examples of themes from previous studies include knowledge-base, previous relationships, collaborative behaviour, geographical proximity, strategic objective of intellectual property management, learning orientation, absorptive capacity in social capital and R&D capability.

Based on these theoretical insights into inter-organisational collaboration, the analysis focuses on discovering constructs relating to the process through which SEs and IIs in dyad successfully select partners, including managerial practice and resource differences. Findings from themes under similarity of firms' mission and managerial practices have been described from the perspective of compatible organisational logics (Hewett et al., 1974) and findings relating to differences in resource type have been linked to shared resource complementarity (Manotungvorapun & Gerdsri, 2016; Sarkar et al., 2001). Our study has found organisational compatibility and resource complementarity aligning with themes across the six cases, which also reveal their pattern of behaviour. The basis for drawing insight from compatibility and complementarity hinges on the fact that the success of any collaboration largely depends on a smart partner selection process (Dhurkari & Nandakumar, 2015; Lambe & Spekman, 1997). It is, therefore, proposed that a similar trend may characterise the process by which SEs and IIs seek to establish partner fit to pursue social and economic objectives across contexts, as is revealed in our study. Two harmonised themes that reflect the six dyads' perceptions and narratives from their collaboration experience are developed in the next section.

5.5 Alignment of Organisational Logics and Managerial Practice

The findings across the six dyadic cases show how SEs and IIs establish partner fit through compatibility. Compatibility of organisational beliefs and managerial practice is the driving force in collaboration. This very much aligns with the definition of institutional logic as "socially constructed, historical patterns of material practices, assumptions, values, believes and rules" (Thornton & Ocasio, 1999: 804). The beliefs and practices across the six cases originated from historical views of the societal problems each organisation set out to address. Thus SEs configure their mission to address such societal ills, and IIs seek engagement with SEs whose mission aligns with their investment goals. These problems emanate from the societal institutional logics of social and economic values manifested within these organisations.

Such practices were thought to be a source of contradiction and incompatibility, based on the scholarly prescription of multiple institutional logics, that is, social and economic logic (Delbridge & Edwards, 2013; Greenwood et al., 2011). However, analytic findings across the six cases align with other streams of research that suggest that organisations can incorporate two or more logics in a relatively compatible fashion, by blending these to create new organisational forms (Rao & Kenney, 2008; Rao et al., 2000). This is why only hybrid social enterprises were analysed here, since their formation aligns with the adoption of societal logic of social and economic value. The findings confirmed that the alignment of organisational goals across the six cases falls within the definition of compatibility by Besharov and Smith (2014) on the extent to which the representation of logic implies consistency and reinforcement of organisational actions. The findings, therefore, extend knowledge on managing dual logic tensions in organisations through logic alignment between hybrid firms with inter-organisational dyadic relations.

5.6 Motivation from Mutual Complementarity of Resource Type

Findings on differences in resource type across the six cases demonstrate another pathway to increasing mutual commitment when two organisations in dyadic relations combine different but complementary resource types to achieve social and commercial goals. This type of behaviour has been described in the literature as resource complementarity in firm alliances (Mitsuhashi & Greve, 2009; Sarkar et al., 2001). It is interesting to note that resource complementarity across the six dyadic cases here varies with the combination of different types of resources. As Dhurkari and Nandakumar (2015) argue, the measure of complementary resources required from parties in alliance for mutual benefit will include differences in tangible and intangible resources, which include physical infrastructure, financial capability, organisational capital, technical capability and technical assets (Dhurkari

& Nandakumar, 2015; Manotungvorapun & Gerdsri, 2016). Miotti and Sachwald (2003) add that collaboration can be successful in any area when a firm cooperates with partners in possession of stronger complementary resources. Similarly, this study has revealed impact investors as contributors of stronger resources, because financial capital represents scarce resources needed by social enterprises. Finance is a scarce resource, because it is short in supply and highly competitive (Martin & Osberg, 2015) and underpins the reason there are some levels of imbalance in terms of complementary resource type across the six cases.

Findings about resource type across the cases align with scholarly findings that resource scarcity has repeatedly manifested as a crucial condition that facilitates the initiation of diverse relationship types (Levine & White, 1961; Pfeffer & Salancik, 2003; Van de Ven, 1976). Our study found that scarcity of resources from traditional sectors such as NGOs and state finance has led a limited number of SEs in Nigeria to adopt a hybrid organisational form in order to attract financial capital from IIs. The findings revealed finance as a complementary type of resource to address social problems by social enterprise with a promising return on investment. IIs; however, were interested in solving difficult social problems, but with organisations that can demonstrate a strong ability to take equity with subsequent returns on investment. SEs and IIs in dyad derive their motivation to a cause for action by engaging in inter-organisational dyadic relations, involving cooperation in tangible and intangible resources for mutual benefit.

The type of relationship in the six dyads analysed has been defined in the literature as corporate financial interlock (Srinivasan et al., 2018; Zona et al., 2018). Corporate financial interlocking occurs when board members of one company serve on another company's board. A model of this type of relationship is meant to reduce the level of uncertainty so as to increase legitimacy by co-opting external representatives to sit on organisations' boards (Oliver, 1990). Analysis from this study found some IIs sitting as board members in some SEs, for example, II4 and SE4. Studies have also revealed that corporate financial interlocks are established for reciprocal purposes (Oliver, 1990), which tends to facilitate mutual borrowing and lending and increase high-quality technical and administrative expertise. Evidence across the six dyads analysed shows that technical expertise from IIs is among the resources they contributed to gain partner fit with SEs. Yet some IIs also examined SEs' technical and managerial capabilities as criteria for choosing SEs to partner, which implies SEs also contributed intangible types of resources to gain partner fit with IIs.

Our study reveals that inter-organisational dyadic relations are prone to asymmetric power dominance by stronger parties through exercise of private rules and conditions which guide exchanges between actors (Rindt & Mouzas, 2015). Although asymmetry has been associated with corporate financial interlocks, the level or degree of such power dominance or control has remained a source of continuing debate (Degryse & De Jong, 2006; Fich & White, 2005; Hernández-Lara & Gonzales-Bustos, 2019; Oliver, 1990). Our analysis found the most appropriate asymmetric level between SEs and IIs to be symbiotic rather than absolute or completely parasitic, as is the case with traditional not-for-profit SEs, because hybrid SEs in this study demonstrate the practical ability to scale business opportunity through profitable financial outcomes. Such outcomes indicate why IIs seek complementary types of resources from SEs in the form of financially viable business models with scalability potential. Inter-organisational relations between SEs and IIs under this arrangement are viewed as one pathway for mutual commitment to achieve common goals.

The findings are supported by scholarly views that uphold the "motives of reciprocity emphasise cooperation, collaboration, and coordination among organisations, rather than domination, power, and control" (Oliver, 1990: 244). It is thus argued that our empirical evidence shows the dyadic relationship is rooted in the contribution of complementary types of resources for mutual benefit. The drive to achieve dual motives of social and economic outcome here revealed the relationship is built on mutual and symbiotic ground. This aligns with a mutual model of inter-organisational relationship, theoretically grounded in social exchange theory (Blau, 1964, 2017; Emerson, 1976; Homans, 1958). Hence, analysis of the cases has provided new knowledge on the type of resources exchanged between hybrid SEs with inter-organisational dyadic relations. It has also extended knowledge of mutuality and reciprocity from the perspective of the symbiotic relationship between hybrid organisations as against traditional asymmetric power.

5.7 Conclusion

This chapter utilised the concepts of organisational compatibility and resource complementarity to demonstrate how SEs and IIs have been guided in Nigeria to establish partner fit. The analysis drew on their mission statements and managerial practice to ascertain organisational or institutional logics that guide either party to establish partner fit. The concept of resource complementarity was used to ascertain the different types of resources that motivate collaboration or partner fit between them. These include tangible and intangible resources considered to possess some measure of value for mutually beneficial exchange. Across the six cases, it is evident that these two concepts greatly influenced, guided and determined the suitability of partnership between SEs and IIs in Nigeria.

Although these findings now offer a broader picture of how the six dyad SEs and IIs successfully established partner fit, it is pertinent to explore specific organisational-level variables that made compatibility and complementarity feasible. This the next chapter addresses.

References

Agrawal, A., & Hockerts, K. (2019). Impact investing strategy: Managing conflicts between impact investor and investee social enterprise. *Sustainability, 11*(15), 4117.

Besharov, M. L., & Smith, W. K. (2014). Multiple institutional logics in organizations: Explaining their varied nature and implications. *Academy of Management Review, 39*(3), 364–381.

Blau, P. M. (1964). *Exchange and power in social life*. Transaction Publishers.
Blau, P. (2017). *Exchange and power in social life*. Routledge.
Brouthers, K. D., Brouthers, L. E., & Wilkinson, T. J. (1995). Strategic alliances: Choose your partners. *Long Range Planning, 28*(3), 2–25.
Chesbrough, H., & Schwartz, K. (2007). Innovating business models with co-development partnerships. *Research-Technology Management, 50*(1), 55–59.
Degryse, H., & De Jong, A. (2006). Investment and internal finance: Asymmetric information or managerial discretion? *International Journal of Industrial Organization, 24*(1), 125–147.
Delbridge, R., & Edwards, T. (2013). Inhabiting institutions: Critical realist refinements to understanding institutional complexity and change. *Organization Studies, 34*(7), 927–947.
Dhurkari, R. K., & Nandakumar, M. (2015). Measures of complementarity and compatibility in strategic alliances for innovation: A review of literature. *The International Technology Management Review, 5*(4), 182–201.
Di Domenico, M., Tracey, P., & Haugh, H. (2009). The dialectic of social exchange: Theorizing corporate—Social enterprise collaboration. *Organization Studies, 30*(8), 887–907.
Emerson, R. M. (1976). Social exchange theory. *Annual Review of Sociology, 2*(1), 335–362. https://doi.org/10.1146/annurev.so.02.080176.002003
Fich, E. M., & White, L. J. (2005). Why do CEOs reciprocally sit on each other's boards? *Journal of Corporate Finance, 11*(1–2), 175–195.
Greenwood, R., Raynard, M., Kodeih, F., Micelotta, E. R., & Lounsbury, M. (2011). Institutional complexity and organizational responses. *Academy of Management Annals, 5*(1), 317–371.
Hernández-Lara, A. B., & Gonzales-Bustos, J. P. (2019). The impact of interlocking directorates on innovation: The effects of business and social ties. *Management Decision*. https://doi.org/10.1108/md-11-2017-1186
Hewett, T. T., O'Brien, G. E., & Hornik, J. (1974). The effects of work organization, leadership style, and member compatibility upon the productivity of small groups working on a manipulative task. *Organizational Behavior and Human Performance, 11*(2), 283–301.
Homans, G. C. (1958). Social behavior as exchange. *American Journal of Sociology, 63*(6), 597–606.
Jackson, A. Y., & Mazzei, L. (2011). *Thinking with theory in qualitative research: Viewing data across multiple perspectives*. Routledge.
Kwon, Y.-C. (2008). Antecedents and consequences of international joint venture partnerships: A social exchange perspective. *International Business Review, 17*(5), 559–573.
Lambe, C., & Spekman, R. (1997). *The bases of alliance derived sustainable advantage: Relationship and resources* (Paper presentation). The American Marketing Association Winter Conference Proceedings.
Levine, S., & White, P. E. (1961). Exchange as a conceptual framework for the study of interorganizational relationships. *Administrative Science Quarterly, 5*(4), 583–601.
Mair, J., & Hehenberger, L. (2014). Front-stage and backstage convening: The transition from opposition to mutualistic coexistence in organizational philanthropy. *Academy of Management Journal, 57*(4), 1174–1200.
Manning, J., & Kunkel, A. (2015). Qualitative approaches to dyadic data analyses in family communication research: An invited essay. *Journal of Family Communication, 15*(3), 185–192.
Manotungvorapun, N., & Gerdsri, N. (2016). Complementarity vs. compatibility: What really matters for partner selection in open innovation? *International Journal of Transitions and Innovation Systems, 5*(2), 122–139.
Martin, R. L., & Osberg, S. R. (2015). Two keys to sustainable social enterprise. *Harvard Business Review, 93*(5), 86–94.
Mason, C., & Kwok, J. (2010a). *Facilitating access to finance*. Discussion paper on investment readiness programmes. OECD. Retrieved from http://www.oecd.org/investment/psd/45324336.pdf
Mason, C., & Kwok, J. (2010b). Investment readiness programmes and access to finance: A critical review of design issues. *Local Economy, 25*(4), 269–292.

Mason, C., & Stark, M. (2004). What do investors look for in a business plan? A comparison of the investment criteria of bankers, venture capitalists and business angels. *International Small Business Journal, 22*(3), 227–248.
Miotti, L., & Sachwald, F. (2003). Co-operative R&D: Why and with whom?: An integrated framework of analysis. *Research Policy, 32*(8), 1481–1499.
Mitsuhashi, H., & Greve, H. R. (2009). A matching theory of alliance formation and organizational success: Complementarity and compatibility. *Academy of Management Journal, 52*(5), 975–995.
Oliver, C. (1990). Determinants of interorganizational relationships: Integration and future directions. *Academy of Management Review, 15*(2), 241–265.
Pache, A.-C., & Santos, F. (2013). Inside the hybrid organization: Selective coupling as a response to competing institutional logics. *Academy of Management Journal, 56*(4), 972–1001.
Pfeffer, J., & Salancik, G. R. (2003). *The external control of organizations: A resource dependence perspective*. Stanford University Press.
Rao, H., & Kenney, M. (2008). New forms as settlements. In R. Greenwood, C. Oliver, & R. Suddaby (Eds.), *The SAGE handbook of organizational institutionalism* (pp. 352–370). SAGE Publications Ltd.
Rao, H., Morrill, C., & Zald, M. N. (2000). Power plays: How social movements and collective action create new organizational forms. *Research in Organizational Behavior, 22*, 237–281.
Rindt, J., & Mouzas, S. (2015). Exercising power in asymmetric relationships: The use of private rules. *Industrial Marketing Management, 48*, 202–213.
Sarkar, M. B., Echambadi, R., Cavusgil, S. T., & Aulakh, P. S. (2001). The influence of complementarity, compatibility, and relationship capital on alliance performance. *Journal of the Academy of Marketing Science, 29*(4), 358–373.
Shields, R., & Watermeyer, R. (2020). Competing institutional logics in universities in the United Kingdom: Schism in the church of reason. *Studies in Higher Education, 45*(1), 3–17.
Solesvik, M. Z., & Encheva, S. (2010). Partner selection for interfirm collaboration in ship design. *Industrial Management, & Data Systems, 110*(5), 701–717.
Spekman, R. E. (1988). Strategic supplier selection: Understanding long-term buyer relationships. *Business Horizons, 31*(4), 75–81.
Srinivasan, R., Wuyts, S., & Mallapragada, G. (2018). Corporate board interlocks and new product introductions. *Journal of Marketing, 82*(1), 132–148.
Thompson, L., & Walker, A. J. (1982). The dyad as the unit of analysis: Conceptual and methodological issues. *Journal of Marriage and the Family, 44*(4), 889–900.
Thornton, P. H., & Ocasio, W. (1999). Institutional logics and the historical contingency of power in organizations: Executive succession in the higher education publishing industry, 1958–1990. *American Journal of Sociology, 105*(3), 801–843.
Van de Ven, A. H. (1976). On the nature, formation, and maintenance of relations among organizations. *Academy of Management Review, 1*(4), 24–36.
Van Fenema, P. C., & Loebbecke, C. (2014). Towards a framework for managing strategic tensions in dyadic interorganizational relationships. *Scandinavian Journal of Management, 30*(4), 516–524.
Zona, F., Gomez-Mejia, L. R., & Withers, M. C. (2018). Board interlocks and firm performance: Toward a combined agency–resource dependence perspective. *Journal of Management, 44*(2), 589–618.

Chapter 6
The Role of Trust in Business Collaboration and Partner Selection at the Organisational Level

6.1 Introduction

This chapter explores factors that enabled collaboration between SEs and IIs in dyad to answer sub-RQ2: "At the organisational level, what factors influence collaboration and partner selection between SEs and IIs in Nigeria?" The study also noted how "trust" played a key role in influencing partner selection for collaboration (Amoako, 2019; Bierly III & Gallagher, 2007).

The entrepreneurship literature reports that trust plays a major role in establishing partnerships between entities (Quince, 2001; Welter, 2012). Trust has been regarded as the essential element in a relationship that enables a problem-free collaboration in inter-organisational dyadic relationships (Thomas & Skinner, 2010). The kind of trust this study examines between SEs and IIs fits the definition of trust as "...the mutual confidence that no party to an exchange will exploit another's vulnerabilities, because opportunistic behaviour would violate values, principles and standards of behaviours that have been internalised by parties to an exchange" (Bierly III & Gallagher, 2007: 138). Trust in a dyadic relationship and the context of this study capture collaborative behaviour that requires a trustworthy impact investor and a trustworthy social enterprise, just as in the case of supplier and buyer relationships (Thomas & Skinner, 2010). The relevance of trust can be explained as a phenomenon that contributes to inter-organisational dyadic business relationships (Svensson, 2005): trust will provide a clear direction to examine factors or conditions in the Nigerian context that lead SEs and IIs to gain mutual trust to establish partner fit. The measure of variables that determine these factors is also in the levels that are defined in terms of mutual and asymmetrical trust.

Success in partner selection is believed to depend largely on how reliable, accessible information can be judged to be right for potential partners to reach an informed decision to collaborate. Bierly III and Gallagher (2007: 147) argued that "Partner selection can be influenced by how quickly another firm can be identified as

J. A. Emmanuel et al., *Social Enterprises and Impact Investors*, Advances in Theory and Practice of Emerging Markets,
https://doi.org/10.1007/978-3-031-59454-0_6

acceptable". Prior research has classified the antecedents to trust in three different broad categories: social networks of firms and individuals that guide the perception of trust between potential partners (Walker et al., 1997), culture and similarity, in the way other firms conduct their business (Barney & Hansen, 1994; Gulati, 1995; Park & Ungson, 1997) and firm reputation as the outcome of legitimacy that can influence trust (Barney & Hansen, 1994; Hill, 1990; Kasper-Fuehrera & Ashkanasy, 2001; Suchman, 1995). It is also noted that positive affect exists in a social situation where collaboration between parties is characterised by trust and mutual friendship (Barry & Oliver, 1996; Eklinder-Frick & Åge, 2020). The analysis here aims to identify organisational-related conditions across collaborating SEs and IIs in Nigerian SEs that influence mutual trust between them.

Consistent with social exchange theory guide for establishing trust in relationship (Leahy & Anderson, 2008), separate interview guides were compiled for SEs and IIs to ascertain organisation-level factors that engendered trust for collaboration. IIs explained factors that enabled them to trust SEs by which they ascertained legitimate SE status before establishing partner fit, while SEs explained factors that enhanced their trust to collaborate with IIs and the processes involved. The first coding process, using NVivo, generated several codes that explain the pattern of perception between SEs and IIs regarding factors that enhance shared trust. The study also captured factors that negatively impacted IIs' confidence to establish partner fit with some SEs (see Table 6.1). Reference to Cluster 3 is limited to its role in future study, since it fell outside this study's frame, consistent with CR philosophy.

Analysis of SE1 and II1 produced shared dyadic themes that explain firm-related factors that enabled them to establish partner fit. These factors are linked to mutual

Table 6.1 Empirical themes on organisational collaboration factors

Empirical cluster—1 Mutual trust legitimacy (44)	Empirical cluster 2 firms' reputation & social network (68)		Cluster 3 lack of investable SEs (26)	
Mutuality & firms' legitimacy of organisations (29)	Ethics and transparent investment pipeline (14)	Technical & Advisory Support (11)	Lack of viable business model (4)	Poor financial record keeping (4)
Alignment of social and economic interest (14)	The size of the organisation (7)	Physical & online verification of company status (3)	Neglect of ethical requirements (3)	The risk of small size organisations (3)
Successful exist and cordiality (1)	Excellent management (3)	Reputation of organisation (4)	Misalignment of business model (4)	Lack of awareness of the potential of impact fund (1)
	Organisation size (5)	Formal & informal network creation (11)	Poor management team (2)	Lack of trust in private capital (1)
	Application—5	Organisational referral (5)	Lack of patience for excellence (2)	Underdeveloped business idea (2)

trust and firms' legitimacy, as revealed in the stage one coding process. On the influence of mutual trust and firm legitimacy on trust level in the collaboration process, II1 linked the source for mutual trust to *genuine intentionality* for social impact, demonstrated by SE1 through the business model's social impact aspect. SE1 linked the source for mutual trust to II1's *belief in their intention* to deliver the required social impact. A belief in SE1's mission by II1 inspired confidence, which further built trust between them. The shared agreement to pursue genuine intentions on social impact demonstrates the influence of mutual trust as a source of strength to their level of trust. This dyad upholds a strong mutual trust in regard to intentions around social impact as the goal of their partnership, which generated mutual commitment that built the required level of trust to establish partner fit. Both parties spoke of their genuine intentionality towards social impact:

> The way we determine the impact potential of a business is we see if the problem that it's solving affects the lives, the wellbeing of the people and apart from just affecting their lives or their wellbeing, we are value-added investors and impact is part of our value proposition, meaning that impact is intentional. (II1)

And:

> II1 saw the need to invest in our organisation, they liked what we were doing, so somewhere along the line we got connected to them, and that was how they ended up investing in SE1. (SE1)

II1's desire to ascertain the genuine intentionality for social impact by SE1 aligns with scholarly research on the effect of social motivation on mutual trust in perception from the context of negotiation (Olekalns et al., 2002; Srivastava & Chakravarti, 2009). This also applies to II1's belief in SE1's intention being genuine, which began by appreciating the social impact potential of SE1 in the impact space. Mutual trust between the two parties to establish partner fit based on genuine social impact intention built the trust towards engagement.

It is also notable that the trust level for collaboration between II1 and SE1 was influenced by firm reputation and social network. In particular, attention is drawn to dyadic themes that demonstrate specific factors that enhance the firm reputation and social network. From the perspective of firm reputation and social network, II1 trust on SE1 has been linked to **firm size** and **proven market opportunity**. The organisational size and the network of impact market opportunities associated with SE1 were considered reputable by II1. That reputation stems from the fact that their activities were considered to be legitimate in view of their societal-wide impact. SE1 linked its trust to II1's reputation and social network from the perspective of **reputation in the space**, as acknowledged by II1. In other words, II1 affirmed that SE1 has a reputation in the impact market space as expected. Both parties have demonstrated how their trust level to collaborate was influenced by firm size, proven market and reputation:

> We don't invest in companies just because they are in Lagos. As I said, we invested in SE1 because they were in an area covering those with the most need. It's just where we see the need and the market opportunity. (II1)

SE1 affirmed their own reputation in the social impact market and its significance:

> In your interaction with II1, you should be able to provide those details… Yes, we are actually driven by the passion to provide a scalable technology for micro finance institutions to directly impact on the different clients that they are providing services to institutions that are operating in hard-to-reach environments like the rural communities. (SE1)

SE1 thus corroborates the information provided by II1 on reputation in the social impact market space. The literature indicates that a firm's reputation tends to influence the degree of being trusted, since a strong reputation means a higher legitimacy to be known and with less uncertainty (Bierly III & Gallagher, 2007; Suchman, 1995). Bierly III and Gallagher (2007: 141) put it thus: "the more positive the reputation, the more likely it is to increase trust". The statement by SE1 clearly showed its consciousness of the positive reputation it has, which has in turn been verified in II1's comment. II1's observation also revealed that a thorough evaluation of social networks of firms, including individuals within firms, can potentially guide the perception of trust for strategic fit between prospective partners (Bierly III & Gallagher, 2007). As II1 stated, there was a thorough evaluation of the market network and opportunities that would come from investing in SE1. Evaluating the investment opportunities and the reputation for doing well within such an opportunity space from past testimonies have increased the trust level between IIs and SEs to establish partner fit.

Analysis of SE2 and II2 generated empirical themes that demonstrate organisation-level factors that influenced the trust level between them for establishing partner fit. Each partner linked mutual trust to specific but different themes, pointing to similar motives that increased their trust level and led to collaboration. For example, from the perspective of mutual trust, II2 linked its ability to ascertain mutual trust to collaborate with SE2 on common interests through applying **due diligence**. Due diligence in the context of SE2's and II2's relationship is the process of building trust through the verification of SE2's legitimacy through physical or online searches. SE2 linked the source of its mutual trust with II2 from the **potential return on investment** after it undertook its due diligence. The level of trust increased when due diligence reports clarified areas of possible doubt about the potential of the partnership. II1 could only invest impact funds in SE2 when the level of trust for a potential return from investing in SE2 had been proven to yield both financial and social returns, and this had been established after due diligence. The comments from II2 and SE2 demonstrate the influence of due diligence on their mutual trust, which also enhanced their trust level to establish partner fit:

> The first thing is their documentation. We want to see if the company [SE2] is registered, if it's a Nigerian company, then we go to CAC. If it's not, then we speak to a lawyer in the country where the company is incorporated to help us conduct a search. We also ask them for their proper documentation. If they have existing investors, we also want to know who those investors are. Sometimes we speak to those investors just to get a sense of the founders' and the investors' long-term vision, what they saw when they were investing in the first instance. The other thing that we typically look out for is, we do reference checks on the founders, [and] not just the founders, [but] the management team on background checks,

> past experiences, companies that they've worked with before, feedback about the team members in those companies. (II2)

SE2 explained the influence of due diligence on their mutual trust that led to partner fit:

> After their [II2] own due diligence...when we were discussing, it was obvious that they were willing to work together, and it was, like, I will say, a perfect match... But having someone who is of very strong character, it goes a long way to assuring them that we are not just going to put our money down the drain but will put money into investment that will bring returns.

The responses from this dyad revealed the influence of the due diligence factor for establishing trust and partner fit. Due diligence as a process of determining the level of trust between parties often guides decisions to establish partner fit. The literature argues that due diligence comprises background checks, credit checks, site visits, cross-checks, and account monitoring by investors (Cumming et al., 2019). The themes from II2 and SE2 revealed that due diligence checks were an instrumental factor for establishing mutual trust and increasing the trust level. Jones and Moncur (2020) define due diligence as actions taken to guarantee that a certain activity is safe; due diligence is mostly carried out by IIs, and it often enables them to build confidence in their investment and trust potential investees. The comment by II2 validates due diligence as a key factor for establishing mutual trust. SE2 also reported that, after due diligence, II2 was more willing to work with it, because the trust level in SE2 had increased—investing in SE2 would lead to financial returns.

Analysis also revealed that collaboration between them had been influenced by firm reputation and social network. Themes from each partner further demonstrate factors linked to these factors that specifically increased their trust level. II2 linked the reputation of SE2 to its size and the verification of the **reputation of its management team**. This was discussed in Chap. 2 as an organisational factor that guides impact investors' decisions in choosing their investee social enterprises. II2 explained the influence of SE2's management reputation on their trust level, exploring that reputation in breadth and depth, both internally with staff and externally with previous partners.

SE2 linked social network influence to the **electronic media platform** factor that provided informal access to establish partner fit with II2:

> We were just on our own when we received an email from an international finance corporation that someone told them about us, and they invited us for a chat and discussions and like, oh! my God ... that a colleague of mine just coming to the country is looking for early-stage start-ups. So, I said, "No problem", so the email was sent out and we reached [out to] (II2)

Bierly III and Gallagher (2007) argue that social networking links influence the development of trust, which comes from the present and past reputation of an organisation. SE2's comment also revealed how their collaboration with II2 started, influenced through informal electronic media social networks. Informal social networks have been influential in market paradigms across the world, particularly in distributing social capital (Horak & Klein, 2016; Huning et al., 2015). The experience has further validated the influence of informal social network for creating social capital for organisations searching for such opportunities.

The collaboration process between II3 and SE3 revealed themes connected to mutual trust and firms' reputation/social network. A close look at the themes around mutual trust shows that II3 achieved mutual trust with SE3 through **advisory and technical support that enhanced belief in SE3**. The process of providing advisory and technical support to SE3 by II3 exemplifies a trust-building process that determines the trust level prior to establishing partner fit. SE3 explained that mutual trust with II3 was developed from **advisory and intentionality for social impact**. Intentionality as a feature of hybrid organisations (see Chap. 2) has also manifested itself in this dyad, just as II3 revealed factors that influenced mutual trust prior to establishing partner fit with SE3 and linked to technical advisory support:

> Normally in accelerator [mode], we pick a few out of the several. But, like the normal processes, we don't throw away models with a problem; we don't throw you away in the first instance. We provide technical support. If we feel the problem you have can be solved, we work with you to solve those problems and prepare you to access the funds. But when you become obstinate with your challenges, and you are not malleable, [then] it becomes a challenge, and we probably might not be able to work with you.

SE3 also explained how mutual trust was built with II3 through advisory support and intentionality, which enhanced the trust level between them:

> As you know, many financial relationships are built on trust, so, up until 2015, I mean there was a lot of buoyancy and trust in the system… We have never at least fallen far in social confidence or [away from] the financial covenant given to us by our investors [that is, II3] … from advisory [through to] terms of structuring some of those deals.

The themes from II3 and SE3 reported the factors that enhanced those mutual trust levels through advisory support and intentionality. This support to SE3 by II3 was meant to build trust in SE3's capability to deliver on the goals of the partnership. It takes a strong belief in a partner to continue to offer technical assistance, even when there is no concrete potential in the current business model. Wu and Tsang (2008) observe that trust building has the potential to influence behavioural intention in relationships. The tenacity demonstrated by II3 in working with SE3 comes from the belief that providing additional advisory services to SE3 will help build the relationship to gain strength for delivering the desired outcome, given the right technical support. Similarly, SE3 revealed it had never fallen short of the social and financial obligations required of it when engaging with II3. This demonstrates the deliberate adherence to intentionality to deliver the expected dual motives based on advisory and technical support provided.

Under "firm reputation and social network", II3 revealed trust levels with SE3 have largely been influenced through **informal social network relations** with SE3. Social network connotes referrals made by other organisations within the social impact space, affirming a social enterprise's legitimacy. Social networks from II3's perspective come from communication with other investors who possess certain information about the history of SE3. SE3 described its trust level with II3 as enhanced through the firm's reputation and social network linked to **CEO overseas**

informal contact with II3. The CEO-SE3 informal contact demonstrates the informal social network connection that established the collaboration process with II3. II3 explained how the trusted social network factor, linked to informal referrals, enhanced their trust level for partner fit with SE3:

> Aside from the fact that we manage assets for impact investors through indirect investment, we also facilitate, based on our network and our relation with our network, that's relations with DFIs, solar investors, creating around effect, people that are investing into impact, based on the fact that we understand the market, we sort of try to facilitate capital relationship and transparent relationship between SMEs in these areas and the investors.

SE3 demonstrated the influence of the informal trusted social network connection on the opportunity to collaborate with II3:

> At the time that SE3 did its trust rating, I think in 2009 or thereabouts, before the institution of the governing council as an organ for policy and advisory guidance for the organisation… the promoters of the organisation had come in contact with the chief executive officer of II3, who already had some extensive connections in the microfinance space in Europe. It was only natural that they offered the services then, I think, under a different organisation, Microfinance Investment Consultancy Services, I think, or something of that nature… they were able to link SE3 to potential funders…

This dyad's comments further revealed how their trust level to collaborate was enhanced through trusted informal social network relationships. II3 revealed how capital investment was facilitated based on its network of relationships with other organisations who provide impact funds and those who need impact funds. "Transparent relationship" is underpinned by the value of SE3's reputation in the social impact space as a key asset to explore benefits in a relationship. It also entails consideration of a firm's reputation as a pre-requisite to gain access for more networking opportunities with impact fund providers. Research has also revealed that a social network of interaction is a constituent of concrete relationships, which may involve direct or indirect material exchange between actors (Maciel, 2018). SE3's comment revealed the influence of informal social networks and how it gained access to II3 through social networks, including the organisation's trust rating, which also points to the firm's reputation in establishing trust to collaborate.

Analysis of SE4 and II4 revealed several key themes that enhanced their trust level. Drawing from these themes in relation to mutual trust, II4 linked the influence of mutual trust to the **due diligence process** used to ascertain whether SE4 could be trusted to establish partner fit. Due diligence from II4's perspective, as with other dyads, enabled it to determine the level of trust to repose in SE4 before establishing partner fit. SE4 revealed that its mutual trust in II4 had been enhanced through **communication factors** that enhanced the trust level. The comments further validate how due diligence and communication factors enhanced mutual trust between them:

> We visit SE4 and local stakeholders to discuss the impact of II4 financing, their business and environmental, social and human rights risks in detail. We continue analysing the business, its financials, the business plan, legal aspects, ESG, the client's tax practices and policies, with our tax department providing expert advice where needed. If we identify gaps in meeting international standards or policies, we develop action plans to mitigate and manage the identified risks and promote positive development in these areas. (II4)

SE4 corroborated this:

> We have a very close relationship with our investors. We actually had one over this week; he left yesterday. So they come and visit us quite regularly, and whenever we are in their area, we go visit them. We are constantly communicating via email.

Both comments validate the themes that increased mutual trust developed through due diligence and communication factors. Constant reciprocal communication between partners in business has been proven to be a key factor for success that increases mutual trust (Bstieler et al., 2017). Due diligence has also been proven to engender trust between partners in business relationships, which is similar to other dyads' experience.

The dyadic theme also demonstrates how firms' reputation and social network influenced their trust level. II4 found that **social network in SE4's domain** was a factor that positively influenced the trust level to collaborate. SE4 operates in agricultural sectors in which its presence in host communities created a strong network with farmers, who also confirmed the reputation of SE4 in the impact space. SE4 noted that its **CEO network with II4, including their reputation in the impact space** was instrumental to the level of trust reposed in it by II4. II4 in turn revealed how the influence of the social network domain of SE4 its reputation increased the trust level:

> Within our mandated strategy, we identify potential opportunities [with SE4] by means of deep-rooted networks in developing countries like [Nigeria].

SE4 affirmed its CEO social network and reputation increased trust level with II4:

> They all kind of work closely with each other, they talk to each other, so they all tend to just say speak to this person, I think this person has a program that might be great for your female farmers, because we have female farmers and there is certain funding that is out there just for women… I also think with an organisation like [SE4], and in the industry that we work in in Nigeria, there are not many SE4s doing what we do. There are not so many people who want to go to areas where there isn't security. So, I think with us, you would find many investors.

The comments further explain the influence of firm reputation and social network as factors that increased the trust level. II4 uses social networks to explore investment opportunities of SE4, demonstrated in the reputation of SE4 as fitting II4's investment beliefs. This approach also aligns with the importance of valuable networks and collaboration for understanding the market for impact investing (Ormiston et al., 2015). SE4 commented that working closely with each other further reiterates the value of social network factors in building mutual trust. This also means impact investors can trust co-investors to recommend social enterprises with promising potential. SE4 revealed that its reputation in the social impact space had engendered the trust level to connect with II4 and several other investors who found the Nigerian agricultural sector an exciting opportunity for impact investment.

Dyadic themes for II5 and SE5 revealed factors that enhanced mutual trust prior to establishing partner fit. These emerged from different perspectives. According to II5, mutual trust that built commitment with SE5 emanated from a factor connected with **expectation of a return on investment and asset-based value rating.** Return from investment is a key factor in the expectation list of IIs, which II5 strongly valued. II5 took a step further to ascertain the level of trust to repose in SE5 by measuring the asset value that SE5 currently possessed. SE5 attributed a **belief in SE5's strategies** as a factor that enhanced its mutual trust with II5. It is also established in the literature that social enterprise business strategies have remained crucial in determining investment potential. A strong and reliable business strategy can build investors' confidence to increase the trust level to commit financial resources into investee SEs. II5 explained how expectation of returns from investment enhanced its mutual trust to commit financial investment on SE5:

> SE5 is another one, not far away from us… Once the business is viable, we'll avail you of funding, believing that, out of that viability, you'll return the principal given to you with the premium added. But down the line, by 2009, II5 realised it was the biggest mistake. First of all, the moment you do that, the average SME player believes that it is part of the national cake. They wouldn't be in a hurry to return that money. So, II5 now shifted and said, yes, viability is important, but there has to be an investment from your part. What do you have in the deal? At least let us see that you have an office, you have paid your rent. Ok, so we say you must have a minimum of 30%, of the amount you're asking invested already in the deal.

SE5 also affirmed that a belief in its business strategies by II5 had enhanced mutual trust to the required level:

> I think [that,] if not for people like II5 that came to our aid, you know this business in Nigeria is not very easy. You don't have access to finance [and] even if you have access, it will be at a cost growth rate.

The comments validate the influence of mutual trust arising from an expectation of a return on investment and asset value as a determinant. II5's expectation of financial returns from SE5 simply shows the relationship is not one-sided or asymmetrical, as has been portrayed by some scholars (Degryse & De Jong, 2006; Rindt & Mouzas, 2015). A belief in SE5's business strategy by II5 also represents a key factor that influenced trust level. The evidence of mutual trust aligns with McEvily et al.'s (2017) argument that two parties in a given relationship mutually determine trust in interfirm exchange. It is important to note there is a power dynamic at work in this dyad that can be termed mutual, but the rallying point for delivery of expectations lies in their trust level. SE5's possession of 30% capital has increased II5's trust level in the potential for a return on investment from SE5. This further shows that SE5 is not "parasitic" but a contributing partner in the relationship. Therefore, it can be deduced that this attribute has enhanced II5's belief in SE5's operation with the potential to deliver the expected returns on investment. It is also important to note the comment by SE5 "if not for II5, who came to our aid…", which revealed an expression of trust that emerged from belief in its business strategy. It is not unlikely that SE5 may have tried several avenues to secure impact investing funds but may not have been trusted at a level demonstrated by II5.

Dyadic themes described factors that influenced firm reputation and social network that increased trust. II5 linked factors connected to firm reputation from the perspective of **SE5's formalisation**. While informality is a big challenge for social enterprises in emerging countries, including Nigeria, identifying SE5, a formalised social enterprise, was a defining factor in its reputation being trusted by II5. SE5 described social network from factors connected to **informal referrals** that led its connection to II5. This study also noted informal relationships had helped organisations sourcing investment capital to achieve their financial needs across some dyads. The comment from II5 below attests to how formalisation of SE5 enhanced its reputation to be trusted within a social network of social enterprises prior to establishing partner fit:

> A lot of these businesses in Nigeria are not formalised, [but] we insist that they must be formalised, that is a no-no for us, you must accept to be formalised before we can invest in your organisation. If you formalise the business, what that means is, they will begin to make returns to CAC. CAC is the Cooperate Affairs Commission. Fine, they begin to make returns to CAC, they will begin to pay taxes, and if they begin to, you are making them worthy citizens. (II5)

SE5 also described how informal referral exemplified social network factors that increased the trust level to collaborate with II5:

> Well, somebody introduced them to us, and we found out they were in our complex. We never knew what they were doing, but somebody introduced [II5] to us, and we connected.

This validates the themes of SE5 formalisation and informal referral of SE5 to II5 as factors that enhanced firm reputation and social network to determine trust level. Several studies in organisational research show that informal social networks constitute various mechanisms that include interpersonal attraction, shared interest, geographical location, etc. (Huning et al., 2015). These factors determine when a firm is considered reputable on a social network. Carter et al. (2002) also reveal a strong correlation between factors that determine reputation and trust, while formalisation and reputation remain excellent steps to begin formalising trust. The desire by II5 to invest in SE5 based on its formality affirmed formalisation as evidence of SE5's reputation.

As noted across other dyads, collaboration between II6 and SE6 has also been influenced by mutual trust. Mutual trust from each partner's perspective revealed deeper knowledge about factors connected to trust that influenced collaboration. From II6's perspective, mutual trust with SE6 was influenced by **due diligence**, which, as demonstrated across other dyads, is a process that generates mechanisms to determine trust levels between partners. SE6 linked factors that influence its mutual trust with II6 to **a belief in its operations, including possession of assets and liabilities**. These assets (similar to Case 5) constitute a factor in mutual trust. II6 did not just trust SE6's ability to generate financial return on investment but also ascertained the asset value that SE6 brought to the partnership as tangible resources. II6 explained how due diligence increased mutual trust:

> What we do is carry out due diligence to ascertain the current state of the company before we invest... We look at the risk level of the project and see if it meet our requirement... It helps most of these companies, because it is a win-win thing, as they are empowering it is helping their supply chain. If you have a factory and you're not meeting your in-store capacity, it will affect your financial returns. These companies are seeing that, as much as they're doing this, we are also gaining from these people.

SE6 also explained how belief in the business strategy, including existing assets, influenced mutual trust:

> ...the thing that is unique is that [II6] is like a multinational and their investment is like being partner in the business. They look at the cash flow of the organisation, looking at the assets and liabilities... Unlike the banks, they are not a partner in the business, they count on their interest and then count on the number of years that you are holding their funds, and the interest keeps accruing and the pressure from them sometimes makes business unbearable. But in this instance, II6, at the end of the day, is concerned about the stakeholders, the profit that accrues from the company on a yearly basis and the period the contract lasts. They will look at how far the company has fared and then, if they are interested, in continuing in the business, they re-invest again and renew the MOU [memorandum of understanding] and business continues. So, the pressure that comes from the bank is not there, because it is like they are part-owners of the business.

This demonstrates how due diligence and belief in the business strategy, including existing assets, influenced mutual trust. II6 revealed how it carried out due diligence before bringing its resources into the partnership and described the relationship as a win-win, which affirmed each other's belief as a source for mutual trust. The comment also affirmed that the relationship is not asymmetrical. It provides evidence of a shared belief that both parties depend on each other to achieve common goals (Lewis, 2007). Comment by SE6 validates the fact that they both work together to achieve common goals. Unlike traditional investors, II6 ensures the interests of SE6 are covered beyond financial gains.

Specific themes from each partner also demonstrate factors linked to a firm's reputation and social network that increased their trust level before establishing partner fit. II6 linked **adherence to ethical standard for operation** as a factor that enhanced the reputation of SE6 to be trusted. Adherence to ethics is a unique identifier of impact investors, since its origin can also be traced to ethical investing. Ethics in the context of this dyad relates to adherence to ethical guideline for operation in poultry farming. SE6 linked factors connected to social network influence to how its **CEO through CBN connects with II6**. Factors connected to SE6's and II6's experience connote a combination of formal and informal network factors for building mutual trust. II6 explains how SE6's reputation linked to adherence to ethical standards:

> My key role is to ensure all our portfolio companies adhere strictly to the environmental social and governance policies and procedures as stipulated by our investors... We would only manage social impact [but] most DFI's are mostly cautious of their reputational damage, these are the things that we take cognizance of before investing. A company that has huge environmental impact and negative social impact, even if the company is doing well financially, we will not go on to work with that company because of reputational damage.

SE6 also described how the social network factor influenced on its partner fit with II6:

> We came to know about [II6] through the CBN. CBN has information about investors that come into the country. I do not know how I will put it now, through the CBN, called Fund for Agricultural Finance in Nigeria, FAFIN. It was through that means we were linked to [II6] through our Chairman, and through the chairman we met jointly with the investors [II6] and other things follow.

The comments further explain factors that influence firm reputation and social network to determine trust level from their experience. II6 aligned the adherence of SE6 to ethical requirements as a factor that measured its reputation to be trusted, and this was aside from presenting a viable business model. SE6 also aligned the influence of both formal and informal social networks as factors that determined the level of trust reposed in them by II6 prior to establishing partner fit.

6.2 Trust in Business Collaboration and Partner Fit

The analysis of organisational factors across the six dyads has produced further evidence of organisation-level factors that influenced mutual trust within the dyad. It was necessary to ascertain these factors, because micro-level processes often drive macro-level outcomes (Coleman, 1990). The more successful and greater the micro-level activities between SEs and IIs, the higher the attention that the macro environment will need to pay, due to their influence on the broader environment. CR has described this process as the effect of agency action on social structure, where agency action resides in SEs and IIs, and can be influenced by or can disrupt the macro environment. Business research, particularly in marketing, has considered the role of personal factors as drivers of inter-organisational business relationships (Barnes et al., 2015; Gligor & Holcomb, 2013). In the same manner, analysis of dyads in this chapter found several factors responsible for building mutual trust across social and economic interest between SEs and IIs. Different dyadic themes emerged from each dyad, and these holistically describe key factors that influence the trust level across the six cases prior to establishing partner fit. These factors have been classified into two specific themes: mutual trust and social network/firm reputation.

From the six cases, themes have emerged as factors that influence mutual trust and social network/firm reputation from each dyad experience, as shown in Fig. 6.1. Under mutual trust, for example, it is evident that mutual trust between II1 and SE1 has been influenced by II1's perception of SE1's genuine intention for impact, while SE1 believes in II1's deliberate intention to achieve an impact outcome. Across the six cases IIs demonstrate that mutual trust with SEs has been influenced from carrying out due diligence in order to ascertain the legitimacy of SEs. SEs mostly linked mutual trust to IIs' belief in their intentions and business strategy.

6.3 Factors That Influence Mutual Trust Between SEs and IIs

All themes arising from the experience of each dyad confirm the emergence of mutual trust as a condition that determines the level of trust between SEs and IIs prior to establishing partner fit in pursuit of social and economic interests. The

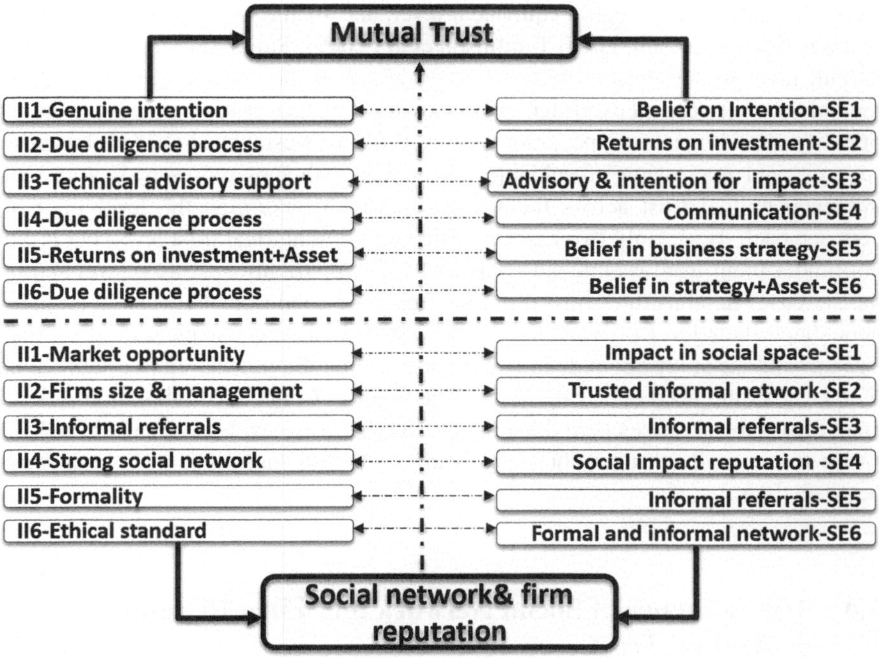

Fig. 6.1 Dyadic factors that influence mutual trust between SEs and IIs

findings about factors that influence mutual trust in dyads validate Liden et al.'s (2016) arguments on how the concept of mutuality remains critical for accurate understanding of dyadic relationship. Thus, searching for factors that influence the level of trust between organisations in dyad can be better understood by exploring factors or conditions connected to mutual trust. This has been revealed through analysis of themes linked to mutual trust. Bstieler et al. (2017) also argue how impossible it would be to establish any successful inter-organisational or dyadic collaboration without mutual trust, because it is a fundamental requirement in building trust in friendship, whether formal or informal.

The analysis in this chapter focuses on dyadic trust defined as "an emergent property of the dyad representing the pattern of trust between two parties" (Korsgaard et al., 2015: 49). As noted in Chap. 2, there are three approaches to examining trust (Korsgaard et al., 2015), reciprocal trust, mutual trust and asymmetrical trust, as key drivers of collaboration between organisations with dyadic relations.

The mutual trust level is ascertained through dyadic view of specific factors that influence mutual trust to establish partner fit within the dyad (Svensson, 2005). It is important to note that social network and/or firm reputation also appear as variables that influence mutual trust between dyadic partners.

According to the literature, mutual trust is the emergent attribute of the dyad wherein parties come together to share a perception or belief in the degree to which they trust each other (Bliese et al., 2007). Mutual trust happens when two parties trust one another at a roughly equivalent level, and such trust may occur in dyadic relationships (Svensson, 2005; Tomlinson et al., 2009). Simply put, it is a trust that is built through consensus. From the analysis across the six cases, the pattern of mutual trust between all dyads has been influenced by factors such as genuine intentionality, due diligence, expectation of return from investment, belief on business strategy, and possession of valuable assets. These themes represent factors that influence mutual trust across the six cases, which determine the level of trust between each dyad. Only two cases revealed an asymmetrical trust level, but it did not hinder them from establishing partner fit. The distribution of trust level across the six cases demonstrates how different factors or conditions between dyad partners shape their level of trust. To discover the negative consequences of mutual trust, a separate study about dyadic relationships that did not end up in establishing partner fit would need to be carried out. The findings from the collaboration experience across the six cases here demonstrate that the trust level between SEs and IIs varies from one dyad to another, depending on factors that influence mutual trust between them.

6.4 The Influence of Social Network and Firm Reputation on Mutual Trust

The second organisational level factor that influences the establishment of partner's has been described as social network and firm reputation. Figure 6.1 reported factors that influence social network and firm reputation prior to the establishment of partner fit. It is important to note that conditions or factors associated with social network and firm reputation also influenced mutual trust across the six cases. This is not surprising, since organisations with a better reputation tend to perform sustainably well over a long period, because good reputation exemplifies intangible resources for competitive advantage (Azeem et al., 2021). The literature has revealed that a firm's reputation, as the outcome of the process of legitimisation emerging from a social construct, influences the survival of the organisation to a large extent (Rao, 1994). It is a behaviour that characterises start-up organisations seeking normative or cognitive justification as entities to gain reputation based on widely shared beliefs and norms (Ranville & Barros, 2021). A social enterprise with good reputation has a better chance of attracting tangible resources from impact investors. This explains why a social enterprise would seek legitimisation within a reputable social network to gain popularity and reputation as key assets.

Studies have reported a positive correlation between reputation and trust (Carter et al., 2002). Bierly III and Gallagher (2007) confirm that a firm's reputation can influence the level to which it can be trusted in two ways: firstly, a stronger reputation will attract higher legitimisation and increase trust with less uncertainty; secondly, a positive reputation will also increase trust between parties. Social network emerged as a factor that also influences the collaboration in the six cases, because informal social relationships have been proven to create potential for social capital between organisations. The experience across the six cases further validates Huning et al.'s (2015) view about the role of information exchange and communication between organisations through trusted social networks. Bierly III and Gallagher (2007) confirm that the social network of the firm also determines and guides the perception of trust between potential collaborating partners.

Analysis across the six cases revealed that the firm's reputation was linked to a range of factors, such as a trusted management team, legitimisation through formality, adherence to ethical standards for operation and identity with the social impact space. Social network has been linked to factors such as formal and informal relations across the media and physical interaction with potential investors. The overall outcome of analysis shows factors that influence mutual trust, the firm's reputation and social network positively define the shared level of trust in the six dyadic cases, which results in established partner fit. It is pertinent to note that the firm's reputation and social network influenced mutual trust, as has been demonstrated in this study.

6.5 Conclusion

This chapter focused on organisation-level factors that influence SEs and IIs to establish partner fit beyond compatibility and complementarity. The study identified several factors and conditions that influenced mutual trust across the six cases, inspiring commitment to establish partner fit. The analysis also found the firm's reputation and social network to have strong correlation with mutual trust, which also facilitates the establishment of partner fit between SEs and IIs. All variables linked to mutual trust and social network and firm reputation highlighted similarities and slight differences across the six cases. The findings provided an organisation-level knowledge of factors that influences the determinants of compatibility and complementarity between SEs and IIs. The next chapter reviews the macro-level factors that enable or constrain partner fit between SEs and IIs in Nigeria.

References

Amoako, I. O. (2019). Trust in interorganisational relationships. In *Trust, institutions and managing entrepreneurial relationships in Africa* (pp. 67–102). Springer.

Azeem, M., Ahmed, M., Haider, S., & Sajjad, M. (2021). Expanding competitive advantage through organizational culture, knowledge sharing and organizational innovation. *Technology in Society, 66*, 101635.

Barnes, B. R., Leonidou, L. C., Siu, N. Y., & Leonidou, C. N. (2015). Interpersonal factors as drivers of quality and performance in Western–Hong Kong interorganizational business relationships. *Journal of International Marketing, 23*(1), 23–49.

Barney, J. B., & Hansen, M. H. (1994). Trustworthiness as a source of competitive advantage. *Strategic Management Journal, 15*(S1), 175–190.

Barry, B., & Oliver, R. L. (1996). Affect in dyadic negotiation: A model and propositions. *Organizational Behavior and Human Decision Processes, 67*(2), 127–143.

Bierly, P. E., III, & Gallagher, S. (2007). Explaining alliance partner selection: Fit, trust and strategic expediency. *Long Range Planning, 40*(2), 134–153.

Bliese, P. D., Chan, D., & Ployhart, R. E. (2007). Multilevel methods: Future directions in measurement, longitudinal analyses, and nonnormal outcomes. *Organizational Research Methods, 10*(4), 551-563.

Bstieler, L., Hemmert, M., & Barczak, G. (2017). The changing bases of mutual trust formation in inter-organizational relationships: A dyadic study of university-industry research collaborations. *Journal of Business Research, 74*, 47–54.

Carter, J., Bitting, E., & Ghorbani, A. A. (2002). Reputation formalization for an information–sharing multi–agent system. *Computational Intelligence, 18*(4), 515–534.

Coleman, J. (1990). *Foundations of social theory*. Belknap Press of Harvard University Press.

Cumming, D. J., Johan, S. A., & Zhang, Y. (2019). The role of due diligence in crowdfunding platforms. *Journal of Banking & Finance, 108*, 105661. https://doi.org/10.1016/j.jbankfin.2019.105661

Degryse, H., & De Jong, A. (2006). Investment and internal finance: Asymmetric information or managerial discretion? *International Journal of Industrial Organization, 24*(1), 125–147.

Eklinder-Frick Jens, O., & Åge, L.-J. (2020). Relational business negotiation – Propositions based on an interactional perspective. *Journal of Business & Industrial Marketing, 35*(5), 925–937.

Gligor, D. M., & Holcomb, M. (2013). The role of personal relationships in supply chains. *The International Journal of Logistics Management, 24*(3), 328–355.

Gulati, R. (1995). Does familiarity breed trust? The implications of repeated ties for contractual choice in alliances. *Academy of Management Journal, 38*(1), 85–112.

Hill, C. W. (1990). Cooperation, opportunism, and the invisible hand: Implications for transaction cost theory. *Academy of Management Review, 15*(3), 500–513.

Horak, S., & Klein, A. (2016). Persistence of informal social networks in East Asia: Evidence from South Korea. *Asia Pacific Journal of Management, 33*(3), 673–694.

Huning, T. M., Bryant, P. C., & Holt, M. K. (2015). Informal social networks in organizations: Propositions regarding their role in organizational behavior outcomes. *Academy of Strategic Management Journal, 14*(1), 20.

Jones, H. S., & Moncur, W. (2020). A mixed-methods approach to understanding funder trust and due diligence processes in online crowdfunding investment. *ACM Transactions on Social Computing, 3*(1), 1–29.

Kasper-Fuehrera, E. C., & Ashkanasy, N. M. (2001). Communicating trustworthiness and building trust in interorganizational virtual organizations. *Journal of Management, 27*(3), 235–254.

Korsgaard, M. A., Brower, H. H., & Lester, S. W. (2015). It isn't always mutual: A critical review of dyadic trust. *Journal of Management, 41*(1), 47–70.

Leahy, J. E., & Anderson, D. H. (2008). Trust factors in community–water resource management agency relationships. *Landscape and Urban Planning, 87*(2), 100–107.

Lewis, J. D. (2007). *Trusted partners: How companies build mutual trust and win together*. Simon and Schuster, The Free Press.

Liden, R. C., Anand, S., & Vidyarthi, P. (2016). Dyadic relationships. *Annual Review of Organizational Psychology and Organizational Behavior, 3*(1), 139–166.

Maciel, C. D. O. (2018). Social network analysis and dyadic identification in the classroom. *RAM. Revista de Administração Mackenzie, 19*(1), 1678–1697.

McEvily, B., Zaheer, A., & Kamal, D. K. F. (2017). Mutual and exclusive: Dyadic sources of trust in interorganizational exchange. *Organization Science, 28*(1), 74–92.

Olekalns, M., Lau, F., & Smith, P. (2002). *Spirals of trust: Identifying the factors that shape and sustain trust in negotiation*. Paper presented at the IACM 15th Annual Conference.

Ormiston, J., Charlton, K., Donald, M. S., & Seymour, R. G. (2015). Overcoming the challenges of impact investing: Insights from leading investors. *Journal of Social Entrepreneurship, 6*(3), 352–378.

Park, S. H., & Ungson, G. R. (1997). The effect of national culture, organizational complementarity, and economic motivation on joint venture dissolution. *Academy of Management Journal, 40*(2), 279–307.

Quince, T. (2001). *Entrepreneurial collaboration: Terms of endearment or rules of engagement?* ESRC Centre for Business Research, University of Cambridge. Retrieved from https://core.ac.uk/download/pdf/7151332.pdf

Ranville, A., & Barros, M. (2021). Towards normative theories of social entrepreneurship. A review of the top publications of the field. *Journal of Business Ethics, 180*, 407–438.

Rao, H. (1994). The social construction of reputation: Certification contests, legitimation, and the survival of organizations in the American automobile industry: 1895–1912. *Strategic Management Journal, 15*(S1), 29–44.

Rindt, J., & Mouzas, S. (2015). Exercising power in asymmetric relationships: The use of private rules. *Industrial Marketing Management, 48*, 202–213.

Srivastava, J., & Chakravarti, D. (2009). Channel negotiations with information asymmetries: Contingent influences of communication and trustworthiness reputations. *Journal of Marketing Research, 46*(4), 557–572.

Suchman, M. C. (1995). Managing legitimacy: Strategic and institutional approaches. *Academy of Management Review, 20*(3), 571–610.

Svensson, G. (2005). Mutual and interactive trust in business dyads: Condition and process. *European Business Review, 17*(5), 411–427.

Thomas, R., & Skinner, L. (2010). Total trust and trust asymmetry: Does trust need to be equally distributed in interfirm relationships? *Journal of Relationship Marketing, 9*(1), 43–53.

Tomlinson, E. C., Dineen, B. R., & Lewicki, R. J. (2009). Trust congruence among integrative negotiators as a predictor of joint-behavioral outcomes. *International Journal of Conflict Management, 20*(2), 173–187.

Walker, G., Kogut, B., & Shan, W. (1997). Social capital, structural holes and the formation of an industry network. *Organization Science, 8*(2), 109–125.

Welter, F. (2012). All you need is trust? A critical review of the trust and entrepreneurship literature. *International Small Business Journal, 30*(3), 193–212.

Wu, J.-J., & Tsang, A. S. (2008). Factors affecting members' trust belief and behaviour intention in virtual communities. *Behaviour & Information Technology, 27*(2), 115–125. https://doi.org/10.1080/01449290600961910

Chapter 7
How the Nigerian Macro Environment Influences Partner Fit Between Social Enterprises and Impact Investors

7.1 Introduction

Having explored the micro-organisational level factors that influence the trust level between SEs and IIs in establishing partner fit to achieve collective social and economic interests, this chapter now examines how the Nigeria macro environment influences collaboration in the six dyadic cases in the study to ascertain factors that enable or constrain the establishment of partner fit between them. Examining the macro-level factors influencing collaboration between these dyad partners was paramount because, as Coleman (1990) posited, macro-level factors often drive micro-level outcomes.

Understanding the full concept of social entrepreneurship requires a complete consideration of contextual factors, since the influence of the macro environment impacts the behaviour of actors (Urban & Kujinga, 2017), like SEs and IIs in the current study. Studies have also proven that a country-specific macro environment that undergoes changes over time can shape and determine desirability, feasibility and social entrepreneurial intentions (Griffiths et al., 2013). Studies on emerging countries like Nigeria are being sought in the literature to gain greater insight into contextual influence on social entrepreneurship (Urban, 2013). This has been linked to the complexity of the African environment, which has strong local and informal institutions that coexist with formal institutions (Zoogah et al., 2015). This can shape social entrepreneurial processes.

As noted earlier, institutions, from the perspective of entrepreneurship literature, represent the economic, social and political set of rules that articulate and organise interaction between individuals and social groups, which has consequences for business activities and socio-economic development (Casero et al., 2005; Veciana & Urbano, 2008). Contextual factors enabling and disenabling social enterprise collaboration with impact investors in Nigeria will be analysed as applied in the field of entrepreneurship. Griffiths et al.'s (2013) perspective of macro-level influence on

J. A. Emmanuel et al., *Social Enterprises and Impact Investors*, Advances in Theory and Practice of Emerging Markets,
https://doi.org/10.1007/978-3-031-59454-0_7

social entrepreneurship also focuses on sociopolitical, cultural and economic factors that can stimulate or impede the emergence of social entrepreneurship across context. Drawing from these perspectives, this analysis will focus on the economic, socio-cultural and political (as governance/regulatory) aspects to analyse and ascertain the macro-level influence on the collaboration experience across the six dyads of SEs and IIs interviewed in Nigeria.

To explore the macro-level factors, a semi-structured interview was administered to SEs and IIs with dyadic relations. The interview guide asked IIs questions relating to factors they consider disenabling or enabling in funding social impact project in Nigeria. SEs, on the other hand, were asked questions relating to factors they considered enabling or disenabling in running their social enterprise projects in Nigeria. Separate, individual interview questions were administered to SEs and IIs (Appendix 8). Responses across the six dyads cases were analysed according to the research method explained in Chap. 4.

Given the Nigerian contextual reality, Griffiths at al.'s categorisation of macro-level factors into governance/regulatory (political), economic, and sociocultural factors was adopted in this analysis. This also aligns with Bird's (1988) categorisation of social, political and economic variables as the contextual factors of entrepreneurship. A coding process involving series of iterations was used to ascertain variables that fall under enabling and disenabling factors from sample data collected across SEs and IIs with dyadic relations in Nigeria. During the coding process, any empirical labels that manifested as macro-level factors from the perception of each dyadic partner were grouped into themes considered to be either enabling or disenabling factors. The first-stage coding process generated several empirical codes associated with enabling and disenabling factors across political, economic and sociocultural dimensions, as shown in Table 7.1, below.

Although all SEs and IIs operate in the same macro environment, the analysis captures the distinct perception of each dyad about its operating environment.

7.2 Macro-Level Analysis Across the Six Cases

The second-stage analysis explored distinct and deeper narratives across the six cases to capture the real meaning of empirical labels generated from stage-one analysis. This approach generated themes that further explained distinctively what the economic, political and sociocultural enabling and disenabling factors across the cases were and how they influenced collaboration in pursuit of collective social and economic goals in Nigeria. It is paramount to indicate that some themes captured did not necessarily link to specific dyad members, as each partner was given the opportunity to reveal their experience about the Nigerian environment beyond their current dyadic relations. The purpose is to capture a wider perspective of the macro-level factors and also reframe participants from limiting responses on their experience to the current dyadic relation.

Table 7.1 Empirical labels linked to SE and II perceptions of the environment

Empirical—Cluster 1a Economic enabling factors	**Empirical—Cluster 2a Political enabling factors**	**Empirical—Cluster 3a Socio-cultural enabling factors**
Large population and economy (2)	Government policy on increase capital base (2)	Opportunity for knowledge sharing experience (4)
Low lending risk due to introduction of BVN (1)	Improved legislation on ease of doing business (1)	Online technology (1)
Regulatory challenges (7)	stability of exchange interest rate (1)	Community support (5)
Empirical—Cluster 1b Economic disenabling factors	**Empirical—Cluster 2b Political disenabling factors**	**Empirical—Cluster 3b Socio-cultural disenabling factors**
High cost of living (5)	Corruption & bureaucratic bottle neck (3)	Inadequate utilisation of technology (2)
High interest rate (6)	Insecurity (1)	Need for stronger community support from organisations (5)
Low consumers purchasing power (3)	Lack of government support tor social enterprise (2)	Need for stronger ecosystem (6)
Poor economic climate (3)	Lack of infrastructure like power and access road (6)	Partial collaboration with government institutions (3)
	Regulatory challenges (5)	
	Unsuccessful policy on SMEs (1)	

Analysis of the Case 1 dyad generates themes that show perceptions about the influence of Nigeria's macro environment on the social entrepreneurship process. The pattern of perception regarding the Nigerian enabling environment shows some agreement about economic opportunities, governance and regulation and some positive agreement about the socio-cultural environmental influence. II1 linked socio-cultural environment influence to a growing potential ecosystem described as welcoming for the growth of social enterprise and economic influence in Nigeria's large market and population. SE1 likewise linked economic and sociocultural environmental influence on Nigeria's supportive community and market opportunity. "Supportive community" implies Nigerians have a positive perception of social enterprise, since they embraced the concept as a strategy to help communities' growth. The comments from both, below, further validate the positive aspects of the sociocultural and economic environment in Nigeria:

> Nigeria is in a unique position because of our population size, arguably the largest economy as well… The stronger the ecosystem is, and the more other companies can look to them and say how do these companies get to where they are and who is behind them, etc. Of course, the stakeholders begin with every single Nigerian, but then the major players would be the enterprises themselves, we have incubators that focus on social enterprises e.g. there are associations such as ANDE (a global organisation but they have their office in Lagos) that focuses on developing enterprises, there are all sorts, investors, accelerators, incubators enterprise. (II1)

SE1 also affirmed the positive aspect of the Nigerian sociocultural environment:

> We have not lost a customer, and I think that losing a customer is a sense of dissatisfaction. We have been in the state for six years and have been providing services to end clients for five years. Our services are also provided through a pricing model subscription that is paid annually… if a customer is not happy at the end of a period, which runs for 12 months, the customer has the right to leave. But all our customers have been renewing their subscription for the past five years."

The comment regarding the influence of the economic environment aligns with Companys and McMullen's (2007) assertion about the attractiveness of social entrepreneurship around existing information regarding the presence of material resources as opportunities for investment. Socio-cultural factors, which the dyads relate to community relationships, align with Thornton et al.'s (2011) argument that entrepreneurship, be it social or mainstream, is embedded and affected by the social context of the environment. Not losing a customer, as SE1 revealed, is a sign that Nigerian communities patronise social enterprise organisations focusing on disadvantaged communities, and are receptive to new social norms of doing things.

On the dimension of disenabling factors, dyadic themes show slight differences from their pattern of perception with regard to socio-cultural disenabling factors, while there is some agreement about economic and political disenabling factors. This dyad linked themes of **poor governance**, **and economic climate and Naira instability to dollars** in Nigeria as disenabling political and economic factors, respectively. Poor governance manifested as governance challenges affecting the development of social enterprises, as well as the instability of the naira, the Nigerian currency for transactions. The comment below further explains how the experience and perception of the Nigerian political and economic environment influenced collaboration:

> Well, Nigeria is where we live, and I think that developing countries all over Africa have challenges; socio-economic challenges that enterprises try to fix… SMEs struggle with getting loans from the banks because apart from the rates banks mostly require collateral…I also think that a lot of businesses do not know about the potential that a private capital can have in growing their business…Well, I started touching on this earlier, demotivating is the same thing that is motivating, the problems are immense, but the potential impacts are also immense. (II1)

SE1 also validates comment by II1 regarding instability of the naira and the economy:

> There are challenges like currency fluctuation. Generally, more or less the harsh environment that you have to cope with in delivering your services because this impacts on both ends, we, as providers and also the clients that are at the receiving end. I mean the microfinance institutions that are interfacing with their clients.

The comments further affirmed the disenabling factors of their collaboration experience in Nigeria. II1 linked social disenabling factors to inadequate awareness of impact funds as alternative sources of capital to traditional loans from banks. No comment was recorded from SE1 regarding socio-cultural disenabling factors, but that does not mean such challenges do not exist, as II1 pointed out; it only shows

SE1's focus on issues that directly impact its enterprise. Thornton et al. (2011) assert that social capital as tangible and virtual resources can facilitate actors' attainment of their unique goals; unfortunately, a lack of knowledge of the potential of impact funds by SEs in Nigeria, as II1 revealed, constitutes an example of a socio-cultural knowledge gap. The economic challenges, which feature an unfavourable economic climate, characterised with instability of the naira, are aligned with the economic challenges of business in emerging economies linked to low standards of living. The political factors feature governance and regulatory setbacks needed to create an attractive environment for social entrepreneurial activities, as Griffiths et al. (2013) posited.

In the analysis of this dyad, themes show slight differences in economic enabling factors and absolute agreement in political and socio-cultural enabling factors. II2 linked economic and socio-cultural influence in their collaboration to the presence of a highly enterprising young population and economic opportunities. An enterprising young population is described as category of young people, within the age bracket of 18 to 35, who are taking up social entrepreneurship opportunities with passion. Economic opportunity is likened to the presence of potential business opportunities to carry out impact projects. SE2, on the other hand, linked economic and social influence to growing market opportunities and networking platforms on social media. The growing market is similar to II1's perception of economic opportunities, while the networking platform represents the gradual development of the social media platform as a medium for social and business interaction between emerging social enterprise organisations. Evidence of the enabling opportunities that linked these themes is supported by comments from both dyads:

> I think that Nigerians are very aggressive, they're very good at, I guess, getting the best for their money, we're hard-working. If I give a Nigerian a 100k for investment, and maybe a Ghanaian, the Nigerian will probably be more creative and will stretch that money maybe a bit more… I share the same comments, it's just that Africa is largely untapped. (II2)

Similar evidence from SE2 reinforces II2's comment on market opportunities and social media platforms:

> On a daily basis you get different needs: "Hi! I want to do a business card"… More people are able to go online and request for anything they want, and in our community, more people don't want to come down to Lagos, to Shomolu, so they just order from where they are and wait for few days and get their products.

This comment further revealed how the economic and socio-cultural enabling factors had supported collaboration in Nigeria. In line with this perception, Asogwa and Dim (2016) argue Nigeria is naturally endowed with human, material and entrepreneurial skills, but as of yet, this potential is grossly underutilised. It is important to note that this dyad partner did not make any comment regarding what constitutes enabling political factors, defined in the context of this analysis as governance and regulatory factors.

From the perspective of disenabling environmental factors, dyadic narratives in this case show some agreement across the three institutional factors. For example, II2 linked disenabling economic factors to high cost of living in Nigeria and lack of funds for start-up social enterprises, political factors to poor regulation, high interest rate and infrastructural deficit, sociocultural factors to brain drain, underdeveloped business ideas and lack of patience among entrepreneurs. SE2 linked disenabling economic factors to past economic recession, political factors to unhealthy government policy, and sociocultural factors to poor internet infrastructure. II2 explains how these themes constitute disenabling factors and its impact on the collaboration experience in Nigeria:

> The cost of living—some of these people just cannot be able to rent office space... so many things are being done around co-working spaces... I think just having more money flowing into start-up ecosystem will be great... There are many issues around the regulatory side, "Oh! We are not sure anymore, we may want to change regulations again", and even for an investor, it does not inspire confidence... Some of the ideas are not well thought through; people do not put their best... There's a bit of impatience, and we're used to quick money... Also infrastructure, I mean access to electricity, access to data... We have the problem of people moving from Nigeria to overseas, because the opportunities are more there. People don't want to work for Nigerian companies because a lot of CEOs or founders have this mindset of "You should not be better than me, and even with professors in the university, they'll not give a first-class because the last time somebody got a first-class it was them."

SE2 corroborated this:

> Recently Nigeria was in recession... One of the disenabling factors is the policy of the government. You can be doing well, and the policy comes out and destroys it... If you look at the country, we have a huge offline market that can serve as an opportunity and a threat.

The narratives here further reinforce more evidence about the negative influence of the economic, political and sociocultural factors on the collaboration experience in Nigeria. Both sets of evidence reveal a deep sociocultural practice that may inspire or demotivate confidence on the part of SEs and IIs. For example, impatience on the part of SEs will not be good for impact investors focusing on sustainability, while lack of infrastructure may be a good opportunity for IIs looking forward to invest in power sectors, etc. Agri et al. (2017) also agree with this evidence, noting that the Nigerian economy has been hit hard by recession, with on-going symptoms. Agri et al. further argue: "Macroeconomic indicators get worse showing that if there is no appropriate policy response, the economy may slip further into depression" (p. 1).

Analysis of dyadic themes in this dyad likewise revealed some agreement about the presence of economic and socio-cultural enabling factors supportive of social entrepreneurship in Nigeria. However, their perception differs slightly with respect to political enabling factors. II3 linked enabling economic influence to the large market for impact projects in Nigeria, political to increased capital base for microfinance and socio-cultural to increasing attention on social impact SMEs. SE3 likewise linked enabling economic factors to the market opportunities for impact investing, political to low lending risk, and socio-cultural to financial inclusion becoming a norm in Nigeria. The enabling market opportunities for impact investing have remained a driving force for social enterprise development and are gradually taking shape. Comments from both partners provide further evidence of how the enabling environment impacted the collaboration experience in Nigeria:

> Nigeria is the largest market in Africa… Recently, the government had to take that bold step of trying to scale up the microfinance to be able to size them up with the new policy. They said they should increase their capital base. So, I think that is the major challenge too that we face in attracting investment. A lot of them are too small compared to what the offshore investors will be interested… There are a lot of commercial banks who are now focusing on SMEs. Sterling Bank, for instance, has a large SME portfolio compared to maybe oil and gas portfolio. (II3)

Comment from SE3 also affirmed the enabling environment from their experience:

> I think enabling factors are the fact that interest rates have been made somewhat stable as the foreign exchange window; the rates have also remained fairly stable. That has created some sort of foreign direct investment to return to the country… Also enabling is the fact that, with innovations or, I would say, advances in information with the BVN and the credit loans, your inclusion agenda being led currently by the central bank and communications commission…

Comments thus demonstrate some evidence about impact of investment opportunities in Nigeria from large market opportunities, enabling government policy on interest rate and reduction from the risk of borrowing funds by small businesses. The success has been attributed to the government's cashless policy and the introduction of the Bank Verification Number (BVN). The BVN is an innovation with technology within the banking system in Nigeria, introduced to check corrupt and fraudulent practices in the financial system. Nwadinobi and Peart (2018) note that the introduction of the BVN in the Nigerian banking system increased social security, customer experience and boosted investor confidence in the banking sector.

Dyadic themes also demonstrate some agreement regarding disenabling macro-factors that negatively influenced the collaboration experience. II3 linked disenabling economic factors to the small size of SEs and risk-averse attitude of indigenous investors; political factors to failed government policies and a lack of investment support for SEs growth, and socio-cultural factors to an underdeveloped ecosystem and family protectionism ideology. Small size of SEs came from a general scanning of the small nature of SEs in Nigeria as against the ideal organisational view of SEs from investors' perspectives. SE3, on the other hand, linked disenabling economic factors to scarcity of foreign exchange, political factors to poor infrastructure, and sociocultural to a lack of indigenous investment funds. These factors affected their collaboration but did not prevent them from establishing partner fit. Narratives in this case have further been supported with evidence about how these disenabling factors influence their collaboration experience in the Nigerian environment:

> One of the key things is the sizes of most of the social enterprises; it is always a challenge. The local financial institutions here are not too strong, so they will rather target their lead trust as a response to rent-seeking investments… Indigenous investors find these enterprises too risky and would say "I'm looking for short-term return, so I would much rather invest in oil and gas"… A few years ago, about 10–15, the Central Bank that's the, our regulatory bank, made a policy that all Nigeria banks (commercial banks) should dedicate a percentage of their profit to finance SMEs. I think they call it SMEEEIS, that was the policy. But over time, the policy was not successful, and that was at a period that the nation was crying for start-up fund for the SMEs… We can't take away the fact that Nigeria is a country of

> about 200 million people in which you have millions of SMEs crying out for lack of support... The ecosystem itself is a challenge, creating an ecosystem for us is very important, there needs to be a network... A lot of Nigerians or a lot of small business owners are very protective of their business and would rather have their wife as the director of finance, and their son as the director of operations. These people may not have the expertise to fill these roles, but you just will not want to give up that position. (II3)

SE3 agreed:

> ...the scarcity of foreign exchange at central bank level meant that they weren't able to repatriate those funds and had a reputational risk for the country as a whole... The other thing is that the infrastructure is not necessarily as advanced enough or widespread to support the implementation of the policy... We have not received any major local funds at least from private equities, but we have done partnership with state government.

This provides further details about the influence of the macro-economic environment on collaboration. It is worthy of note that the challenges for the growing impact of investing viability of SEs start when the government creates the required enabling environment. Stability in the exchange rate, then support funds for start-up SEs are revealed in the comments above. II3 also observed that most SEs in Nigeria are small, meaning they do not have the capacity to accommodate the investment appetite that most foreign impact investors usually bring. For instance, impact investors operating offshore usually prefer investing in large portfolios that can generate greater financial return than small portfolios. Travelling from the US or UK only to invest in small organisations will not always be worth the risk from an offshore investor's perspective. The political factors related to poor infrastructure are linked to the difficulty of doing business in Nigeria due to lack of infrastructure facilities, which include good roads, electricity and stable data service providers. Family protectionism constitutes a setback to impact investors seeking to make major changes in social enterprise with management challenges, such as lack of capacity in financial management and administration. Since having a good management team is a key criterion for investors in SE models, the absence of good management expertise can prevent them from establishing partner fit with some SEs.

Analysis of themes revealed some agreement, with minor differences on the positive influence of economic, political and socio-cultural factors in the collaboration experience. II4 linked enabling economic, political and socio-cultural factors to large market for impact investment, provision of farm input, and community network support, respectively. SE4 linked their success to the rich agricultural land in Nigeria as an economic factor, government reduction of interest rates for farmers as political factors, and cooperation with farmers as a socio-cultural factor. The analysis also found some evidence linked to themes that further validates how the Nigerian macro environment enabled the collaboration experience:

> Nigeria is a large market with about 200 million population... The provision of cost effective farm inputs—we visit the client and local stakeholders to discuss the impact of II4 financing, their business, and environmental, social and human rights risks in detail. (II4)

SE4 further affirmed the impact of enabling macro factors in their collaboration:

...agriculture was the one he felt was most relevant and would really have a lot of impact... The Nigerian government has some programmes out there that organisations like SE4 can access to get cheaper funding. There are quite a few programmes that CBN has rolled out; there is RSSF [Real Sector Support Fund]. Those are different packages that CBN has put together to avail cheaper funding to people in the agricultural sector and other sectors that are making impact in the economy... We operate primarily in the north: Kaduna, Kano, Katsina region. Honestly, I would say, the communities there are so receptive to us.

The comments also revealed the economic, political and sociocultural-related factors in the Nigerian macro environment that positively influenced their collaboration experience. Both parties alluded to the large market, rich agricultural farmland, and some government support for local farmers. This dyad perceived the sociocultural enabling environment from community cooperation and reception while relating with the community stakeholders on their investment strategies and implementation. Some studies situate Nigeria's business environment in the context of a weak institutional void (Amaeshi et al., 2016), meaning the absence of established governance support. It would be interesting to know how this dyad successfully navigates social institutional immunity in the collaboration experience.

From the perspective of a disenabling macro environment, there are great similarities in the narratives regarding the disenabling factors for doing social impact business in Nigeria. In particular, II4 linked these economic factors to the devaluation of the naira, political factors to insecurity and poor infrastructure, and sociocultural factors to inadequate access to social investment finance. SE4 likewise linked disenabling economic factors to insecurity, political factors to governance setbacks on security and sociocultural factors to increasing youth restiveness. Disenabling and enabling factors, as perceived by this dyad, have remained the biggest barrier to change in the shift of Nigeria to become a full-fledged industrial nation. Unfortunately, this is still not the case, as evidence provided validates how the disenabling nature of the Nigerian environment influenced the collaboration:

The challenge we face investing in Nigeria began at the macro level with the devaluation of the Naira... II4 does not have an office in Nigeria but operates from the home office in Netherland... [With] poor access to finance, inadequate cash flow, lack of extension services and limited access to good markets, Nigerian smallholder farmers continue to remain at the base of the pyramid. (II4)

SE4 agreed:

...at [that] time, they were dealing with lots of security challenges, it was something that he noticed and wanted to find a solution to the problem, as well as recognising the need for jobs for young people in the country... So there was quite a distinct link between the increase in the youth population and the increase in insecurity with the birth of Boko–Haram [terrorist group].

Comments revealed the disenabling macro factors for social entrepreneurship, starting with insecurity as the top challenge. However, one may wonder why this dyad simply went ahead to collaborate despite the various risks, including insecurity. In reality, sociocultural challenges across the world are perceived as opportunities for both impact investors and social enterprises (Majercakova & Kocisova, 2016). This is true of Nigeria, as one informant remarked: "demotivating is the same things that are motivating for impact investing in Nigeria" (II2). In essence, what people considered a risk or problem is also counted as a motivation for social enterprise and impact investors passionate about collaborating to devise a solution. Unemployment, as revealed by SE4, was a challenging problem; however, it also presents the opportunity to create jobs through farming to address insecurity in the northern part of Nigeria triggered by the activities of Boko-Haram.

Analysis shows a number of similarities, with a slight margin of differences from perceptions regarding the enabling influence of the economic, political and socio-cultural factors in the collaboration experience. This case did not record any opinion about the influence of political factors on the collaboration experience. II5 linked enabling economic factors to huge market opportunities and sociocultural factors to many socially driven businesses. SE5 likewise linked economic factors to Nigeria's large market and socio-cultural factors to a large network of workforce spread across 36 states. It is not debatable that countries with a huge labour force and market opportunities will always attract investment opportunities due to low labour costs and those market opportunities. Supporting evidence from this dyad further explains how these factors influenced collaboration:

> First of all, Nigeria is a huge market. Let's not talk about that; I'm sure you're familiar with the saying that "every fourth African is a Nigerian". If you say every fourth African is a Nigerian, what that means is that you have huge energy. If you get it right in Nigeria, you would have solved the problem of Africa by at least 25%. That's actually one of the reasons we birthed in Nigeria. (II5)

SE5 reiterated the Nigerian enabling environment:

> We have different categories of customers: we have doctors, we have pharmacy shops, and we have the patient meeting group… We are increasing our sales force and we are creating employment…

Comments from both dyad further revealed the reality and the enormous economic potential for impact investing in Nigeria and how it inspired their collaboration experience. Besides the huge market, labour is also not in short of supply because of a teeming population of young people ready to work. Having a workforce at an affordable rate enhances industry creation.

From the dimension of disenabling factors, this dyad held similar perceptions about the disenabling nature of the Nigerian environment from their experience. II5 linked disenabling economic factors to weak consumers' purchasing power and high cost of doing business in Nigeria, political factors to poor electricity, road infrastructure and corruption, and socio-cultural factors to the large number of informal SEs. SE5 linked disenabling economic factors to consumers' low economic status, political factors to poor regulation, electricity and road infrastructure and sociocultural factors to inadequate access to social investment finance. The problems highlighted by this dyad have been widely reckoned as the major challenges for growing the Nigerian impact investing sector. Comments from this dyad further explain how these factors influenced their collaboration experience in the Nigerian macro environment:

> The economic situation in the country is not helping them [social enterprises]. First, because of the economic situation, the ability to purchase is affected… Secondly, as I have repeatedly said, infrastructure, absence of infrastructure is a major issue. If they can address infrastructure and successfully reduce the cost of doing business in Nigeria, I'm sure a whole lot of people would be happy… Cost of doing business gets quite high—if you go to register in cooperate affairs, you can't believe it. You have come, you have a property, the bank or the financial need security, you pledge the property. To even get to the documentation required in the land offices, with all the corruption there, and so on and so forth. That increases the cost of doing business, and they don't find it funny, those are part of the problems… A lot of these businesses in Nigeria are not formalised. When they go to conventional financial institutions to access funds, the conditions given to them are difficult to meet. No bank will give them money. (II5)

SE5 confirmed this disenabling influence:

> You know this business in Nigeria is not very easy. You don't have access to finance, and even if you have access, it will be at a high cost. Meanwhile, in the pharmaceutical business, the barrier to entry now is low, unlike in some countries with regulations. The regulatory authorities are trying their best, but we find out that the barriers to entry are low… Well, apart from that, the low economic status of people in Nigeria, the buying power is low. Many people are going to churches to seek for miracles, whereas they could have gone for medical treatment… I told you about regulatory [problems], the border is porous, people are bringing in products from everywhere. But in the midst of that, the issue of power, the issue of infrastructure, those are challenges also, because we also use do some local products: you find out that we are not competitive, because of infrastructures that are on ground.

Comments thus further validate existing facts that the cost of doing business in Nigeria has remained high, despite several years of government efforts to create an enabling environment. The comment by SE5 corroborates experience with II5 regarding partnering as investors with a common purpose to help navigate institutional voids to address societal challenges. The "low economic status of many people now seeking miracle in places of worship" explains why the hope of the common person in some parts of the developing world will always remain with their Creator. However, the question is, if they have all the resources needed to afford medical help when sick, will they still hope in God? The question of lack of regulation aligns with Madison's (1996) assertion that Nigeria has had all the resources and time but lacked adequate technocrats who will make these factors contribute to long-term economic growth and wellbeing. Thus, it is argued that lack of technocrats may not be the main problem of regulation in Nigeria, as there are several qualified Nigerians operating those institutions. The most significant setback lies in poor leadership and enforcement of regulatory guidelines, although this was expressed as opinion only.

Analysis of themes revealed some similarities regarding enabling economic factors that influence collaboration between them and slight differences under political and socio-cultural factors. The agreement and differences from the narratives show their distinct perceptions of how macro-level factors influenced the collaboration experience. II6 linked enabling economic factors to the wide spread of impact opportunities with increasing financial returns, political factors to partnership with government, and socio-cultural factors to changing businesses' mindset to social impact. SE6 linked enabling economic factors to the large consumer market for poultry, and socio-cultural factors to great admiration for their product by consumers. Comments reiterate how these factors influenced the collaboration experience:

> First is the financial return, another thing is we are well spread… Nigerian government is part of our investors… The federal Ministry of Environment focus on companies, ensuring they carry out EIA while monitoring the process… We are changing the mindset of business promoters, that it's not just about financial returns, but you have to impact the people…. (II6)

SE6 made similar comments:

> Well, we are being encouraged, one, for the fact you have a product that is being admired. You have a product that is being chased after. You have a product that your target audience, that is the consumers are always in need at any given point in time. It's not a product you produce, you keep, and you don't have market for; the market is there. For the fact that we are always under pressure most of the time, so we find every means towards meeting up with the demand by the consumers.

The comments further demonstrate how enabling economic, political and sociocultural factors influenced collaboration. II6 linked enabling political factors to the fact that the government is one of the investors. SE6, however, did not give any acknowledgement to any government enabling support to their operation as an SE. It can thus be inferred, indirectly, that the government supports SEs, since the government partners with impact investors like II6 who invest in SEs such as SE6. However, it is understood from SEs' perspective that government direct support in the form of start-up grants may be inadequate. Details about this are discussed under disenabling factors.

From the perspective of a disenabling environment, perceptions in this dyad show both similarities and differences, particularly under sociocultural factors. No record of any perception from II6 regarding the sociocultural factors implies there was no comment regarding II6's experience about disenabling sociocultural factors. II6 linked disenabling political factors to poor regulation and compliance and sociocultural factors to most social enterprises' small size. SE6 linked disenabling economic factors to unpredictable economic climate, political factors to inadequate financial support for SMEs, and sociocultural factors to an underdeveloped ecosystem. Comments further demonstrate how disenabling macro factors impacted negatively on collaboration:

> The environment is still very tough because of the very low level of compliance… From the level of compliance, our regulatory agencies need to sit up to make sure that things are looked into more… A large company in Nigeria is a small company in America… (II6)

SE6 also explained how the disenabling factors impacted on its experience:

> Well, the major thing with doing business in Nigeria is the financial climate. Last year (2017), we had a very tough time in the poultry sector. Almost 25–30% of those involved in poultry had to fold up. Why? Because they could not carry on with their business because of the recession… The agricultural sector need a lot of support and encouragement from the government. The previous government tried to do something about it, but since the coming of this government, in fact all they will tell you is, go and insure your farm… There must be an ecosystem, as one cannot operate individually or in isolation.

These comments further revealed each partner's experience and how the disenabling macro factors influenced their collaboration. It is noticeable that II6 did not give an account of disenabling factors from the perspective of economic factors but from the political aspect, which hinges on regulation and compliance. Regulation and compliance can be a big setback to impact investors who adhere strictly to ethical standards, as II6 revealed. Indeed, II6's partnership with the government may have impacted its ability to critique Nigeria's economic performance. SE6, however, argued that the previous government made efforts to improve the agricultural sector, while the present government did not show interest in sustaining such policies. Analysis of Nigeria's agricultural imports and exports between 2013 and 2015 by Ogunmodede (2019) revealed that Nigeria exported more agricultural produce in 2014 compared to 2016, with a sharp decrease in 2015. There seems to be some agreement about SE6's narrative with Ogunmodede's finding on the decrease in government attention to the agricultural sector.

7.3 Summary of the Findings

Analysis of macro-level factors that influenced collaboration in the six Cases has enabled this study to ascertain what constitutes enabling and disenabling macro factors in social entrepreneurship processes in an emerging country context. Narratives also demonstrate how these factors influenced their collaboration. It is also important to note analysis across the six cases explored dyadic themes from each dyad experience, which further provided specific narrative about each partner's experience with enabling and disenabling factors. There were similarities and slight differences from each dyad's experience, which further enriched perception of the collaboration process from diverse macro factors specific to Nigeria. The themes across the six cases have been grouped into two broad themes and used to explain SEs' and IIs' perceptions about the Nigerian macro environment's influence—political, economic and sociocultural—on social entrepreneurship. The findings showed Nigeria as a large market with middle-range sociopolitical advantage from enabling the macro environment. Yet the disenabling perspective characterised Nigeria as an example of a developing country with challenges of an institutional void that cut across political and socio-economic barriers to investment opportunities. While an institutional void could be labelled a barrier to impacting investment flow, it also represents opportunities for investors with a passion to deliver measurable social impacts.

In Table 7.2, the study presents a summary of the similarities and slight differences across the six cases regarding their perception of the enabling dimension of the Nigerian macro environment. The first and fifth columns contain names of the cases interviewed. Columns 3 and 4 contain dyadic variables or themes linked to the

Table 7.2 Summary of dyadic themes linked to macro enabling factors

IIs	Macro factor	Dyadic themes	Dyadic themes	SEs	Remarks
II1	Socio-cultural	Potential ecosystem	Supportive community	SE1	No input on political Agreement on all other factors
	Economic	Population & Market	Market opportunity		
II2	Economic	Economic opportunities	Market opportunities	SE2	No input on political but agreement on all other factors
	Socio-cultural	Young population	Networking platforms		
II3	Economic	Large market	Market opportunities	SE3	Agreement all other factors. No input on socio-cultural from II3.
	Political	increased capital base	Low lending risk		
	Socio-cultural	-	Social inclusion norms		
II4	Economic	Large market	Rich farmlands	SE4	Agreement across all variables
	Political	Farm input support	Low agricultural interest rate		
	Socio-cultural	Community network	Cooperation with farmers		
II5	Economic	Huge market	Large market	SE5	Agreement on all other factors. No input under political
	Socio-cultural	Potential social enterprises	Large workforce network		
II6	Economic	Investment opportunities	Large poultry market	SE6	Agreement on social and economic. No input under political
	Political	Government partnership	-		
	Socio-cultural	Social impact mindset	Product patronage		

macro level factors in column 2, i.e. political, socio-cultural, and economic factors. Most cases agreed that Nigeria has enormous market opportunities for impact investment. Spaces with no variables show the dyad did not provide a response regarding socio-cultural and political variables. Details of the findings are discussed in the next section.

Socio-economic Opportunities for Impact Investing in Nigeria

Analysis of the six cases interviewed revealed that impact investing opportunities abound in Nigeria, as found in the table of variables linked to the enabling macro factors in Table 7.2. Perception across the six cases linked enabling macro-economic factors to variables describing the opportunities for impact investing, such as a huge population and market for impact investment, a very high enterprising young population, rich agricultural farmland, etc. Undoubtedly, just like mainstream or traditional investors, impact investors also tend to flood into an environment where opportunities abound. A study by Jadhav (2012) on foreign direct investment (FDI) in Brazil, Russia, India, China and South Africa found that market size and natural resources constitute the main economic attraction for FDI flow. One point to note is that an impact investor interviewed observed that "what is demotivating for impact investing in Nigeria is the same things that are motivating"' (II2). This comment implies that the bigger the social challenges, the greater the opportunities for impact investing in a country where such opportunities exist.

The sociocultural factors, as constituents of the macro environment, also formed the basis for collaboration and exchange between Nigeria's social entrepreneurial actors (Du, 2018). A conducive socio-cultural environment often stimulates innovative activities that act as motivation for transforming societal challenges into opportunities. Analysis also shows that Nigeria's socio-cultural environment played some significant roles in attracting impact investors. The enabling socio-cultural factors revealed in Table 7.2 include variables such as a potential ecosystem for social entrepreneurship, a supportive community, growing social networking platforms, socially focused SMEs and a shift in mindset towards social innovation by some mainstream businesses. The enabling aspect of the sociocultural environment for social entrepreneurship stems from the fact that people are increasingly beginning to believe in the ideology of social enterprise as organisations, set up to solve difficult social problems unattended to by traditional or purely commercial businesses. A study by Adepoju and Akinwale (2019) reveals a large proportion of MSMES in Lagos are creating more awareness on reducing greenhouse gases through renewable energy technologies. Similarly, Thorgren and Omorede (2018) carried out an empirical study of 37 social enterprise leaders in Nigeria and found a growing awareness on the value that social enterprise leaders can bring to shaping the future of social enterprise organisation through trust and commitment. There is no doubt that the sociocultural environmental factors have been perceived as enabling factors in all six cases.

The political enabling factor for social enterprise and impact investing in Nigeria from the perspective of this study comprises the regulatory and governance mechanisms. The enabling perspective of SEs' and IIs' collaboration from the political angle is centred around legislation and regulatory issues that encourage social enterprise development. In the analysis, only Cases 3 and 4 provided variables linked to political enabling factors. SE6 did not provide any variables to correspond to II6. Although the political environment is key to SE and II processes, perceptions across the cases did not show that political factors played significant roles in their collaboration. A few cases linked political enabling factors in Nigeria to variables such as an increased capital base for microfinance, low lending risk, some forms of partnership with government and provision of farm input. Some of the changes is the reform in the banking sector. For example, a cashless policy was introduced through technology to reduce lending risk due to tightened security that blocked corrupt practices.

Uduji et al. (2019) allude to the provision of technologically enhanced media for accessing credit by farmers in rural areas in Nigeria that has further strengthened transparency in the financial system. A programme called the Growth Enhancement Support Scheme (GESS) introduced by the government has also enabled smallholder farmers to access farm credit. Although the initiative is a right step towards the goal of building an enabling environment for social enterprise, its impact has not been widely felt. It underpins why a major criticism of the Nigerian government, both past and present, hinges on a lack of priority programmes for the poor population across social welfare, economic, education and health sectors (Holmes et al., 2012; Olokundun et al., 2018). Table 7.3 provides a summary of shared perceptions across the six cases on variables linked to the disenabling nature of the Nigerian macro environment. Information in the table shows some similarities and slight differences across the dyads regarding their perception of the disenabling dimensions. The first and fifth columns contain names of the cases interviewed. Columns 3 and 4 contain dyadic variables or themes linked to the macro level factors in column 2, i.e. political, sociocultural, and economic factors. Most dyad cases agree that Nigeria's biggest barrier for impact investment hinges around political factors. Only II6 did not link economic factors to any variable. Details on these variables are discussed under the theme of governance and socio-economic barriers to investing in Nigeria.

7.4 Governance and Socio-economic Barriers to Impact Investing in Nigeria

In the context of the disenabling macro environment, several variables have been linked to political, economic and sociocultural factors that influence collaboration in this study. As shown in Table 7.3, there are context-specific variables linked to the disenabling factors from SEs' and IIs' collaboration experiences. A disenabling political environment centred around regulatory and governance setbacks. Although there are greater benefits to derive from creating an enabling environment for social entrepreneurship, barriers in governance corridors have remained a big dilemma in Nigeria. Several variables linked to Nigeria's disenabling political environment include unhealthy and failed policies, poor regulatory practices, lack of investment support for start-up SEs, poor infrastructure facilities such as power and roads, and insecurity and corruption.

The findings reflect the reality of many developing countries living in poverty, characterised by a difficulty in driving economic opportunities due to weak or absent institutional support (Mair & Marti, 2009). The presence of institutional voids amidst huge market opportunities remains a major concern in Nigeria. These challenges were classified as governance and regulatory setbacks because the Nigerian government controls the largest share of key sectors believed to drive enabling investment opportunities. The narratives across the six cases are reflected

Table 7.3 Summary of dyadic themes linked to macro disenabling factors

IIs	Macro factor	Dyadic themes	Dyadic themes	SEs	Remarks
II1	Political	Governance challenges	Poor governance	SE1	No input on socio-political. Agreement on all other factors
	Economic	Poor economic climate	Naira instability to dollars		
II2	Economic	High living cost/ startup funds	Economic recession	SE2	Agreement across all disenabling factors
	Socio-cultural	Brain drain/lack of patience	Poor social facilities (Data)		
	Political	Poor regulations/ high interest	Unhealthy government policy		
II3	Economic	Small size of Nigerian SEs	Scars foreign exchange	SE3	Agreement all disenabling factors in different perspective
	Political	Failed government policies	Poor infrastructure		
	Socio-cultural	Underdeveloped ecosystem	Few local investors		
II4	Economic	Devaluation of Naira	Insecurity	SE4	Agreement across all variables from different perspectives
	Political	Insecurity & infrastructure	Poor regulation/ Insecurity		
	Socio-cultural	Poor access to social funds	Youth restiveness		
II5	Economic	Poor purchasing power	Low economic status	SE5	Agreement across all variables from different perspectives
	Socio-cultural	Informality of SEs	Poor access to social funds		
	Political	Poor infrastructure/ corruption	Poor regulations		
II6	Economic	–	Unstable economic climate	SE6	Agreement on all variables. No input under economic from II6
	Political	Poor regulations/ compliance	Inadequate SEs finance		
	Socio-cultural	Small size of Nigerian SEs	Underdeveloped ecosystem		

in Nigeria's overall ranking of 131 out of 190 economies, with a scale of 56.9 on the ease of doing business (Doing Business, 2020). The World Bank Doing Business Indicator measures the regulatory and country policy assessments to determine countries with the most attractive investment environment. Contractor et al. (2020) affirm the impact of regulatory variables similar to those perceived across the six cases in this study as determinants of FDI. Although investors are known to be risk takers, there is a limit to the risk they might be willing to take, particularly when the propensity for a return on investment is below average, no matter the potential for social impact.

The sociocultural environment in this study is essentially the home condition and the general perceptions that people hold about social enterprise, particularly with regard to the notion of blended value creation. Variables linked to Nigeria's sociocultural environmental factors include brain drain, underdeveloped business ideas, lack of patience, absence of a strong eco-system, lack of home investors, youth restiveness, family protectionism, informality and inadequate access to social investment funds. As earlier discussed, most indigenous impact investors lack the patience to invest in start-up SEs but often invest in businesses that have the least social impact on society due to immediate financial returns on investment. Family protectionism, as conceived in Nigeria, is a situation where a CEO would prefer to have his or her family members in the managerial team of an organisation, even if they may not have the required qualifications and skills to perform such a role. Social business owners addicted to family protectionism do not give room for external expertise and innovative ideas. Such situations constrain investors from advocating changes that may lead to excellent business performance. As identified in Nigeria, lack of a strong ecosystem is evidence that overall societal perception of the concept of social entrepreneurship being driven by social enterprise and impact investing organisations is still at an infant stage. The question of informality hinges on the inability of foreign or indigenous investors to entrust their funds to ventures that do not meet the legal requirements for doing social impact business.

Finally, disenabling variables linked to Nigeria's economic environment include currency fluctuations and interest rates, economic recession, small sizes of SEs, and economic uncertainty. The economic realities in Nigeria are contrary to Cleeve (2012), who asserts that large market size, the growth rate of the economy, high skills, and openness of economics are key drivers of FDI. Variables linked to Nigeria's disenabling political environment did not completely deter investors from coming to Nigeria. This situation aligns with Cleeve's (2012) discovery that institutional and political risk variables have been found to impact positively on FDI inflows into sub-Saharan African countries where Nigeria is also located. This assertion may be contradictory to previous studies alluding to these factors as impediments to FDI inflow (Contractor et al., 2020; Noorbakhsh et al., 2001). However, in the context of impact investing, the presence of social challenges constitutes motivating factors for impact investing. It underpins the reason experience across the six cases did not include significant setbacks in disenabling economic factors. The most devastating blow to Nigeria's investment prospects has been impacted by interest rate fluctuations (Jadhav, 2012). As impact investing constitutes FDI inflow, it is important to realise that economic factors affecting traditional businesses also affect investors' drive to come to Nigeria. Studies by Agri et al. (2017) and Ezeanyeji et al. (2019) also affirm that economic recession has negatively impacted the macroeconomic indicators in Nigeria, as some dyads in the analysis revealed.

7.5 Conclusion

Analysis of the Nigeria's macro environment has revealed several context-specific variables linked to both enabling and disenabling factors hampering social entrepreneurship development. Some of the factors revealed by SEs and IIs centred on lack of enabling governance and socio-economic support. All variables linked to these factors have been discussed in this chapter. Because SEs and IIs often navigate institutional voids as potential market opportunities for social and economic gains, dyads in this study have successfully established partner fit despite the unfavourable economic climate. The next chapter unpacks the learning experience from the micro and macro influences on SEs and II experiences to predict future collaboration prospects.

References

Adepoju, A. O., & Akinwale, Y. O. (2019). Factors influencing willingness to adopt renewable energy technologies among micro and small enterprises in Lagos State Nigeria. *International Journal of Sustainable Energy Planning and Management, 19*, 69–82.

Agri, E. M., Mailafia, D., & Umejiaku, M. R. I. (2017). Impact of economic recession on macroeconomic stability and sustainable development in Nigeria. *Science Journal of Economics*, 1–12.

Amaeshi, K., Adegbite, E., & Rajwani, T. (2016). Corporate social responsibility in challenging and non-enabling institutional contexts: Do institutional voids matter? *Journal of Business Ethics, 134*(1), 135–153.

Asogwa, O. S., & Dim, E. (2016). Entrepreneurship development and unemployment reduction in Nigeria. *International Journal of Business and Management Review, 4*(8), 27–43.

Bird, B. (1988). Implementing entrepreneurial ideas: The case for intention. *Academy of Management Review, 13*(3), 442–453.

Casero, J. D., Pulido, D. U., & Mogollón, R. H. (2005). Teoría económica institucional y creación de empresas. *Investigaciones europeas de dirección y economía de la empresa, 11*(3), 209–230.

Cleeve, E. (2012). Political and institutional impediments to foreign direct investment inflows to sub-Saharan Africa. *Thunderbird International Business Review, 54*(4), 469–477.

Coleman, J. (1990). *Foundations of social theory*. Belknap Press of Harvard University Press.

Companys, Y. E., & McMullen, J. S. (2007). Strategic entrepreneurs at work: The nature, discovery, and exploitation of entrepreneurial opportunities. *Small Business Economics, 28*(4), 301–322.

Contractor, F. J., Dangol, R., Nuruzzaman, N., & Raghunath, S. (2020). How do country regulations and business environment impact foreign direct investment (FDI) inflows? *International Business Review, 29*(2), 101640.

Doing Business. (2020). *Comparing business in 190 economies: Region profile Sub-Saharan Africa*. Retrieved from https://www.doingbusiness.org/content/dam/doingBusiness/media/Profiles/Regional/DB2020/SSA.pdf

Du, Z. (2018). A literature review on institutional environment and technological innovation. *American Journal of Industrial and Business Management, 8*(9), 1941–1950.

Ezeanyeji, C., Imoagwu, C. P., & Ifeako, M. (2019). Impact of recession on economic growth in Nigeria. *International Journal of Economics Commerce and Management, 7*(4), 207–221.

Griffiths, M. D., Gundry, L. K., & Kickul, J. R. (2013). The socio-political, economic, and cultural determinants of social entrepreneurship activity: An empirical examination. *Journal of Small Business and Enterprise Development, 20*(2), 341–357.

Holmes, R., Akinrimisi, B., Morgan, J., & Buck, R. (2012). Social protection in Nigeria. In *Mapping programmes and their effectiveness*. Overseas Development Institution (ODI). Retrieved from https://www.odi.org/sites/odi.org.uk/files/odi-assets/publications-opinion-files/7582.pdf

Jadhav, P. (2012). Determinants of foreign direct investment in BRICS economies: Analysis of economic, institutional and political factor. *Procedia-Social and Behavioral Sciences, 37*, 5–14.

Madison, M. A. (1996). Orthodox strategies. In A. Grammy, A. P., & C. K. Bragg (Eds.), *"Disenabling" environment: Politico-economic decline. United States-Third world relations in the new world order*. California State University, Nova Science Publishers.

Mair, J., & Marti, I. (2009). Entrepreneurship in and around institutional voids: A case study from Bangladesh. *Journal of Business Venturing, 24*(5), 419–435.

Majercakova, D., & Kocisova, L. (2016, September 1–2). *Impact investing–opportunity for creative investment*. Paper presented at the Cconomic and Social Development (Book of Proceedings), 16th International Scientific Conference on Economic and Social Development, Split.

Noorbakhsh, F., Paloni, A., & Youssef, A. (2001). Human capital and FDI inflows to developing countries: New empirical evidence. *World Development, 29*(9), 1593–1610.

Nwadinobi, E., & Peart, A. (2018). E-government development in Nigeria, bank verification no (BVN) an anti-corruption tool. *World Academy of Science, Engineering and Technology, International Journal of Computer and Information Engineering, 5*. https://doi.org/10.29007/h2tr

Ogunmodede, A. M. (2019). *The past, present and future contributions of small-scale and local food supply systems to Nigeria's food security: A critical appraisal* (pp. 1–14). Royal Agricultural University.

Olokundun, A. M., Moses, C., Falola, H. O., Ibidunni, A. S., Salau, O. P., & Oluremi, O. A. (2018). The role of social entrepreneurship and the state in propelling national development in Nigeria: A conceptual approach. *International Journal of Entrepreneurship, 22*(1), 1–6.

Thorgren, S., & Omorede, A. (2018). Passionate leaders in social entrepreneurship: Exploring an African context. *Business & Society, 57*(3), 481–524.

Thornton, P. H., Ribeiro-Soriano, D., & Urbano, D. (2011). Socio-cultural factors and entrepreneurial activity: An overview. *International Small Business Journal, 29*(2), 105–118.

Uduji, J. I., Okolo-Obasi, E. N., & Asongu, S. A. (2019). Electronic wallet technology and the enabling environment of smallholder farmers in Nigeria. *Agricultural Finance Review, 79*(5), 666–688.

Urban, B. (2013). Influence of the institutional environment on entrepreneurial intentions in an emerging economy. *The International Journal of Entrepreneurship and Innovation, 14*(3), 179–191.

Urban, B., & Kujinga, L. (2017). The institutional environment and social entrepreneurship intentions. *International Journal of Entrepreneurial Behavior & Research, 23*(4), 638–655.

Veciana, J. M., & Urbano, D. (2008). The institutional approach to entrepreneurship research. Introduction. *International Entrepreneurhsip Management, 4*(4), 365–379.

Zoogah, D. B., Peng, M. W., & Woldu, H. (2015). Institutions, resources, and organizational effectiveness in Africa. *The Academy of Management Perspectives, 29*(1), 7–31.

Chapter 8
Key Learning Experience from SEs' and IIs' Collaboration

8.1 Introduction

Analysis in Chaps. 5, 6 and 7 shows how SEs and IIs in Nigeria collaborate to pursue dual motives for addressing social and economic problems. The findings also shed light on how the concepts' compatibility and complementarity guide collaboration between SEs and IIs vis-à-vis the influence of the micro (organisational context) and macro (external environmental context) factors on the collaboration process. This chapter aims to identify the perceived learning experience from the collaboration process across the six cases. According to Franco and Pessoa (2014), the overall outcome of an experience can potentially inspire or discourage further attempts by either SEs or IIs to collaborate with other SEs or IIs in Nigeria or elsewhere with similar contexts. The learning experience also aims to demonstrate the role of mutual trust in achieving a collaboration process characterised by cooperation with minimal tension. It has been established in Chap. 2 that trust plays a key role in minimising potential conflict in strategic business alliances (McEvily et al., 2017; Zaheer et al., 1998). It is necessary, too, to establish the role of mutual trust for building sustainable relationships from the perspective of hybrid organisations. Studies also show trust has increased sustainable performance in inter-organisational relationships (Davis & Love, 2011; Golinelli et al., 2011).

8.2 Learning Experience

In the literature review in Chap. 2, several authors posit that previous partnering experience has great potential to influence decision-making and the potential for actors to engage in new forms of partnership (Dyer & Singh, 1998; Montoro-Sánchez et al., 2009; Teng & Das, 2008). A social enterprise's perceived learning

J. A. Emmanuel et al., *Social Enterprises and Impact Investors*, Advances in Theory and Practice of Emerging Markets,
https://doi.org/10.1007/978-3-031-59454-0_8

experience with impact investors during their collaboration process is important for predicting a potential for future engagement with similar partners. Because the process entails building mutual trust for commitment, some experience may involve negative perspectives, which could hinder future engagements (Franco & Haase, 2013). Unpacking the perception from the six cases in this study could generate either positive or negative perceptions about future collaboration potential between SEs and IIs in Nigeria.

To achieve this objective, the study asked, "*What is the perceived learning experience from the collaboration and partner selection between SEs and IIs with dyadic relations in Nigeria*?" To answer this, interview guides were designed that sought what IIs considered rewarding and learning experience from their collaboration and what improvements could be proposed. The responses provided evidence whether the collaboration experience was rewarding or not, including the learning experience. If the experience was rewarding, this is an indication of a possibility for either partner wishing to continue collaborating with the current partner or engage in a new partnership. If the experience was not rewarding for some reason connected to each partner's experience, such responses may be useful for suggesting future study research directions. The outcome will also reveal the role of mutual trust in future collaboration. The first-stage analysis in the NVivo coding process generated a cluster of empirical codes that provide an overview of perception across the six cases regarding learning experience. Table 8.1 shows the empirical code cluster associated with SEs' and IIs' learning experience.

Clusters 1–3 distinctively represent the experience and perception across the six cases regarding the collaboration process. Twenty-nine reference codes linked to collaboration prospects being higher suggest that the six SEs and IIs in the dyad see the potential to continue to address difficult social problems in Nigeria. Sixteen codes linked to sustainable mutual experience suggest collaboration was characterised by minimal tension and conflict. One code (only) linked to potential tension suggests that, to a large extent, that collaboration across the six cases was almost tension-free. The unlikely potential for tension across the cases validates the pre-investment process of establishing partner fit between SEs and IIs that is guided by

Table 8.1 Empirical code on learning experience across the six cases

Empirical Code Cluster 1 Collaboration prospect (29)
Future collaboration potential (11) **Learning on innovation and scalability (11)** **Positive contribution to economy growth (7)**
Empirical Code Cluster 2 Sustainable mutual experience (16)
Great social impact and financial returns (11) **Good business models, managerial and technical support (5)**
Empirical Code Cluster 3 Potential Tension (1)
Financial return tension (1)

organisational compatibility and resource complementarity and is key to matching the right SEs with the right IIs.

8.3 Analysis of the Cases

The second-stage analysis sought deeper meaning from each case's narrative about perceptions, including key variables linked to experience. These variables have been reduced to dyadic themes between each case, explained with empirical evidence. It is important to note the analysis was not limited to specific dyadic relations; participants were encouraged to share their experience regarding other partners outside the current dyad used in this study. The approach is to capture detailed data about SEs' and IIs' collaboration experience in Nigeria. The next section analyses the themes across the six cases.

The collaboration experience between II1 and SE1 led to a dyadic relationship of over 2 years. This dyad shared experience of some rewards and learning experience derived from the collaboration process which resulted in established partner fit. Although II1 observed collaboration with SE1 was successful, there is a need for greater innovation and more demonstration of the scalability of business models across SEs in Nigeria. II1 also observed that the Nigerian social enterprise ecosystem remains in its infancy in development, and needs support from all stakeholders. II1's perception and learning experience with Nigerian SEs is as follows:

> Well, as I said, it can only get better, so we are not satisfied. We need to see more; we need to see higher quality, we need to see people doing things differently, we need to see innovations with business models, we need to see companies that appreciate scales and know how to get there. We need to see innovations in different sectors; we need to see people taking more advantage of technology… The stronger the ecosystem is and the more other companies can look to them and say how do these companies get to where they are and who is behind them, etc.

Comment by II1 provides an overview of the learning experience from its engagement with SE1 and other social enterprises in Nigeria. II1 revealed a lack of satisfaction from the experience and suggested areas that need improvement moving forward and how this can be achieved. For example, greater innovation and scalable business model are necessary for continuing engagement. Studies have also revealed developing a scalable business model as a pathway to prevent failure in social enterprise, particularly social enterprises at the growth-stage level (Nair & Blomquist, 2019). The second area cited by II1 is the need for a stronger ecosystem. Although impact investing opportunities abound in Nigeria, studies also support II1's experience that funding is just one part of a thriving ecosystem. Strengthening other domains can help the ecosystem grow sustainably (Owoade, 2016). This is an area where the government and other stakeholders need to step in to develop the ecosystem to achieve sustainable growth.

SE1 perceived its collaboration with II1 has brought about greater sustainability and business expansion. The theme of sustainability and business expansion from the account of SE1's experience shows some improvement and satisfaction from the collaboration experience. Evidence of satisfaction is supported:

> We have not lost a customer… I think losing a customer is a sense of dissatisfaction. We have been in the state for six years and have been providing services to end-clients for five years, so we have not lost a customer. Our services are also provided through a pricing model subscription that is paid annually. It was also a deliberate strategy not to lock in customers for 3, 4, 5 years. If a customer is not happy at the end of a period, which runs for 12 months, then the customer has the right to leave. But all our customers have been renewing their subscription for the past five years. (SE1)

SE1 affirmed it made sustainable progress for a period over 5 years in dyadic relations with II1. It shows the enterprise has remained sustainable as a result of the technical and financial support received from II1. Sustainability does not come by just receiving financial support but also by the social enterprise's ability to balance its business model from several perspectives that require attention and better management (Jabłoński, 2016). SE1, in this instance, has been able to manage the profitability of its enterprise, as well as social impact, which justified its sustainability and expansion over the years of its experience with impact investors in Nigeria. It is, therefore, clear engagement in the future is potentially more likely.

Emerging themes from the collaboration experience between II2 and SE2 revealed some important lessons which could improve the experience for potential collaborating partners in the future. Although II2 had a fruitful collaboration with SE2 for an ongoing period of 5 years, II2 observed that the start-up space for social enterprises in Nigeria needs more attention in the form of support from stakeholders in order to increase SEs' viability to attract IIs. This study captured the positive experience:

> We hope to attract more strong business ideas and founders in the start-up space. It's even more rewarding to be able to invest in a company that has a significant impact on the economy. We've done some, education, and tech investment, we've done health, the one I talked about [i.e., SE2]. They're specific sectors where, whatever it is you do, you're impacting. You'll impact even more than other sectors, like education, healthcare, financing to some extent, but, like I said, I think, the people are trying to solve the most basic problems that would automatically create impact for everybody. (II2)

II2 had a good experience with SE2, informing the desire to attract more social enterprise with particular reference to the start-up space in Nigeria. Start-up space involves SEs at the growth stage, whose business model can scale but may require smaller funding. II2's choice of a start-up social enterprise shows the positive impact of its experience with SE2. Most impact investors usually do not have the patience to invest in start-up social enterprises (Battilana, 2018), which may be linked to the time it takes for such enterprises to start yielding profit or making financial returns. SE2 revealed that its collaboration experience with II2 has resulted in greater scalability of its business model:

> More people can go online and request for anything they want, and in our community, more people don't want to come down to Lagos…, they just order from where they are and wait for few days and get their products. Yes, the impact has been good, and hopefully, it will be getting bigger every day.

This revealed how the enterprise scaled its social business impact through collaboration with II2. Investing in SE2 has led to better innovation with technology, which now attracts online printing service delivery to clients across all locations in Nigeria. If SE2 has achieved scalability through its collaboration with II2, it also means it met the financial returns obligation to II2. Therefore, this dyad had a positive experience. However, II2 observed that more attention should be given to growing the start-up social enterprise space in Nigeria.

Analysis of the collaboration experience in this dyad shows they had a fruitful experience over a period of two ongoing years in their partnership. II3 linked the good experience it had to the impact of technical assistance provided to SE3, which had a trickle-down effect on the enterprise's social and financial performance. Seeing the investment portfolio gain improvement with impact beyond financial returns was a good experience, as II3 recorded:

> There's room for improvements, and that's why we're very keen and very interested in the technical assistance part of the things that we do because we just don't want to give you money. Yes, we will get our returns, and everybody can move on, but we want to see that these things grow and that they're replicated, and we can do more, we want to be able to do more.

II3 affirmed its interest in the scalability of SE3 and other social enterprises it invested in in the past. Providing technical assistance was a great learning experience from this dyad, as it enabled SE3 to grow in line with II3's expectations. Studies reveal that beyond the personal experience that most social enterprise owners bring into the business, they rely on expert support from a variety of networks (Allen, 2020). The technical assistance given to SE3 is a typical example of the kind of support social enterprises leverage across networks to enhance their performance and experience.

SE3 also revealed some learning experience linked to its collaboration. Two strategic learning experiences included improving internal capability through technical support and opportunity for capital formation. It will be recalled the need for technical support and access to finance dominated the complementary goals of several SEs who desired to collaborate with IIs. The learning experience from SE3 affirmed the achievement of such goals, as revealed in their improvement:

> Oh yes, like I said, we've pulled technical assistances and all of that—especially we have had technical assistance in the area of risk management, in the area of rural development, and it is always good to learn, you know, exchange knowledge, and so I would say there have been direct influences from those partnerships in the increase in capacity at organisational level. (SE3)

This comment demonstrates the specific areas where SE3 gained improvement in terms of technical support, which also enhanced the enterprise's capability. For example, risk management from impact investors' perspectives constitutes a key knowledge area where IIs would like to see greater improvement from their investee to be sure their investment does not run into losses. SE3 likewise revealed its improvement in capital formation as part of the learning experience they linked to collaborating with II3. Capital formation entails the process of creating funds to pursue the missions of social enterprise. II3 provides evidence:

> There is a great opportunity for impact investment to do some of the things that the government cannot do. Everybody knows about public-private partnerships and how we can also drive development from the private sector. Capital formation in Nigeria is still evolving: I mean we are now talking about, for instance, trying to see how we can engage the pension funds in terms of engaging the secondary capital market. Some microfinance institutions have tried to raise funds from that level in terms of capital formation; there is still a lot to learn. But investors can come in and give buoyancy to the institutions that are already in space so we can continue to make impact at our level. I think collectively there is still much work to do there, but I will say there is still a very clear future for impact investing.

The comment clearly shows the bright future for impact investing in Nigeria, particularly in the area of capital formation.

SE3 revealed the government has been inadequate in supporting social enterprises seeking growth in terms of funding. Much more funding can be drawn from impact investors' engagement with other stakeholders in Nigeria's existing financial institutions. Studies also show it is no longer debatable that private capital can change the equation of government strategy in managing a variety of social problems bedevilling any nation (Brambila-Macias & Massa, 2010; Caceres, 2017). Leveraging private capital has been proven to help grow economies in times of economic recession.

In this analysis, II4 perceived its collaboration with SE4 had yielded some rewarding learning experience that informed its desire to continue to engage with social enterprises looking forward to scaling their social and financial impact. A key learning experience for II4 was the impact of technical support on SE4's performance. II4 revealed how technical support provided to SE4 had increased the value of financial investment in the overall collaboration experience:

> While providing technical support to our investees to some extent, we are satisfied but will always look forward to better performance of the companies we invest. For example, SE4 contributes to higher productivity in the Nigerian agricultural sector, which accounts for 22% of the country's GDP, resulting in higher economic growth.

The learning experience from II4 demonstrates how the provision of technical support to SE4 had contributed to the enterprise's performance. In the long run, the technical support has benefited both parties in proven financial and social impact, as reflected in the increase in agricultural contribution to Nigeria's GDP. Satisfaction by II4 affirms that the collaboration experience was positive, as this has yielded good returns on investment. However, since scalability remains the goal of every impact investor, providing technical support would be a useful tool to expand the capability of SE4 to even do better in the future.

From SE4's perspective, the learning experience in collaboration has been linked to improved capability in best practice environmental social impact. The achievement came from the technical support provided by II4 during the period of 2 years' ongoing relationship. Bringing the expertise of II4 into their mission has enhanced the performance of SE4 with the latest farming technology. It is not surprising that the impact of SE4 has contributed to the overall economic performance in the

Nigerian agricultural sector. II4's technical support has influenced the performance of SE4:

> Some of these investors in Europe or the United States are quite knowledgeable of best practice farming methods, and they helped us in terms of best practices environmental issues. In Africa, we may not be as concerned about preserving a national park, for example. These investors can question and put metrics in place so that you are making an impact, but you are also not damaging the environment, or you are also not taking advantage of a farmer, things like child labour. All those things are things that they request and require, because they are putting their investment in our trust. They have to ensure that we are deploying it in a manner which they would. Also, as an organisation, we have our internal policies which arise from the initiatives of these investors. Internally, we have to shape them ourselves, so we do not engage in any child labour or anything like that. (SE4)

This further validates the interesting learning experience SE4 had. Beyond financial investment made, there is also evidence that technical support specifically tailored towards managing agricultural farming without harming the environment has shaped the farming methods of SE4. Akinrotimi et al. (2011) argue that besides regulatory activities from governing authorities, engaging expert advice from knowledgeable investors will ensure that farmers conform to national policy and international standards for preserving the environment.

Themes from II5 and SE5 show their 3-year collaboration was fruitful, with expressed satisfaction from the process. II5 revealed that collaboration has resulted in an increased number of portfolios funded by the organisation, that is, they have been attracted to more social enterprises in Nigeria. Secondly, II5 had received several awards in recognition of its impact on SEs' funding in Nigeria. II5 expressed the rewards thus:

> SE5 has gone beyond haywire [beyond expectation], he's introduced some other people, some relations of his. One is Havilah: that's the number one library manager in this country, he models libraries for universities, for banks, He's doing very well… Almost yearly II5 has been winning awards for doing what it is doing…

The comment indicates some great learning experience and rewards, showcasing the profitability of activities with SEs in Nigeria. The impact investor also revealed increasing numbers of portfolios arising from collaboration with SE5. The long list of awards received by II5 in Nigeria validates the saying that "a good product will always market itself". The progress achieved by SE5 prompted the enterprise to invite other SEs facing funding challenges to enter into partnership with II5.

It is also important to note that II5 also had some tension with a different social enterprise but not with SE5. The tension arose from the inability of the SE to return the initial capital invested in the business by II5, even when the social enterprise had made a profit and was scaling its projects across Nigeria. This was why II5 introduced a criterion that will ensure trust in SEs does not stop at the scalability or viability potential of a business model: The enterprise must also present 30% worth of assets as investment into the partnership.

SE5 affirmed collaboration has been fruitful. Increase in financial capability to scale has been revealed by SE5 as a major improvement from the dyadic relationship. Successful collaboration between SE5 and II5 demonstrates how SEs facing financial challenges can succeed when they leverage resources from organisations with stronger resources through hybrid forms of organising (Doherty et al., 2014). Indeed, collaboration with II5 has enabled SE5 to attain greater financial sustainability and scalability:

> We have been able to have more people come on board, at least with the fund given we are increasing our sales force, and we are creating employment also. We are looking at going to the West African sub-region, we are thinking of expansion. (SE5)

The progress and opportunity for SE5 expansion evolved from the enterprise's funding support from II5. Recall that the progress made by SE5 has produced multiple effects from referrals that also benefited from II5, employment generation and a potential to scale beyond the Nigerian environment.

The last dyad's learning experience revealed fruitful collaboration from its 3 years' ongoing relationship. Some outcomes connected to collaboration include the ethical impact on SE6 strategies and sustainable returns on investment resulting from resourceful capability building by II6. The learning experience from this outcome validates the assertion that profit with purpose is attainable when two organisations combine different resources in a fashion that can be managed for the benefit of both (Mongelli et al., 2019). Comment from II6 demonstrates the learning outcome from its experience:

> Doing business in the right way as most of them [SE6] have seen, it pays. Empowering and employing is important, but you can't go above your employment limit. It is like employing two drivers for one car, it's not possible... We focus on empowerment because...it helps most of these companies, it is a win-win thing, as they are being empowered. It is helping their supply chain.

This revealed the impact of providing technical support to SE6 and other enterprises in II6's investment portfolio. Doing business the right way, as the investor noted, pays both parties in the form of return on investment. II6 also declared its dyadic relation with SE6 had to remain beneficial for both because "it has been a win-win thing". Emphasis on ethics aligns with the key purpose of impact investing, which is also derived from ethical investing. Priority is placed on the impact of investment into the wider society against the pursuit of profitability, which distinguishes impact investing from mainstream businesses.

The narrative from SE6 further affirmed this dyad had achieved their intentions based on their collaboration experience. SE6 linked its improvement to capability development in business strategy gained from II6, which led to its scalability in poultry farming in Nigeria. SE6 demonstrates the learning experience and specific improvement gained from its collaboration:

> While we were operating as a company singly, the rate of our thinking, the rate of our operations, the strategy to reach out to larger society was a little bit myopic. But partnering with the impact investors [II6], we've been exposed to many things such that we're not only thinking about our immediate environment, but we're also thinking of reaching out to the totality of Nigeria. Nigeria is a very large country, and we have the people in terms of population, and with the large population Nigeria is an excellent market opportunity.

SE6 corroborates that collaboration with II6 has positively influenced SE6's capability to think innovatively along the lines of the possibility of expanding operations beyond their current limits. Knowledge exposure builds critical capability to innovate in every business venture. Urban (2015) describes capability improvement of the SE6 kind as an example of self-efficacy, a construct that illustrates conviction about the ability to perform at a designated level of credibility.

8.4 Key Findings of the Analysis

Analysis of the six cases has enabled the study to ascertain variables that describe the perceived learning experience across SEs' and IIs' collaboration in Nigeria. The learning experience also demonstrates the role of mutual trust in a hybrid inter-organisational relationship. It revealed areas where success had been recorded, as well as areas that need improvement in future collaboration. Based on the empirical references generated from the cases' perception of the learning experience, variables linked to collaboration prospects, outcomes of mutual trust, and potential tensions have been summarised in Table 8.1. It is evident that all cases had a fruitful learning experience linked to the pre-investment collaboration process. Column 1 (from the left) presents the impact investor in a dyad with social enterprise in column 2 (from the right). Column 2 (from the left) presents the learning experience measure from collaboration prospect, the outcome of mutual trust and potential tension. Columns 2 and 4 present the variables linked to learning experience across the six cases. As there was no potential tension across most of the cases, except for Case 5, with a partner different from the current dyad, only one tension was recorded (Table 8.2).

It has been noted investee SEs who failed to return funds invested in the business signalled potential tension arising from a breach of trust between collaborating partners. The perception across the cases is explained in one central theme in the next section.

8.5 The Role of Mutual Trust on SE and II Performance and Sustainability

Across the six cases, each partner's dominant learning experience has come from mutual trust gained from inter-organisational exchange of tangible and intangible resources. Technical support from IIs featured as significant intangible resources tailored towards capability development necessary for the growth of SEs. The provision of such resources engendered SEs to trust IIs' intention for genuine impact. This study views IIs' capability support for SEs as some form of learning opportunities that social enterprise organisations may or may not have, but require in order to

Table 8.2 Variables on learning experience

IIs	Learning experience	Dyadic variables	Dyadic variables	SEs	Areas for improvement
II1	**Collaboration prospect**	Positive	Positive	**SE1**	**Scalability of business model**
	Outcome of mutual trust	Establish partner fit/sustainability	Sustainability & expansion		
II2	**Collaboration prospect**	Positive	Positive	**SE2**	**Start-up SEs need more attention**
	Outcome of mutual trust	Fruitful collaboration	Scalability of business model		
II3	**Collaboration prospect**	Positive	Positive	**SE3**	**Scalability of business model start-up funding**
	Outcome of mutual trust	Financial returns	Technical support		
II4	**Collaboration prospect**	Positive	Positive	**SE4**	**More technical support for SEs**
	Outcome of mutual trust	Good performance sustainability	Capability on best practice		
II5	**Collaboration prospect**	Positive	Positive	**SE5**	**Evaluation of SEs assets as capital contribution SEs formality**
	Outcome of mutual trust	Increase in portfolio companies	Sustainability & Scalability		
	Potential tension	Financial return (different partner)	No tension (with II5)		
II6	**Collaboration prospect**	Positive	Positive	**SE6**	**Ethical compliance**
	Outcome of mutual trust	Ethical practice on SEs strategies	Scalability and capability		

achieve their goals, aside from any financial investment considerations (Weaver, 2018). The kind of support being provided to SEs by IIs is likened to what Weaver (2018) calls capability dispersion, meaning the choice or opportunities provided by an institution through services and programmes. Weaver's idea of capability dispersion is similar to Giddens' (1979) conception of structuration theory, which suggests that institutions exist to address specific human or organisational needs that build confidence in the recipient.

It is also evident from analysis that providing technical capability support to SEs not only benefited the social enterprise alone but impact investors. As a result, SEs and IIs had a unique experience which emerged from the role of mutual trust on performance and sustainability of dyadic relations.

The performance of social enterprises as hybrid organisations combining social and economic interest in this study has been attributed to innovation achieved through collaboration with impact investors, although some impact investors did acknowledge the level of innovation displayed by some SEs was not at a satisfactory level and there was room for improvement. The most successful social enterprise presents an innovative business model that can demonstrate profit, sustainability and scalability. Ebrahim and Rangan (2014: 122) argue that impact investors measure the outcome and impact of funds invested into social enterprises to help them see "what bang they are getting for their buck". Across the six cases, several IIs linked the performance of social enterprises to the scalability of the enterprise mission in line with their own investment motives. As defined in Chap. 2, scalability is the ability to replicate a solution to a problem across local, regional, national and global environments. From experience across the dyad cases, some IIs were more willing to invest more in SEs because they trusted the enterprise's scalability potential on a unique business idea beyond a particular context. Scalability is evidence of profitability and, by extension, a sign that investment made into SEs will generate financial return. In summary, learning experience across the six dyads shows IIs' technical capability support has increased mutual trust in SEs' performance, evidenced in the scalability of the enterprise's innovative business idea.

Sustainability is the second instance of evidence of the role of mutual trust between SEs and IIs. Most impact investors provided technical support to their investee social enterprise to build mutual trust because they do not want their financial investment to turn into a loss. Sustainable mutual experience is underpinned by the fact that these dyads complement mutual trust in each other across the different resources brought into the partnership. IIs provided technical capability, ranging from financial risk management to technology and sector-specific-related investment guidance, including finance. SEs likewise traded with these resources with a viable business model that generated financial returns to IIs. Sustainability as a learning experience across the six dyads found impact investors manifested as socially minded financiers, who supported social enterprise to attain scalability and sustainability. Sustainability as a learning experience across the cases has, therefore, validated Roth's (2019) assertion that it is better to support social enterprise through impact investing than providing a grant. Investing in social enterprise with a profit motive engenders discipline on the part of SEs due to the cost of their financier's capital. SEs in these cases acknowledged the impact of IIs' financial and technical support on their sustainability. IIs also agreed they had received financial returns from their investment in SEs. This was why the IIs in the six dyad cases agreed to positive future collaboration with more SEs in Nigeria and other regions, based on the financial returns and social impact achieved. Indeed, mutual trust is the linkage across social enterprise sustainability, taking account of impact investors' provision of technical capabilities, including financial investment.

8.6 Conclusion

This chapter demonstrates the learning experience from the pre-investment collaboration process in Nigeria. That experience can inspire and guide potential investors and SEs seeking partners to leverage both the positive and negative experience for future benefits. This chapter's most exciting lesson is validating the concepts of organisational compatibility and resource complementarity as panaceas to forestall potential tension between SEs and IIs. The next chapter discusses the main findings of the study and demonstrates how the research questions have been answered, the contribution to knowledge of the study and future research directions.

References

Akinrotimi, O., Abu, O., & Aranyo, A. (2011). Environmental friendly aquaculture key to sustainable fish farming development in Nigeria. *Continental Journal of Fisheries and Aquatic Science, 5*(2), 17–31.

Allen, R. A. (2020). Sources of expertise in social enterprises. *Strategic Change, 29*(4), 447–458.

Battilana, J. (2018). Cracking the organizational challenge of pursuing joint social and financial goals: Social enterprise as a laboratory to understand hybrid organizing. *Management, 21*(4), 1278–1305.

Brambila-Macias, J., & Massa, I. (2010). The global financial crisis and Sub-Saharan Africa: The effects of slowing private capital inflows on growth. *African Development Review, 22*(3), 366–377.

Caceres, L. R. (2017). Economic openness and stagnation in Central America. *Journal of Developing Areas, 51*(1), 373–389.

Davis, P., & Love, P. (2011). Alliance contracting: Adding value through relationship development. *Engineering, Construction and Architectural Management, 18*(5), 444–461.

Doherty, B., Haugh, H., & Lyon, F. (2014). Social enterprises as hybrid organizations: A review and research agenda. *International Journal of Management Reviews, 16*(4), 417–436.

Dyer, J. H., & Singh, H. (1998). The relational view: Cooperative strategy and sources of interorganizational competitive advantage. *Academy of Management Review, 23*(4), 660–679.

Ebrahim, A., & Rangan, V. K. (2014). What impact? A framework for measuring the scale and scope of social performance. *California Management Review, 56*(3), 118–141. https://doi.org/10.1525/cmr.2014.56.3.118

Franco, M., & Haase, H. (2013). Firm resources and entrepreneurial orientation as determinants for collaborative entrepreneurship. *Management Decision, 51*(3), 680–696.

Franco, M., & Pessoa, N. (2014). University sports partnerships as collaborative entrepreneurship: An exploratory case study. *Administration & Society, 46*(8), 885–907.

Giddens, A. (1979). *Central problems in social theory* (pp. 49–95). Palgrave.

Golinelli, G. M., Pastore, A., Gatti, M., Massaroni, E., & Vagnani, G. (2011). The firm as a viable system: Managing inter-organisational relationships. *Sinergie Italian Journal of Management, 58*(58), 65–98.

Jabłoński, A. (2016). Scalability of sustainable business models in hybrid organizations. *Sustainability, 8*(3), 194.

McEvily, B., Zaheer, A., & Kamal, D. K. F. (2017). Mutual and exclusive: Dyadic sources of trust in interorganizational exchange. *Organization Science, 28*(1), 74–92.

Mongelli, L., Rullani, F., Ramus, T., & Rimac, T. (2019). The bright side of hybridity: Exploring how social enterprises manage and leverage their hybrid nature. *Journal of Business Ethics, 159*, 301–305.

Montoro-Sánchez, Á., Ortiz-de-Urbina-Criado, M., & Romero-Martínez, A. M. (2009). The decision to use alliances as corporate entrepreneurship: The role of resources and skills. *Group Decision and Negotiation, 18*(5), 431.

Nair, S., & Blomquist, T. (2019). Failure prevention and management in business incubation: Practices towards a scalable business model. *Technology Analysis & Strategic Management, 31*(3), 266–278.

Owoade, A. (2016). *Entrepreneurial ecosystem development: Learning from successes* (Master's thesis). Retrieved from https://www.diva-portal.org/smash/get/diva2:952310/FULLTEXT01.pdf

Roth, B. (2019). Impact investing: A theory of financing social enterprises. In *Harvard business school entrepreneurial management working paper* (p. 20-078). Retrieved from https://www.hbs.edu/faculty/Publication%20Files/20-078_8f45e8dc-fbcf-43d9-90fd-d3a6ba59d4c5.pdf

Teng, B.-S., & Das, T. (2008). Governance structure choice in strategic alliances: The roles of alliance objectives, alliance management experience, and international partners. *Management Decision, 46*(5), 725–742.

Urban, B. (2015). Evaluation of social enterprise outcomes and self-efficacy. *International Journal of Social Economics, 42*(2), 163–178.

Weaver, R. L. (2018). Re-conceptualizing social value: Applying the capability approach in social enterprise research. *Journal of Social Entrepreneurship, 9*(2), 79–93.

Zaheer, A., McEvily, B., & Perrone, V. (1998). Does trust matter? Exploring the effects of inter-organizational and interpersonal trust on performance. *Organization Science, 9*(2), 141–159.

Chapter 9
The Impact of the Study on Academic and Practice

9.1 Introduction

The overall purpose of this study is to explore how organisational compatibility and resource complementarity guide social enterprises and impact investors to establish partners fit in pursuit of social and economic interests in Nigeria. The study also examines how and what micro and macro institutional factors influence collaboration between SEs and IIs in dyadic relationships in Nigeria. This purpose can also be interpreted as exploring how IIs select SEs to establish partners fit for collective or common interest. The findings in Chaps. 5, 6, 7 and 8 have enabled the study to answer the four sub-questions by innovatively integrating the concepts of organisational compatibility from institutional logics and resource complementarity from social exchange theories. These concepts were used to explain how SEs and IIs were guided to establish partner fit to pursue their social and economic interests vis-à-vis the influence of the Nigerian micro- and macro-environmental factors and the perceived learning experience in the process. The overall purpose of this chapter, therefore, is to discuss the main findings in relation to the literature on the partner fit selection process from the dimensions of resource complementarity and organisational compatibility, and the implications of the findings in relation to contribution to theory and practice. Other sections of the chapter provide recommendations, study limitations, research translation, and directions for future study.

The study utilised a qualitative, semi-structured interview based on CR exploration of agency's deeper reality in inter-organisational dyadic business relationships as social constructs governed by structure and institutionalised belief and practice. The primary goal was to explain how hybrid organisations such as SEs and IIs align compatible institutional logics to exchange complementary resources in pursuit of their unique interests across contexts. The learning experience from their collaboration experience in Nigeria, either positive or negative, is believed to shape future exchange relationships between potential partners. Consistent with the study

J. A. Emmanuel et al., *Social Enterprises and Impact Investors*, Advances in Theory and Practice of Emerging Markets,
https://doi.org/10.1007/978-3-031-59454-0_9

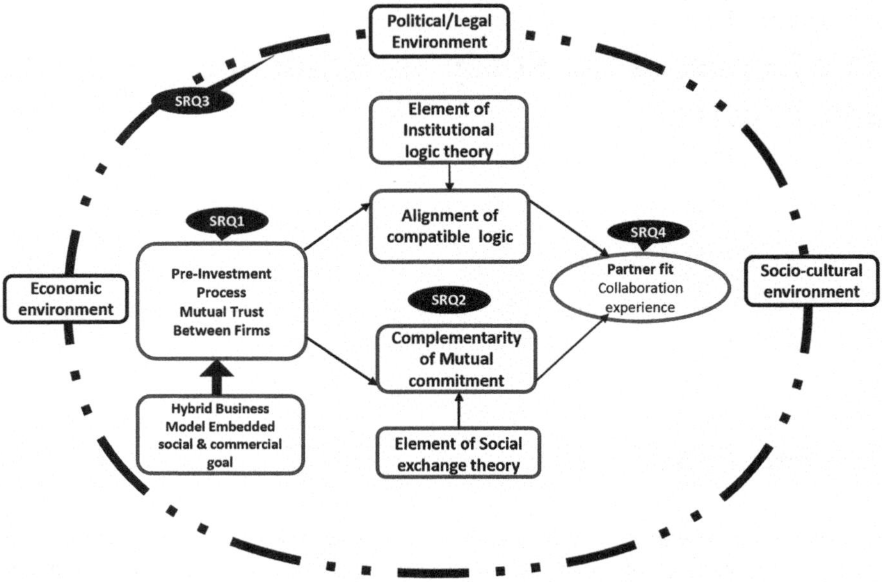

Fig. 9.1 Research framework with key themes

framework in Fig. 9.1 (compare Chap. 3), the discussion of the findings follows the analysis approach according to sub-questions for the study. The improved research framework demonstrates across each sub-question key themes that emerged from using a specific theoretical framework, i.e. the compatibility and complementarity concepts in the analysis.

9.2 SE and II Partner Fit in Pursuit of Common Social and Economic Interests

Sub-question 1 explores how SEs and IIs are guided when selecting partners to collaborate, using the concepts of organisational compatibility and resource complementarity, to pursue their social and economic interests in Nigeria. The objective is to gain deeper knowledge of how they establish partner fit by aligning similar organisational beliefs, practices, and operations, including leveraging different types of resources. It reads: "*In the process of collaboration, how do the SEs and IIs establish partner fit in pursuit of their social and economic interests in Nigeria*?"

Knowledge Extension on Establishing Partner Fit Between SEs and IIs

Drawing insight from the concepts of organisational compatibility and resource complementarity has afforded this study the opportunity to combine insight from institutional logic and social exchange theories to demonstrate how hybrid organisations can align similar logics collaboratively to pursue social and economic interests in Nigeria. Findings on how SEs and IIs align similar organisational missions to pursue common goals fall within literature on institutional logic (Thornton & Ocasio, 2008; Thornton et al., 2012; Zhao & Lounsbury, 2016). According to the findings, the behaviour of SEs and IIs in Nigeria falls within scholarly descriptions of such practices as hybridisation, rooted in the pursuit of competing institutional logics of social and economic interests (Battilana & Dorado, 2010; Pache & Santos, 2013; Reay & Hinings, 2009). All cases investigated in this study incorporated social and economic logic while pursuing common goals.

Contrary to a tendency towards conflicts of interest, which appear inevitable, findings reveal that SEs and IIs can overcome potential conflicting interests through pre-investment collaboration processes that align similarities and differences. This ensures that SEs and IIs determine partners that are compatible and complementary in strengths to establish partner fit. However, the good the intentions of potential partners are, if they cannot establish partner fit with organisations with similar value propositions, collaboration may be impossible or ineffective. Partner fit from the perspective of organisational compatibility in this study shows that aligning similar institutional logics between SEs and IIs is the first requirement for establishing collaboration. The pre-investment practice of aligning similar or compatible logics can create better understanding between SEs and IIs intending to pursue competing social and economic interests. The study has, therefore, empirically demonstrated how SEs and IIs can establish partner fit through alignment of compatible institutional logics, despite organisational differences in beliefs, practice and operations. This approach can potentially guide hybrid organisations towards overcoming conflicting interests and enhancing sustainable relationships when pursuing competing logics.

Knowledge Extension on Partner Selection from Resources Motivation

Findings on how SEs and IIs are guided to combine different types of resources in a way that allows them to achieve mutual and reciprocal social impact with economic returns align with the matching theory of resource complementarity (Mindruta et al., 2016; Vissa, 2011). According to Mitsuhashi and Greve (2009), the logic behind that theory stems from the notion that organisations form alliances with organisations with mutual resources. Mutual resources fit in this context means complementary benefits from resources' contribution to a cause of action. The literature reveals that complementarity between organisations occurs when partners leverage tangible and intangible resources complementarily to jointly create additional value between them (Hamel, 1991; Hamel & Prahalad, 1993). This hinges on the fact that, for a match to occur, "it is not enough that a given organisation needs to obtain a certain resource – an organisation holding that resources must also need something that the given organisation can provide in return" (Mitsuhashi & Greve, 2009: 977). Findings from different types of resources between SEs and IIs in this study situate SEs as organisations that need financial and technical expertise from IIs, while IIs also need SEs with innovative and profitable business models. SEs therefore present themselves as hybrid organisations and fall within the spectrum of for-profit entities: their hybrid nature and structure situate them within the category of for-profit organisations and explain why impact investors collaborate with them, since they can also give something in return for the finances and technical expertise invested in them. They are different from traditional social enterprises that largely fall within the non-profit spectrum configured with an NGO structure. In particular, all SEs in the current study make profits from a viable business model that delivers both social impact and financial return to impact investors.

Findings on resource differences between SEs and IIs described in the matching theory of resource complementarity are situated within social exchange literature. Complementarity in social exchange theory refers to differences between partners' resources in relation to each firm's capabilities (Kale et al., 2000; Sarkar et al., 2001). Partner fit in terms of complementarity is often motivated by the need to leverage resources between exchange parties, based on the perceived benefits to derive from the relationship (Blau, 2017; Homans, 1958; Levine & White, 1961). As revealed in the six cases here, resource leverage occurs when IIs' complementary expertise and financial resources are joined with SEs' financially viable and scalable business models to create additional value for collaborating firms (Mongelli et al., 2019). Hence the study posits that the strength of SEs and IIs lies in the valuable innovative business model versus the financial resources and technical expertise as types of resources that both parties exchange in the relationship. These resources, be they tangible or intangible, have formed the basis of and a solid foundation for a successful collaboration across the cases analysed. The findings have therefore extended knowledge about different types of resources exchanged at the organisational level of inter-firm collaboration. The different types exchanged between these actors have also revealed the level of mutual trust and power balance between them, linked to the level of differences in resource type exchanged. This insight extends knowledge of power relations between hybrid organisations, based on empirical examples, which can be either mutual or asymmetric. The findings contribute to prior debate regarding the level of power balance between SEs and financial contributing partners (Oliver, 1990; Tomlinson et al., 2009), which has remained unclear as to whether this is equal or unequal.

9.3 Organisational Factors That Influence Collaboration and Partner Selection Between SEs and IIs

Sub-question 2, *"At the micro-level, what organisational factors influence collaboration and partner selection between SEs and IIs in Nigeria?"* explores micro-organisation-related factors that influence the collaboration process. The intention was to understand the micro level or organisational factors that enable SEs and IIs to develop mutual trust (Lewis, 2007) before establishing partner fit. At the same time, the analysis took note of factors that negated the opportunity for other SEs to collaborate with IIs. Although the study's focus is on SEs and IIs that have successfully established partner fit, the analysis also found factors that hindered other SEs from establishing partner fit with IIs. These outcomes were not discarded because CR philosophy of retroduction affirms that they embed explanatory power of possible theoretical explanations that may be relevant for future studies (Hu, 2018; Wynn Jr & Williams, 2012).

Knowledge Extension on the Influence of Mutual Trust in Hybrid Dyads

Findings in Chap. 6 provide organisational-level variables explaining factors that influence compatibility and complementarity across the six case organisations. While knowledge on partner selection may not be new in inter-organisational relationships, particularly in mainstream business (Manu, 2014; Ryan & O'Malley, 2006; Solesvik & Encheva, 2010; Thorgren et al., 2012), collaboration knowledge in hybrid organisations like SEs and IIs is still emerging (Mersland et al., 2020). Dominant research draws insight from social exchange theory in exploring inter-organisational relationships based on transactional cost and reward that influence firms' behaviour (Homans, 1958; Montoro-Sánchez et al., 2009; White & Klein, 2008). These insights are valuable, as they guide organisations in making informed decisions on the potential gains from intending partnership. It is also well-established that reciprocal trust plays a major role in inter-organisational relationships involving cost transaction (Blau, 1964; Molm, 2010; Vanneste, 2016). The premise of the theoretical implications for transactions between organisations involving dual motives is missing and needs to be fully understood, because the world is being shaped by social phenomena linked to the failure of mainstream business and not-for-profit entities in addressing the most difficult societal problems. Application of SET in hybrid inter-organisational exchange relationships can bring better insight into managing differing interests from a combination of different types of resources, including power dynamics between actors.

Findings here extend knowledge regarding factors that can influence partner selection in hybrid organisations, rather than purely commercial enterprises, in relation to cost and rewards. The results found mutual and asymmetric trust to be the building blocks for inter-organisational relationships between hybrid organisations like SEs and IIs in Nigeria. The study finds the first level of mutual trust between SEs and IIs in dyad emerging from the alignment of compatible institutional logics. The alignment of similar logics between SEs and IIs develops trust that leads to commitment towards the delivery of collective interest between these organisations. These findings align with the literature definition of mutual trust as an emerging attribute within dyads that enable collaborating partners to come together based on the degree of perception and belief in trusting each other (Bliese et al., 2007): across the six cases, trust patterns emerged from factors linked to genuine intentionality, expectation of return on investment, and due diligence.

The second level of trust emerged from the alignment of complementary resource type that could be tangible or intangible. In some cases, impact investors carried out due diligence to determine tangible resource type owned by social enterprises to build trust: e.g. possession of building and equipment by some SEs was found to be a tangible resource type that motivates IIs to trust SEs. The findings on how mutual trust is built from dyadic examples in this study have shed light on Liden et al.'s (2016) assertions on the critical nature of mutuality for an accurate understanding of dyadic relationships between organisations. Fulfilment of certain conditions by SEs to build trust with IIs also validates Svensson's (2005) assertion that mutual trust in dyadic view will require the fulfilment of specific conditions of trust in business relationship dyad. As demonstrated across the six cases, trust within each dyad was developed by fulfilment of certain conditions measured by aligning organisational compatibility and resource complementarity. That is, two organisations trusted each other based on compatible logics and complementary resource type that they believe to be mutually beneficial. Another interesting discovery from the measure of power balance between inter-organisational dyads in this study is asymmetric trust. Thomas and Skinner (2010) report that trust asymmetry is a common attribute for understanding inter-organisational relationships, but its exploration is lacking. Since asymmetrical trust has been shown to explain power imbalance between dyad partners due to type of resources contributed, it possesses the explanatory power of factors that could lead to relationship failure in hybrid inter-organisational relationships.

Knowledge Extension on Power Balance in Hybrid Organisations

The study draws upon empirical examples of SEs and IIs in dyad to demonstrate a practical understanding of what asymmetric trust in dyadic relationships entails and how it can be ascertained in hybrid arrangements. It responds to studies seeking further knowledge on the level of power imbalance between SEs and IIs under cooperate financial interlocks, characterised by motives of asymmetry, i.e. the exertion of dominance, power and control by one party (Oliver, 1990). Therefore, findings in this study have provided better clarity on asymmetrical trust, which remains a source of debate requiring a better understanding of variables that surround its existence (Korsgaard et al., 2015; Oliver, 1990). The source of debate over the type of relationship between hybrid organisations characterised by social and economic logics has been in the areas of power dominance in relation to type of resource contribution. This study found some variables determining the level of trust and power balance between investors and investees. From SEs' perspective, these variables include possession of viable and scalable business models with financial returns and innovative ideas, including non-financial capital. For IIs, financial resources in the form of equity or debt and technical expertise constitute variables that are used to measure the level of power balance with their investee. It is notable that some dyads in the study shared asymmetrical trust due to uniqueness of resources and wealth of resources both partners bring to the negotiating table.

This research provides valuable insight that shows the trust level between SEs and IIs is not parasitic, as is the case with not-for-profit social enterprises. Empirical evidence across the six cases has shown the share level of trust to be mostly mutual.

Knowledge Confirmation on Factors Influencing Mutual Trust

This research discovered informality was a unique contextual factor that enhanced social enterprise legitimisation in Nigeria. The results confirmed existing knowledge about the role of informality as a form of interaction that leads to the creation of social capital in hybrid organisations (Blau, 1964; Redmond, 2015). According to Huning et al. (2015), informal social relationships as potential sources of capital for organisations can happen through the exchange of valuable information. Indeed, this study shows that informal arrangements have become a vital avenue for sourcing finance, particularly in the emerging field of hybrid arrangements. For example, several SEs described how their relationships began in informal settings with leaders of different impact investing organisations but ended in fruitful partnerships. This result confirmed Huning et al.'s (2015: 23) argument that "informal social relationships have potential to create social capital for the individual as well as the organisation via exchange of information and communication". In the current study, Case 2 revealed having received an email through informal arrangements, which eventually led to conversation that established partner fit between them.

The findings also confirmed related studies on the role of a firm's reputation in building trust, legitimacy, and social capital (Carroll & Carroll, 2013; Carter et al., 2002; Preston, 2004). The results show organisational-level factors that enhanced collaboration with IIs and, by extension, access to financial resources were rooted in SEs reputation. Reputation among SEs that inspired trust validates impact investing strategy as deeply rooted in ethical approaches as a source of firms' legitimisation. This outcome counters the tendency to develop a sense of isomorphism in order to gain legitimacy (Beckert, 2010). Reputation is what organisations earn from their activities as endorsed by their societies and their records of accomplishment. In Nigeria, adherence to reputation has been proven to be a source of credibility in the process of legitimisation of SEs, where stiff competition always results in corrupt practices in order to access limited impact funds.

9.4 Key Factors Enabling or Constraining Establishment of Partner Fit Between SEs and IIs

Sub-question 3, *"How does the Nigerian macro environment influence collaboration between SEs and IIs, and what factors enable or constrain the establishment of partner fit between them?"*, focused on the influence of Nigeria's macro environment in the collaboration process between SEs and IIs and sought to understand what and how contextual factors influence social entrepreneurship in emerging economies. The motive for examining Nigeria's macro environment hinges on the fact that social entrepreneurship is a context-driven phenomenon: it means different things to people across regions (Agafonow, 2015; British Council, 2016; Defourny et al., 2011; Griffiths et al., 2013). Therefore, it is necessary to explore how the Nigerian context perceived social entrepreneurship and what factors enabled or disenabled the collaboration process between SEs and IIs.

Knowledge Confirmation on Contextual Influence on Social Enterprise

This study finds the influence of the external environment to SEs' and IIs' collaboration across socio-cultural, economic and political/legal factors. Findings across these three factors from the experience of SEs and IIs in dyad confirm that Nigerian economic environment has remained attractive for motivating the flow of impact capital across West Africa. They confirm studies positing that population size and market opportunities are key drivers of impact investing in emerging markets (Carmody et al., 2011; Cetindamar & Kozanoglu, 2014; Liu, 2012; Santi & Sennett, 2016). This also underpins the allocation of impact funds to West Africa and Nigeria taking the largest investment opportunities.

Findings regarding disenabling economic factors show this is the least disenabling factor preventing investors from investing in Nigeria. Variables linked to the disenabling nature of the economic environment include instability in exchange rates, the small size of Nigeria's social enterprises, and economic instability. The variables aligned with Mersland et al.'s (2020) argument that, although impact investors are interested in context with institutional voids, they will avoid context with high-risk factors that could result in shortfall of expected financial returns. Despite the fact that investment opportunities with promising social impact and financial returns exist in Nigeria, some investors will not take risks that will result in financial losses.

This study also confirms knowledge in relation to disenabling political context of collaboration. The presence of institutional void in Nigeria was the greatest setback for the development of social entrepreneurship. Variables that linked the political and legal environment also revealed examples of disenabling factors (see Chap. 7). While political and legal institutional void acts as a constraint to having investable social enterprises, that void also serves as an opportunity for private capital to deal with difficult social problems with a business mindset. The biggest contentions likely to arise from the absence of institutional support include poor regulatory practices, lack of investment support for start-ups, insecurity, poor infrastructure and corruption. Similarly, Kareem et al. (2020: 498) link "poor or absence of infrastructure, unstable power supply, corruption and insufficient capital, poor managerial experience, high level of illiteracy, lack of relevant skills, and motivation of owner/managers", as challenges bedevilling small businesses in Nigeria.

From these factors, this study extends knowledge by demonstrating the negative effect of institutional void. Some cases revealed that institutional void has also led to brain drain, where intelligent Nigerians move overseas because of lack of home support. Several businesses that could have been established in the Nigerian soil have been established overseas, because Nigerian social entrepreneurs want to thrive in an environment where innovations and skills are well appreciated and adequately remunerated.

Findings on social environment factors also show that social entrepreneurship is still in its infancy specifically due to lack of awareness regarding the benefits of impact investing compared to traditional funding sources—banks and overseas development assistance. This aligns with Ademola et al.'s (2019) research, which shows impact investing as an innovative option for financing social enterprises remains underdeveloped. Yet the study here also extends knowledge which shows the level of awareness regarding impact investing is not widespread across Nigeria. As shown in Chap. 4, the demographics of most SEs and IIs interviewed revealed they operated mainly in Lagos State, compared with the 35 other states. A lack of spread of the hybrid entrepreneurial concept hinges upon concentration of business and economic activities in urban cities, which also underpins uneven development in Nigeria.

This study extends knowledge about some embedded socio-cultural beliefs and practices in Nigeria that can positively and negatively affect the development of social entrepreneurship. On the positive side, Nigeria is a highly religious country, endowed with passionate entrepreneurs willing to sacrifice personal interest in pursuit of social and economic advantageous causes for societal benefit, as evidenced under socio-cultural enabling factors (Chap. 7), where Case 2 adverted to the existence of a highly enterprising young population in Nigeria. This with Thorgren and Omorede (2018), who highlighted how Nigeria's enabling socio-cultural environment is characterised by passionate, entrepreneurial leaders. On the negative side, this study found adherence to religious practices does not favour some healthcare-related enterprises. Evidence from Case 5 shows that many customers opted to go to prayer houses to get healing due to their poor economic status for affording innovative healthcare drugs. This aligns with Kareem et al.'s (2020) empirical work that revealed spirituality as one of the factors that can affect small-scale enterprise development.

On political and legal environmental factors, perceptions across the six cases revealed the absence of a legal framework that provides formal regulatory guidelines for hybrid social enterprise operations. This finding aligns with existing studies across emerging countries where non-existence of specific legal frameworks for social enterprise underpins the prevalence of institutional void (Mair & Marti, 2009; Mersland et al., 2020; Stephan et al., 2015). Developed countries such as the United Kingdom, the US, Italy, South Korea and recently France have put in place legal arrangements suitable for the operation of hybrid social enterprises (Battilana, 2018; Triponel & Agapitova, 2017). Despite this institutional setback, this study found some measures have been put in place to create an enabling environment for private organisations in Nigeria. Examples of these measures include increased capital bases for microfinance institutions and low-lending risk that is meant to reduce corruption tendencies. Unfortunately, variables linked to political factors also show that Nigeria's political and legal environment has influenced collaboration between SEs and IIs negatively.

9.5 Perceived Learning Experience from Collaboration and Partner Selection

Sub-question 4 was *"What is the perceived learning experience from the collaboration and partner selection between SEs and IIs with dyadic relations in Nigeria?"*. This focused on understanding the perceived outcome of the collaboration process and the learning experience to ascertain the role of mutual trust in collaboration. Understanding the learning experience from the collaboration process is essential for developing the social entrepreneurial ecosystem in Nigeria. The learning experience can also be replicated across other emerging economy contexts, whether in Africa or elsewhere. Based on the learning experience across the six cases, it is anticipated that some insight could have emerged capable of extending, developing, challenging or confirming existing knowledge in the collaboration literature of social entrepreneurship. The next section discusses the contribution of findings regarding the experience of the six cases.

New Knowledge on the Role of Mutual Trust in Hybrid Tension

The study provides new knowledge regarding the role of mutual trust on sustainability and performance between SEs and IIs. Findings regarding the learning experience from the collaboration experience revealed collaboration was predicated on the strength of business model viability and scalability. Narratives affirmed that collaboration with SEs in pursuit of social and financial returns resulted in achieving the set objectives for the partnership. These achievements were possible because of mutual trust between dyadic partners. The achievements have, therefore, set hybrid SEs apart from not-for-profit SEs, and they also challenge existing framing of their partnership with IIs as dominantly asymmetrical in nature, i.e., characterised by power imbalance in terms of the type of resources contributed to the relationship (Oliver, 1990). As Chap. 8 shows, learning outcomes on sustainability across SEs validate the expectation of some scholars who would rather see different types of SEs seeking support through impact investing funds compared to absolute dependence on grants and donations (Agrawal, 2018; Brown et al., 2019; Bugg-Levine & Emerson, 2011; Roth, 2019; Roundy et al., 2017). These findings challenge existing debate about the question of what type of resources set SEs apart in terms of the defining lines of power balance between them and their investors.

Another area in which the findings extend knowledge is in the list of variables that define SEs' sustainable status. Analysis between SEs and IIs in Chap. 8 demonstrated how provision of technical support and financial investment enhanced SEs' performance. On the other hand, performance of SEs which occurred through provision of finance and technical support met the expectations of impact investors in terms of meeting the latter's social and financial expectations. It is paramount to note the performance of SEs had been earlier predicated by IIs on the viability and scalability of the business model through a due diligence process that assessed the legitimacy of SEs in the social impact space, past experience, the management team, the level of innovative ideas and assets owned. These variables were discussed in Chap. 5 from the perspective of organisational compatibility and resource complementarity as a prior measure for determining the social impact and financial viability of SEs. The level of satisfaction from IIs' perspective is indicative that a satisfactory level of balance in their goals has been achieved. Evidence across the six dyadic cases regarding learning experience generated more positive outcomes than negative outcomes, which was attributed to the role of mutual trust in the process. As revealed in Chap. 8, some of the learning experience include social impact and financial returns, future collaboration potential, improved model from managerial and technical support, improved learning with innovation, and scalability.

This learning experience now challenges existing literature, which envisages tension between hybrid organisations coming together to pursue similar goals with different interests (Gillett et al., 2019; Mitzinneck & Besharov, 2019; Mogapi et al., 2019; Ozanne et al., 2016; Smith et al., 2013). Through empirical examples, this study demonstrates how SEs and IIs can achieve tension-free collaboration, challenging dominant research on tensions between them. The findings have also addressed the study gap in scholarship which shows insufficient attention to managing relationships in hybrid organisations with external stakeholders that comprise funders, intermediaries, and governmental institutions (Battilana, 2018; McMullen & Warnick, 2016; York et al., 2016). This study focused on the pre-investment process of engagement between SEs and IIs, but believes further research is needed to examine the outcome of dyadic relations between SEs and IIs in the period of contractual agreement.

9.6 The Key Insights from the Research Findings

Chapter 1 outlined the aim of this research: to explore how SEs and IIs to establish partner fit to pursue their social and economic interests in Nigeria. The study focuses on how SEs and IIs are guided to determine their compatibility in organisational logic and type of complementary resources before establishing partner fit for collective goals. The study also examined the influence of organisational level (micro) and the Nigeria's macro environmental factors in the process. It demonstrates that activities between SEs and IIs are a well-established model recognised as legitimate hybrid organisations but with potential risks (Battilana, 2018). This underpins why the hybrid organising process currently faces many contradictions in its creation of partnerships because partners have to deal with institutionalised complexity for managing different logics and identity to gain acceptance. It has also been established that, in order to gain sustainability, SEs need to effectively combine and balance different practices, structures, values, beliefs and objectives connected with dual logics that are beneficial for social and commercial outcomes (Battilana, 2018; Battilana & Lee, 2014).

First, this study identified collaboration activities between SEs and IIs as agency action, which comes from intentional and unintentional drives to create social change through unconventional approaches. It demonstrates in Chap. 5 that IIs are intentional about social impact and economic outcome and are classified as impact-first investors. There are also investors who do not have a deliberate intention for social impact but are making an impact. This category of investors has been classified as financial-first investors. For example, Case 2 exemplifies financial-first impact investors in this study.

This research has also demonstrated how hybrid organisations establish partner fit to pursue collective interests, drawing insight from the concept of organisational compatibility and resource complementarity (Mitsuhashi & Greve, 2009). From the concept of organisational compatibility in partner fit literature (Dhurkari & Nandakumar, 2015; Manotungvorapun & Gerdsri, 2016), the study draws insight from an institutional logics perspective to gain understanding of how social and commercial logic can be combined by SEs and IIs to achieve their interests in Nigeria. By definition, institutional logics connect agency action and cognition with systems that are socially constructed, referred to as institutionalised practice and rules (Reay & Hinings, 2009; Thornton, 2015). Studies have revealed that hybrid organisations pursuing competing logics to meet social welfare and commercial goals often face severe difficulties in balancing the tensions created at the strategic level of the organisation (Bruneel et al., 2016; Davies & Chambers, 2018). In response to this dilemma, this study demonstrated in the six cases how SEs and IIs established partner fit through a process of aligning compatible logics that comprises organisational values, mission, beliefs and practice. It is therefore argued that, by establishing partner fit through deliberate alignment of compatible institutionalised practices between intending partners, potential conflict that may arise from competing or conflicting institutional logics can be overcome.

Similarly, from the concept of resource complementarity in partner fit literature, the study draws insight from literature on dyadic inter-organisational exchange relationships (Di Domenico et al., 2009; Larson, 1992; McEvily et al., 2017) to understand how SEs and IIs combine different types of resources to pursue their social and commercial interests. It was notable that a social enterprise as an innovative and emergent hybrid organisation often struggles to access the resources needed to accomplish its intentions (Di Domenico et al., 2010). IIs have emerged as organisations with financial resources and technical expertise seeking to invest in an organisation that can generate social impact with financial return on investment (Bugg-Levine & Goldstein, 2009; Martin & Lohin, 2017). Partnership between SEs and IIs is believed to help them achieve the financial resources needed to pursue their objectives, while also generating financial returns to their investors in a sustainable manner (Cohen, 2011). For these two organisations to achieve their unique goals, Di Domenico et al. (2009) have proposed collaboration objectives between them will require alignment of organisational objectives and contribution is to be valued by each partner. However, due to the nascency of literature on SE and II collaboration, some scholars have raised questions about the type of resources and capability needed to determine exchange value in such partnerships, and the influence on power dynamics (Clark, 2015; Doherty et al., 2014). The study has produced findings addressing these gaps.

From the six cases, this research has laid the foundation for examining the types of resources determining exchange value between SEs and IIs, and how the value of such resources can be used to ascertain the influence of different power dynamics between them. The premise in which this study examines types of resources exchange between SEs and IIs stems from Husted's (2003) assertion of hybrid SEs as unique types of organisations operating with a business mindset and capable of contributing commercial value to their business partners in a manner that ensures long-term progress and sustainability. Evidence abounds on how SEs in the US, the United Kingdom and other regions have demonstrated financial sustainability with profitability (Bhattarai et al., 2019; Briar-Lawson et al., 2020; Ryan & Lyne, 2008; Young, 2001). Through the six cases here, this study provides further evidence of the valuable type of resources exchanged between SEs and IIs in Nigeria, as Clark (2015) suggested.

Figure 9.2 illustrates the main findings of this study, showing how SEs and IIs establish partner fit through alignment of compatible institutionalised logic, that began with mutual trust between firms in social network, motivated by

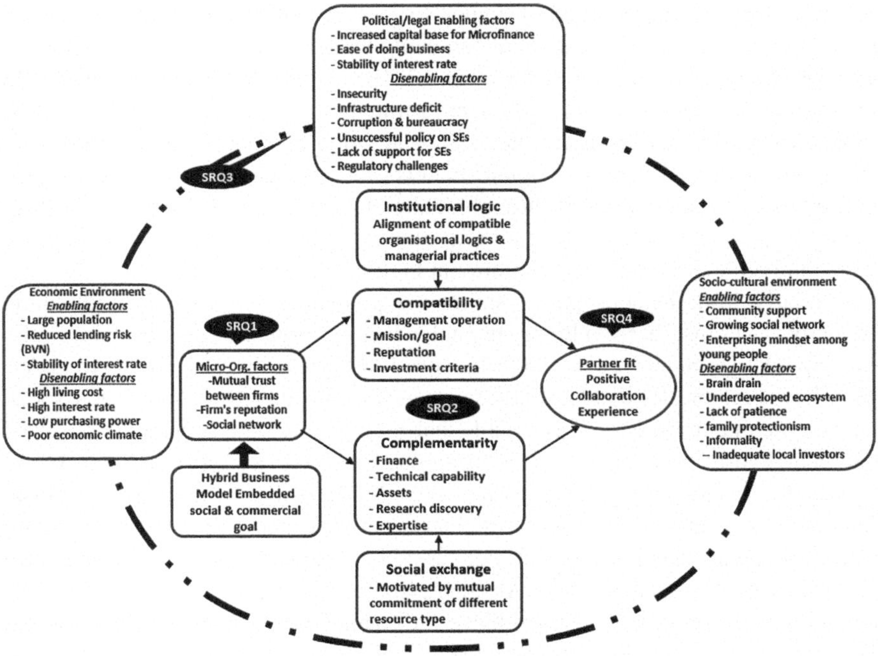

Fig. 9.2 Research framework with summary of findings

complementary resource type between actors to gain partner fit. The study also finds that the process has also been influenced by the micro-organisational level and macro-environmental factors in Nigeria. At the micro- organisational level, the study demonstrates factors that influence mutual trust between SEs and IIs, including social network and firm reputation, to achieve compatibility and complementarity as a guide for partner fit. As demonstrated in Chap. 6, several factors also impede finding investable social enterprises, such as poor financial records, lack of awareness of impact capital fund, underdeveloped ideas, etc. These factors are not discussed in detail here, as they do not constitute the key area of focus in this study. They do, however, form the basis for further research seeking to know why only a few SEs collaborate with IIs in Nigeria, despite opportunities offered. From the Nigerian macro environment, the study also demonstrates several context-specific variables that both enable and constrain the collaboration process between SEs and IIs, and are linked to political, economic and socio-cultural factors, as shown in Fig. 9.2.

Collaboration experience across the six cases judged to be sustainable demonstrates the role of mutual trust and validates the outcome of the collaboration process, underpinned by alignment of compatibility organisational logics, and motivated by mutual commitment of different types of complementary resources. The overwhelming interest to connect with more SEs in Nigeria by IIs in the findings in Chap. 8 affirm the attainment of their investment goals across social impact and financial returns. Results of the collaboration experience between SEs and IIs from micro and macro perspectives validate existing studies showing how SE funding and creation can be influenced by factors related to both the macro environment and characteristics of the enterprises (Battilana, 2018; Fauchart & Gruber, 2011; Pache & Santos, 2013; Powell & Sandholtz, 2012).

9.7 Research Implications and Contributions to Theory and Practice

The main research findings make a number of theoretical contributions to collaborative hybrid entrepreneurial, institutional logic and social exchange theories, and the practice of social enterprise and impact investing. The study implications are further discussed below.

Matching Theory of Inter-organisational Collaboration

Scholars have acknowledged that collaborative entrepreneurship has been fundamentality shaped by the institutionalised rules, practices and resources in the field of dyadic relationships (Oliver, 1990; Phillips et al., 2000; Ryan & O'Malley, 2006). Dominant studies on collaborative social entrepreneurship have focused on the tensions that arise from combining conflicting logics to achieve common goals (Bruneel et al., 2016; Pache & Santos, 2013; Reay & Hinings, 2009). A few have examined the decision-making process involved in the collaboration between social enterprise and its business partners (Clark, 2015; Di Domenico et al., 2009; Huybrechts & Nicholls, 2013). These latter studies found the commercial competencies of social enterprises can enhance their exchange value and balance the power dynamic between partners (Agrawal & Hockerts, 2019; Clark, 2015). This study advances such limited studies that examine how SEs and IIs align their organisational interests and resources in a manner that demonstrates types of complementary resources and compatible logics determining the power dynamics between them (Oliver, 1990; Woldesenbet Beta & Storey, 2019; Yunxia et al., 2016). Applying the matching theories of compatibility and complementarity will guide SEs and IIs in establishing partnership with minimal tension, paramount for managing sustainability to achieve their set targets. Findings in this study have taken the first step to providing a novel insight explaining how SEs and IIs establish partner fit to pursue social and economic interests (Clark, 2015). The study achieved this objective by integrating knowledge from institutional logics and social exchange theories in line with research direction in providing novel insights in management (Mayer & Sparrowe, 2013). The novel insight of the research hinges on integrating interdisciplinary theories to explain how SEs and IIs establish partner fit despite institutionalised complexity to exchange different type of resources relevant for social and economic outcomes.

The first implication of this study relates to challenging existing knowledge about collaboration between hybrid organisations, often characterised by potential conflict and power dominance by one party (Saz-Carranza & Longo, 2012). Across the six cases, it is evident that establishing partner fit by alignment of compatible organisational logics, motivated by complementary resource type, serves as checks and balances that can avert potential conflict. This finding also validates similar discovery from Clark (2015: 210): "…SE-Business partnerships have the potential to involve balanced arrangements characterised by reciprocated resources contributions, trust, and the creation of shared value".

The second implication of collaborative social entrepreneurship provides novel insight into the process of ascertaining the value and type of resources being exchanged in the partnership to determine the power dynamic between SEs and IIs. Findings in Chap. 6 demonstrate the level of power balance between SEs and IIs through the illustration of how compatible organisational logics and resource complementarity shaped mutual trust between SEs and IIs. It is notable that not all dyads had balanced or mutual trust; some trust levels were asymmetrical. The finding in this regard responds to Clark's (2015) proposed need for studies that could determine exchange value between a social enterprise and its business partner. It is not surprising that the finding of this study falls within the prediction of Clark (2015), who noted that achieving a power dynamic between SEs and their business partners may be influenced by the nature of partnerships established and resources exchange value of social enterprise. As discovered in this study, establishing partner fit between SEs and IIs in Nigeria has been guided and determined by measuring organisational compatibility and the type of complementary resources each partner possesses. This approach has also helped in determining the nature of partnership in terms of power dynamic, and types of resources exchanged between actors. The differences in power dynamic across mutual and asymmetrical resources were determined by types of resources, and the level of trust each partner brought to the relationship. For example, in Chap. 6, of the six cases four had partnerships that were mutual, meaning the same level of trust, while two were asymmetrical, characterised by imbalance. The differences in terms of power dynamic in the partnership were determined by the value and level of trust linked to both tangible and intangible resources each partner brought to the relationship.

Integrating Institutional Logic and Social Exchange Theory

Combining sociological and psychological theories to examine collaborative entrepreneurship in hybrid organisations is not a coincidental approach. Just as SEs and IIs need to collaborate to address the world's most difficult problems, Mayer and Sparrowe (2013) argue that scholars may need to draw insight from different theories to address what neither theory can independently address. Combining institutional logic and social exchange theory in this study has responded to critiques of their being deterministic, unable to delineate between organisational relationships with the influence of the environment (Johnson Jr, 1995; Vincent, 2008). This accounts for why organisations are forced to engage in exchange relations with other organisations in their environment. This study has demonstrated that social exchange and institutional logic can mutually fill this gap, because each holds promise to inform the other. As institutional logic fills a theoretical gap regarding the influence of values, practice and cultural context on exchange behaviour of organisations, social exchange theory can help better specify the process and mechanisms through which patterns of social collaboration can shape and reproduce organisational identities and practices constitutive of institutional logic (Pirkey, 2016). This study has demonstrated the applicability of this assertion through empirical evidence on how SEs and IIs in Nigeria are guided to align compatible institutional logic and complementary resource type needed to pursue their collective interest. The study also has extended knowledge in terms of type of resources exchanged at the organisational level against the individualistic context of exchange (Di Domenico et al., 2009; Hald, 2005; Van de Ven, 1976; Zeitz, 1980). For example, the study demonstrates the exchange of both tangible and intangible resources between SEs and IIs.

Similarly, across several studies, the institutional logic perspective has provided the framework for understanding overarching principles, rules and practices that determine how organisations understand their realities, shape behaviour, and are influenced by the sociocultural, political and economic environment (Thornton & Ocasio, 1999; Urban, 2013). This study has demonstrated empirical findings on institutionalised complexity factors that impede or enable social entrepreneurial processes in an emerging country context, challenging dominant academic focus on the US, the United Kingdom and Europe. This insight has now extended knowledge on the micro- and macro-institutional determinants of SEs' and IIs' collaboration, bringing the disparate voices of emerging markets into the social entrepreneurship discourse, as scholars suggest (George et al., 2016; Greenwood et al., 2011). These findings also validate the agency effect on social structure from an emerging country context and demonstrates CR philosophy's appropriateness in explaining the social entrepreneurial process from both institutional and social exchange perspectives (Leca & Naccache, 2006; Vincent, 2008). Combining social exchange and institutional theory in this study has also responded to the call for the juxtaposition of institutional theory with other theories (Bamberger, 2008; Mayer & Sparrowe, 2013; Oliver, 1997). The approach has also met the demand for greater insight into social movements that create institutional change embedded in agency action, as demonstrated in SEs' and IIs' collaboration experience.

The emergence of impact investing in the wake of the 2008 global financial crisis redefined the social enterprise structure from not-for-profits to hybrid organisations. Among the various sources of funding for social enterprises, impact investing stood out over the years as a more sustainable approach for funding social enterprises across developed and emerging markets. Unfortunately, in emerging economies and some developed countries, there is still lack of knowledge about how SEs and IIs establish partner fit to pursue social and economic interests (Cetindamar & Kozanoglu, 2014; Diouf, 2015; Donnelly & Wynn-Jones, 2017). Knowledge of how social business relationships develop between hybrid organisations such as investors and investees will benefit several social enterprises currently operating as not-for-profit entities due to a lack of knowledge on how to establish partner fit with impact investors.

As demonstrated in Chap. 5, this study provides practical knowledge beneficial to organisations desiring to collaborate with impact investors on the process involved. Understanding how compatible organisational logics result in mission alignment will guide potential SEs to direct their strengths in modelling a hybrid organisational structure capable of attracting potential investors' interest. Impact investors can also draw on knowledge of hybrid organisational experience to guide the structuring of their investment portfolio in a manner that could benefit social enterprises operating in an emerging country. Understanding the type of complementary resources possessed by each actor will guide both SEs and IIs in determining the level of power dynamic in terms of the value of resources being exchanged between them. It is important to note the value of resources contributed to establishing partner fit is not a hard fit rule but depends on the intended outcome of such a partnership. Collaboration built on financial impact first will be different from collaboration coming from social impact-first investors. This study has laid a foundational knowledge required for a sustainable collaboration between SEs and IIs accessible to any single SEs or IIs for use as a model.

9.8 Limitations and Directions for Future Study

Despite the key findings and insights presented in the previous chapters, this study has a number of limitations. Firstly, while it uses dyadic data, it could only carry out individual interviews where the SEs and IIs in the dyads were interviewed separately. Conducting dyadic interviews in the future research that bring two participants together for conversation in one meeting can stimulate ideas that might not have been recognised or recalled through individual interviews (Morgan et al., 2013, 2016). Dyadic interviews will also provide the opportunity for wider and in-depth social interaction with the researcher according to CR philosophy (Aastrup, 2000; Fleetwood & Ackroyd, 2004; Leca & Naccache, 2006).

Secondly, the study has also been limited by the difficulty in finding social enterprises with dyadic relations in Nigeria, due to the nascency of the phenomenon in an emerging country. Future study should consider dyadic interviews in a context where impact investing has reached an advanced stage, such as in developed economies like the United States, Europe, United Kingdom, and some Asian countries.

Finally, this study has also opened several avenues to make cross-disciplinary theoretical contributions to the social entrepreneurship literature, as demonstrated by the integration of institutional logics and social exchange theories. More studies are needed to demonstrate the applicability of the concepts of compatibility and complementarity across other contexts, developed economies in particular, where social enterprise and impact investing have reached an advanced stage. This will further provide empirical evidence of the synergy between social exchange and institutional theories, as Pirkey (2016) has argued, given the potential synergy in their use in management studies.

9.9 The Innovation of Study Translation

Research in social enterprise and impact investing constitutes a timely innovative field of studies, with several opportunities to effect positive impact on industry practice. This study has been tested and proven through the principal author's engagement with the industry. The translation of this study to practice followed a process of innovation involving three stages: "…leveraging knowledge to generate ideas (idea creation), communicating about the adequacy of novel ideas to the top management based on firm's strategic goals (idea translation), and making innovative products and processes a reality (idea implementation)" (Rodriguez-Montemayor, 2013: 329). Innovative ideas from this study were presented at conferences: the 7th Annual International Conference for Sustainable Development (ICSD), New York, the 16th International Conference on Business Management (ICBM), British Academy of Management Conference (BAM), etc. Ideas from this study led to the development of a social business model that competitively won a team start-up grant awarded by Monash Sustainable Development Institute (MSDI). The recipient of the grant jointly co-founded a start-up social enterprise in Melbourne, Australia, in 2018, by name "ONE LOVE AUTRALIA".

9.10 Conclusion

This book has explored the emergence of social enterprise and impact investing as examples of hybrid organisations operating at the crossroads between social and commercial logics. These two organisations hold enormous potential for transforming how difficult societal challenges are addressed in both developed and emerging economies. The study integrates institutional logic and social exchange theories to demonstrate how SEs and IIs in Nigeria align compatible logics and complementary types of resources to establish partner fit. These theories make cross-disciplinary contributions by providing empirical evidence on how hybrid organisations can collaboratively work together through pre-investment strategies that address source of potential tension.

References

Aastrup, J. (2000). *Change in networks-A critical realist interpretation* (Paper presentation). The 16th Industrial Marketing and Purchasing (IMP) Conference, Copenhagen. Retrieved from https://www.impgroup.org/?show=all

Ademola, A. H., Olajide, O. P., Ayodele, A. Y., & Olusola, A. J. (2019). An examination of financing practices of social entrepreneurs in Nigeria: A study of selected non-governmental organisations. *Academy of Entrepreneurship Journal, 25*(2), 1–17.

Agafonow, A. (2015). Value creation, value capture, and value devolution: Where do social enterprises stand? *Administration & Society, 47*(8), 1038–1060.

Agrawal, A. (2018). Impact investing: Framework and future research avenues. *Social Business, 8*(3), 293–317.

Agrawal, A., & Hockerts, K. (2019). Impact investing strategy: Managing conflicts between impact investor and investee social enterprise. *Sustainability, 11*(15), 4117.

Bamberger, P. (2008). From the editors beyond contextualization: Using context theories to narrow the micro-macro gap in management research. *Academy of Management, 51*(5), 839–846.

Battilana, J. (2018). Cracking the organizational challenge of pursuing joint social and financial goals: Social enterprise as a laboratory to understand hybrid organizing. *Management, 21*(4), 1278–1305.

Battilana, J., & Dorado, S. (2010). Building sustainable hybrid organizations: The case of commercial microfinance organizations. *Academy of Management Journal, 53*(6), 1419–1440.

Battilana, J., & Lee, M. (2014). Advancing research on hybrid organizing–Insights from the study of social enterprises. *The Academy of Management Annals, 8*(1), 397–441.

Beckert, J. (2010). Institutional isomorphism revisited: Convergence and divergence in institutional change. *Sociological Theory, 28*(2), 150–166.

Bhattarai, C. R., Kwong, C. C., & Tasavori, M. (2019). Market orientation, market disruptiveness capability and social enterprise performance: An empirical study from the United Kingdom. *Journal of Business Research, 96*, 47–60.

Blau, P. M. (1964). *Exchange and power in social life*. Transaction Publishers.

Blau, P. (2017). *Exchange and power in social life*. Routledge.

Bliese, P. D., Chan, D., & Ployhart, R. E. (2007). Multilevel methods: Future directions in measurement, longitudinal analyses, and nonnormal outcomes. *Organizational Research Methods, 10*(4), 551–563.

British Council. (2016). *Social enterprise in a global context: The role of higher education institutions insight with Playmouth University*, Country Brief, California.

Briar-Lawson, K., Miesing, P., & Ramos, B. M. (2020). Social Entrepreneurship and Enterprises in Economic and Social Development: *USA: Oxford University Press*.

Brown, K., Wood, D., & Paetzold, F. (2019). *Impact investing for the next generation: Insights from young members of investor and business families*. World Economic Forum. Retrieved from http://www3.weforum.org/docs/WEF_Impact_Investing_for_the_Next_Generation.pdf

Bruneel, J., Moray, N., Stevens, R., & Fassin, Y. (2016). Balancing competing logics in for-profit social enterprises: A need for hybrid governance. *Journal of Social Entrepreneurship, 7*(3), 263–288.

Bugg-Levine, A., & Emerson, J. (2011). Impact investing: Transforming how we make money while making a difference. *Innovations, 6*(3), 9–18.

Bugg-Levine, A., & Goldstein, J. (2009). Impact investing: Harnessing capital markets to solve problems at scale. *Community Development Investment Review, 2*, 30–41.

Carmody, L., McCarron, B., Blinch, J., Prevatt, A., & Arosio, M. (2011). *Impact investing in emerging markets*. Responsible Research. Retrieved from https://thegiin.org/research/publication/impact-investing-in-emerging-markets

Carroll, C. E., & Carroll, C. E. (2013). *The handbook of communication and corporate reputation*. John Wiley & Sons, Incorporated.

Carter, J., Bitting, E., & Ghorbani, A. A. (2002). Reputation formalization for an information–sharing multi–agent system. *Computational Intelligence, 18*(4), 515–534.

Cetindamar, D., & Kozanoglu, H. (2014). *Fostering impact investment in developing countries.* Paper presented at the Proceedings of PICMET'14 Conference: Portland International Center for Management of Engineering and Technology; Infrastructure and Service Integration, Portland.

Clark, S. (2015). *Social enterprise-business partnerships: Exploring the influence of institutional logics upon social enterprise partnership experiences and decision-making* (Doctoral dissertation). Retrieved from https://eprints.utas.edu.au/23155/1/Clark_whole_thesis.pdf

Cohen, R. (2011). *Harnessing social entrepreneurship and investment to bridge the social divide.* Paper presented at the EU conference on the social economy.

Davies, I. A., & Chambers, L. (2018). Integrating hybridity and business model theory in sustainable entrepreneurship. *Journal of Cleaner Production, 177*, 378–386.

Defourny, J., Kuan, Y. Y., & Kim, S. Y. (2011). Emerging models of social enterprise in Eastern Asia: A cross-country analysis. *Social Enterprise Journal, 7*(1), 86–111.

Dhurkari, R. K., & Nandakumar, M. (2015). Measures of complementarity and compatibility in strategic alliances for innovation: A review of literature. *The International Technology Management Review, 5*(4), 182–201.

Di Domenico, M., Tracey, P., & Haugh, H. (2009). The dialectic of social exchange: Theorizing corporate—Social enterprise collaboration. *Organization Studies, 30*(8), 887–907.

Di Domenico, M., Haugh, H., & Tracey, P. (2010). Social bricolage: Theorizing social value creation in social enterprises. *Entrepreneurship Theory and Practice, 34*(4), 681–703.

Diouf, D. (2015). Exploring the barriers to impact investing in the sustainable energy area in West Africa. In *Decentralized solutions for developing economies* (pp. 177–183). Springer.

Doherty, B., Haugh, H., & Lyon, F. (2014). Social enterprises as hybrid organizations: A review and research agenda. *International Journal of Management Reviews, 16*(4), 417–436.

Donnelly, F., & Wynn-Jones, S. (2017). *Impact investing – What does it mean for Hong Kong?* Retrieved from https://thepurposebusiness.com/impact-investing-what-does-it-mean-for-hong-kong/

Fauchart, E., & Gruber, M. (2011). Darwinians, communitarians, and missionaries: The role of founder identity in entrepreneurship. *Academy of Management Journal, 54*(5), 935–957.

Fleetwood, S., & Ackroyd, S. (2004). *Critical realist applications in organisation and management studies* (1st ed.). Routledge.

George, G., Corbishley, C., Khayesi, J. N., Haas, M. R., & Tihanyi, L. (2016). Bringing Africa in: Promising directions for management research. *Academy of Management Journal, 59*(2), 377–393.

Gillett, A., Loader, K., Doherty, B., & Scott, J. M. (2019). An examination of tensions in a hybrid collaboration: A longitudinal study of an empty homes project. *Journal of Business Ethics, 157*(4), 949–967.

Greenwood, R., Raynard, M., Kodeih, F., Micelotta, E. R., & Lounsbury, M. (2011). Institutional complexity and organizational responses. *Academy of Management Annals, 5*(1), 317–371.

Griffiths, M. D., Gundry, L. K., & Kickul, J. R. (2013). The socio-political, economic, and cultural determinants of social entrepreneurship activity: An empirical examination. *Journal of Small Business and Enterprise Development, 20*(2), 341–357.

Hald, K. S. (2005). *Managing inter-organizational relationships: Using the force of partner attraction.* Copenhagen Business School. Retrieved from https://research-api.cbs.dk/ws/portalfiles/portal/58880103/4.pdf

Hamel, G. (1991). Competition for competence and interpartner learning within international strategic alliances. *Strategic Management Journal, 12*(S1), 83–103.

Hamel, G., & Prahalad, C. K. (1993). Strategy as stretch and leverage. *Harvard Business Review, 71*(2), 75–84.

Homans, G. C. (1958). Social behavior as exchange. *American Journal of Sociology, 63*(6), 597–606.

Hu, X. (2018). Methodological implications of critical realism for entrepreneurship research. *Journal of Critical Realism, 17*(2), 118–139.
Huning, T. M., Bryant, P. C., & Holt, M. K. (2015). Informal social networks in organizations: Propositions regarding their role in organizational behavior outcomes. *Academy of Strategic Management Journal, 14*(1), 20.
Husted, B. W. (2003). Governance choices for corporate social responsibility: To contribute, collaborate or internalize? *Long Range Planning, 36*(5), 481–498.
Huybrechts, B., & Nicholls, A. (2013). The role of legitimacy in social enterprise-corporate collaboration. *Social Enterprise Journal, 9*(2), 130–146.
Johnson Jr, B. L. (1995). *Resource dependence theory: A political economy model of organizations*. Retrieved from https://eric.ed.gov/?id=ED387871
Kale, P., Singh, H., & Perlmutter, H. (2000). Learning and protection of proprietary assets in strategic alliances: Building relational capital. *Strategic Management Journal, 21*(3), 217–237.
Kareem, A. O., Jiboye, T. F., Adejumo, O. O., & Akinyosoye, M. O. (2020). Socio-cultural factors and performance of small-scale enterprise in agro-allied manufacturing firms in Nigeria. In *The Palgrave handbook of agricultural and rural development in Africa* (pp. 495–512). Springer International Publishing.
Korsgaard, M. A., Brower, H. H., & Lester, S. W. (2015). It isn't always mutual: A critical review of dyadic trust. *Journal of Management, 41*(1), 47–70.
Larson, A. (1992). Network dyads in entrepreneurial settings: A study of the governance of exchange relationships. *Administrative Science Quarterly, 37*, 76–104.
Leca, B., & Naccache, P. (2006). A critical realist approach to institutional entrepreneurship. *Organization, 13*(5), 627–651.
Levine, S., & White, P. E. (1961). Exchange as a conceptual framework for the study of interorganizational relationships. *Administrative Science Quarterly, 5*(4), 583–601.
Lewis, J. D. (2007). *Trusted partners: How companies build mutual trust and win together*. Simon and Schuster, The Free Press.
Liden, R. C., Anand, S., & Vidyarthi, P. (2016). Dyadic relationships. *Annual Review of Organizational Psychology and Organizational Behavior, 3*(1), 139–166.
Liu, H., & Yeung. (2012). *Impact investing in SMEs capital deployment for Cambodia's future* [Press release]. Retrieved from http://prog.global-inst.com/downloads/press%20room/Invest%20in%20Cambodia%20-%20GIFT.pdf
Mair, J., & Marti, I. (2009). Entrepreneurship in and around institutional voids: A case study from Bangladesh. *Journal of Business Venturing, 24*(5), 419–435.
Manotungvorapun, N., & Gerdsri, N. (2016). Complementarity vs. compatibility: What really matters for partner selection in open innovation? *International Journal of Transitions and Innovation Systems, 5*(2), 122–139.
Manu, E. (2014). *Supply chain management practices in construction and inter-organisational trust dynamics* (Doctoral dissertation), University of Wolverhampton. Retrieved from http://hdl.handle.net/2436/333133
Martin, R., & Lohin, R. (2017). Impact investing: Tracking the adoption of a financial (and social) innovation. *Rotman Management*, 64–69.
Mayer, K. J., & Sparrowe, R. T. (2013). Integrating theories in AMJ articles. *Academy of Management Journal, 56*(4), 917–922.
McEvily, B., Zaheer, A., & Kamal, D. K. F. (2017). Mutual and exclusive: Dyadic sources of trust in interorganizational exchange. *Organization Science, 28*(1), 74–92.
McMullen, J. S., & Warnick, B. J. (2016). Should we require every new venture to be a hybrid organization? *Journal of Management Studies, 53*(4), 630–662.
Mersland, R., Nyarko, S. A., & Sirisena, A. B. (2020). A hybrid approach to international market selection: The case of impact investing organizations. *International Business Review, 29*(1), 101624.

Mindruta, D., Moeen, M., & Agarwal, R. (2016). A two-sided matching approach for partner selection and assessing complementarities in partners' attributes in inter-firm alliances. *Strategic Management Journal, 37*(1), 206–231.

Mitsuhashi, H., & Greve, H. R. (2009). A matching theory of alliance formation and organizational success: Complementarity and compatibility. *Academy of Management Journal, 52*(5), 975–995.

Mitzinneck, B. C., & Besharov, M. L. (2019). Managing value tensions in collective social entrepreneurship: The role of temporal, structural, and collaborative compromise. *Journal of Business Ethics, 159*(2), 381–400.

Mogapi, E. M., Sutherland, M. M., & Wilson-Prangley, A. (2019). Impact investing in South Africa: Managing tensions between financial returns and social impact. *European Business Review, 31*, 397–419.

Molm, L. D. (2010). The structure of reciprocity. *Social Psychology Quarterly, 73*(2), 119–131.

Mongelli, L., Rullani, F., Ramus, T., & Rimac, T. (2019). The bright side of hybridity: Exploring how social enterprises manage and leverage their hybrid nature. *Journal of Business Ethics, 159*, 301–305.

Montoro-Sánchez, Á., Ortiz-de-Urbina-Criado, M., & Romero-Martínez, A. M. (2009). The decision to use alliances as corporate entrepreneurship: The role of resources and skills. *Group Decision and Negotiation, 18*(5), 431.

Morgan, D. L., Ataie, J., Carder, P., & Hoffman, K. (2013). Introducing dyadic interviews as a method for collecting qualitative data. *Qualitative Health Research, 23*(9), 1276–1284.

Morgan, D. L., Eliot, S., Lowe, R. A., & Gorman, P. (2016). Dyadic interviews as a tool for qualitative evaluation. *American Journal of Evaluation, 37*(1), 109–117.

Oliver, C. (1990). Determinants of interorganizational relationships: Integration and future directions. *Academy of Management Review, 15*(2), 241–265.

Oliver, C. (1997). Sustainable competitive advantage: Combining institutional and resource-based views. *Strategic Management Journal, 18*(9), 697–713. Retrieved from https://www.jstor.org/stable/3088134

Ozanne, L. K., Phipps, M., Weaver, T., Carrington, M., Luchs, M., Catlin, J., et al. (2016). Managing the tensions at the intersection of the triple bottom line: A paradox theory approach to sustainability management. *Journal of Public Policy & Marketing, 35*(2), 249–261.

Pache, A.-C., & Santos, F. (2013). Inside the hybrid organization: Selective coupling as a response to competing institutional logics. *Academy of Management Journal, 56*(4), 972–1001.

Phillips, N., Lawrence, T. B., & Hardy, C. (2000). Inter-organizational collaboration and the dynamics of institutional fields. *Journal of Management Studies, 37*(1), 23–43.

Pirkey, M. (2016). *Being, doing, & creating community: Social exchange & the microfoundations of institutional logics* (Paper presentation). Academy of Management Proceedings. https://doi.org/10.5465/ambpp.2016.10979abstract

Powell, W. W., & Sandholtz, K. W. (2012). Amphibious entrepreneurs and the emergence of organizational forms. *Strategic Entrepreneurship Journal, 6*(2), 94–115.

Preston, L. E. (2004). Reputation as a source of corporate social capital. *Journal of General Management, 30*(2), 43–50.

Reay, T., & Hinings, C. R. (2009). Managing the rivalry of competing institutional logics. *Organization Studies, 30*(6), 629–652.

Redmond, M. V. (2015). *Social exchange theory*. English Technical Reports and White Papers. Retrieved from https://lib.dr.iastate.edu/engl_reports/5

Rodriguez-Montemayor, E. (2013). The positive 'Premium' of genuine software: A macroeconomic approach. INSEAD working paper no. 2013/40/TOM, Available at SSRN: https://ssrn.com/abstract=2236684 or https://doi.org/10.2139/ssrn.2236684

Roth, B. (2019). Impact investing: A theory of financing social enterprises. In *Harvard business school entrepreneurial management working paper* (p. 20-078). Retrieved from https://www.hbs.edu/faculty/Publication%20Files/20-078_8f45e8dc-fbcf-43d9-90fd-d3a6ba59d4c5.pdf

Roundy, P., Holzhauer, H., & Dai, Y. (2017). Finance or philanthropy? Exploring the motivations and criteria of impact investors. *Social Responsibility Journal, 13*(3), 491–512.

Ryan, P. W., & Lyne, I. (2008). Social enterprise and the measurement of social value: Methodological issues with the calculation and application of the social return on investment. *Education, Knowledge & Economy, 2*(3), 223–237.

Ryan, A., & O'Malley, L. (2006). *Conceptualising dyadic inter-organisational relationships as complex adaptive systems* (Paper presentation). 22nd Imp Conference, Boconni University, Milan, San Diego, California. Retrieved from https://eprints.lancs.ac.uk/id/eprint/46867

Santi, E., & Sennett, L. (2016). Impact investing in Africa. In *Principles and practice of impact investing: A catalytic revolution*. Routledge.

Sarkar, M. B., Echambadi, R., Cavusgil, S. T., & Aulakh, P. S. (2001). The influence of complementarity, compatibility, and relationship capital on alliance performance. *Journal of the Academy of Marketing Science, 29*(4), 358–373.

Saz-Carranza, A., & Longo, F. (2012). Managing competing institutional logics in public–private joint ventures. *Public Management Review, 14*(3), 331–357.

Smith, W. K., Gonin, M., & Besharov, M. L. (2013). Managing social-business tensions: A review and research agenda for social enterprise. *Business Ethics Quarterly, 23*(3), 407–442.

Solesvik, M. Z., & Encheva, S. (2010). Partner selection for interfirm collaboration in ship design. *Industrial Management, & Data Systems, 110*(5), 701–717.

Stephan, U., Uhlaner, L. M., & Stride, C. (2015). Institutions and social entrepreneurship: The role of institutional voids, institutional support, and institutional configurations. *Journal of International Business Studies, 46*(3), 308–331.

Svensson, G. (2005). Mutual and interactive trust in business dyads: Condition and process. *European Business Review, 17*(5), 411–427.

Thomas, R., & Skinner, L. (2010). Total trust and trust asymmetry: Does trust need to be equally distributed in interfirm relationships? *Journal of Relationship Marketing, 9*(1), 43–53.

Thorgren, S., & Omorede, A. (2018). Passionate leaders in social entrepreneurship: Exploring an African context. *Business & Society, 57*(3), 481–524.

Thorgren, S., Wincent, J., & Örtqvist, D. (2012). Unleashing synergies in strategic networks of SMEs: The influence of partner fit on corporate entrepreneurship. *International Small Business Journal, 30*(5), 453–471.

Thornton, P. H. (2015). Culture and institutional logics. In *International encyclopedia of the social and behavioral sciences*. Elsevier.

Thornton, P. H., & Ocasio, W. (1999). Institutional logics and the historical contingency of power in organizations: Executive succession in the higher education publishing industry, 1958–1990. *American Journal of Sociology, 105*(3), 801–843.

Thornton, P., & Ocasio, W. (2008). Institutional logics. In R. Greenwood, C. Oliver, & R. Suddaby (Eds.), *The SAGE handbook of organizational institutionalism* (pp. 99–128). SAGE Publications Ltd.

Thornton, P. H., Ocasio, W., & Lounsbury, M. (2012). *The institutional logics perspective: A new approach to culture, structure, and process*. Oxford University Press on Demand.

Tomlinson, E. C., Dineen, B. R., & Lewicki, R. J. (2009). Trust congruence among integrative negotiators as a predictor of joint-behavioral outcomes. *International Journal of Conflict Management, 20*(2), 173–187.

Triponel, A., & Agapitova, N. (2017). *Legal framework for social enterprise: Lessons from a comparative study of Italy, Malaysia, South Korea, United Kingdom, and United States*. World Bank.

Urban, B. (2013). Influence of the institutional environment on entrepreneurial intentions in an emerging economy. *The International Journal of Entrepreneurship and Innovation, 14*(3), 179–191.

Van de Ven, A. H. (1976). On the nature, formation, and maintenance of relations among organizations. *Academy of Management Review, 1*(4), 24–36.

Vanneste, B. S. (2016). From interpersonal to interorganisational trust: The role of indirect reciprocity. *Journal of Trust Research, 6*(1), 7–36.

Vincent, S. (2008). A transmutation theory of inter-organizational exchange relations and networks: Applying critical realism to analysis of collective agency. *Human Relations, 61*(6), 875–899.

Vissa, B. (2011). A matching theory of entrepreneurs' tie formation intentions and initiation of economic exchange. *Academy of Management Journal, 54*(1), 137–158.

White, J., & Klein, D. (2008). The social exchange and rational choice framework. *Family Theories, 3*. Retrieved from https://www.sagepub.com/sites/default/files/upm-binaries/17262_Chapter_3.pdf

Woldesenbet Beta, K., & Storey, J. (2019). Navigating competing institutional logics in a developing economy. *Africa Journal of Management, 5*(1), 24–46.

Wynn, D., Jr., & Williams, C. K. (2012). Principles for conducting critical realist case study research in information systems. *MIS Quarterly, 36*, 787–810.

York, J. G., Hargrave, T. J., & Pacheco, D. F. (2016). Converging winds: Logic hybridization in the Colorado wind energy field. *Academy of Management Journal, 59*(2), 579–610.

Young, D. (2001). *Social enterprise in the United States: Alternate identities and forms.* Paper presented at the international conference on social enterprise.

Yunxia, Z. H. U., Rooney, D., & Phillips, N. (2016). Practice-based wisdom theory for integrating institutional logics: A new model for social entrepreneurship learning and education. *Academy of Management Learning & Education, 15*(3), 607–625.

Zeitz, G. (1980). Interorganizational dialectics. *Administrative Science Quarterly, 25*(1), 72–88.

Zhao, E. Y., & Lounsbury, M. (2016). An institutional logics approach to social entrepreneurship: Market logic, religious diversity, and resource acquisition by microfinance organizations. *Journal of Business Venturing, 31*(6), 643–662.

Bibliography

Aguinis, H., & Solarino, A. M. (2019). Transparency and replicability in qualitative research: The case of interviews with elite informants. *Strategic Management Journal, 40*(8), 1291–1315.

Austin, J. E. (2006). Three avenues for social entrepreneurship research. In J. Mair, J. Robinson, & K. Hockerts (Eds.), *Social entrepreneurship*. Palgrave Macmillan.

Easton, K. L., McComish, J. F., & Greenberg, R. (2000). Avoiding common pitfalls in qualitative data collection and transcription. *Qualitative Health Research, 10*(5), 703–707.

Eisenhardt, K. M., & Graebner, M. E. (2007). Theory building from cases: Opportunities and challenges. *Academy of Management Journal, 50*(1), 25–32.

Marx, K., & Engels, F. (1845). The ruling class and the ruling ideas. In *Media and cultural studies: Key works* (Vol. 9). https://we.riseup.net/assets/102142/appadurai.pdf

J. A. Emmanuel et al., *Social Enterprises and Impact Investors*, Advances in Theory and Practice of Emerging Markets,
https://doi.org/10.1007/978-3-031-59454-0

The manufacturer's authorised representative in the EU is Springer Nature Customer Service Centre GmbH, Europaplatz 3, 69115 Heidelberg, Germany. If you have any concerns regarding our products, please contact ProductSafety@springernature.com

Printed and bound by CPI Group (UK) Ltd, Croydon, CR0 4YY
01/10/2026
02225950-0004